Dr ALEXANDER BUCHNER

# MUSICAL INSTRUMENTS THROUGH THE AGES

*TRANSLATED BY IRIS URWIN*

SPRING BOOKS
LONDON

KT-413-920

*Graphic design by Metod Kaláb*

*This edition first published 1958*

*Second impression 1961*

*Third impression 1964*

781.9109 BUC (OVERSIZE)

THE BRITISH MUSEUM WITHDRAWN
THE PAUL HAMLYN LIBRARY

*Designed and produced by Artia for*

SPRING BOOKS

*WESTBOOK HOUSE · FULHAM BROADWAY · LONDON*

© *1961 by Artia*

*Printed in Czechoslovakia*

*S-1540*

# CONTENTS

# ACKNOWLEDGEMENTS

Ancient Egyptian Paintings, Chicago-London 1936 67, 68
Archives of the State Office for the Preservation of Historical Buildings (Vladimír Fyman, Vladimír Hyhlík, František Stöber and Čestmír Šíla) 6, 7, 74, 75, 95, 96, 107, 121—128, 130—133, 137, 145, 146
British Museum, London 66, 76
Brok, Jindřich, Prague 171—174
Brückner, Dr. Rudolf, Coburg 122
Buchner, Dr. Alexander, Prague 241
Chinese Institute of National Music, Peking 42—44
Czechoslovak Chamber of Commerce (Karel Vykysalý and Alfred Kramer) 147—149, 152—157, 162—165, 186—189, 192—195, 198, 199, 202, 204, 209, 231—236, 239, 240, 246, 247, 249, 256—259. 262, 275—293, 295, 314, 322, 323
Egyptian Museum, Berlin 69
Ehm, Josef, Prague 138
Encyclopédie photographique de l'Art, Paris 1936—1938 65
Forman, Werner, Prague, 33—37, 46, 54, 57
Fotografia, Prague (Glogar branch) 294
Haščák, Josef, Košice 310
Hickmann, Dr. Hans, Cairo 70—72
Hirmer, Munich 73
Honty, Tibor, Prague 15, 24—32, 52, 55, 88—91, 118—120, 159—161, 220, 271, 272, 298, 316, 317, 320, 321
Illek and Paul, Prague 92, 94, 100—104, 134, 139
Kolowca, Stanislav, Cracow 230
Krahulec, Jan, Prague 14, 16—23, 47, 48, 179, 182, 201, 216, 217, 221, 225—227, 251, 260, 263, 264, 301, 302, 305, 306, 309, 311, 312
Kruckenhauser, Stefan 140, 141
Kus, Lev, Prague 243
Metropolitan Museum of Art, New York 210, 211
Moravian Museum, Brno 1—5, 8, 9, 59—63
Museum of Art, Vienna 150, 166, 203, 215, 218, 228
Musical Instruments, Hipkins, Edinburgh 1886 212
National Gallery, Prague 303
National Museum, Copenhagen 10—13
National Museum, Naples 82, 84—86
National Museum of Antiquities, Bucharest 83
Neruda, Josef, Prague 200, 273, 274, 296, 299, 300, 313
Orbis, National Corporation, Prague 38—41, 45, 49—51, 56, 58, 77—81, 87, 93, 99, 108—117, 129, 136, 142—144, 151, 158, 177, 183—185, 190, 191, 213, 219, 223, 224, 229, 237, 238, 242, 244, 245, 250, 252—255, 261, 268—270, 297, 304, 307, 315, 318, 319
Revue d'Assyriologie, Paris 1912 64
Slovak National Museum, Martin 308
State Library, Vienna 53
University Library, Prague 97, 98, 135

The score reproduced in illustration No. 267 was drawn by Josef Milota, Prague.

# LIST OF PLATES

songs of Zurich, the Codex of the Manesse family from the beginning of the fourteenth century. University Library, Heidelberg.
100 Shepherd's horns; Velislav's Bible, 1340. University Library, Prague.
101 Decachordum (ten-stringed), *crot*, horn and trumpets; Velislav's Bible, 1340. University Library, Prague.
102 Psaltery and fiddles; Velislav's Bible, 1340. University Library, Prague.
103 Psaltery harp, bell chimes and psaltery; Velislav's Bible, 1340. University Library, Prague.
104 Bohemian wing *(ala bohemica)*, *cetera*, fiddle and psaltery; Velislav's Bible, 1340. University Library, Prague.
105 Psaltery harp; a breviary of 1343. Monastery Library, Rajhrad.
106 Organ; Bologna breviary of the middle of the fourteenth century. University Library, Prague.
107 Psaltery; Roudnice psalter, fourteenth century. Chapter Library, Prague.
108—109 Lute and *lira da braccio*; detail of a frame of a Madonna by Thomas of Modena; fourteenth century. Karlštejn.
110—111 Beaked flute and shawm; wall painting, fourteenth century. Karlštejn.
112—113 Horn with fingerholes and bagpipes; wall painting, 14th century. Karlštejn.
114—115 Cromorne with bladder and shepherd's horn; fourteenth century wall painting. Karlštejn.
116 Bladder-pipe; fourteenth century wall painting. Karlštejn.
117 Handbells, mandora, fiddle and Bohemian wing *(ala bohemica)*; Thomas of Štítný, Six Little Books on Christian Matters, c. 1376. University Library, Prague.
118—120 Fourteenth century oliphant, and details. National Museum, Prague.
121 *Crots*; Scriptum super apocalypsim, from the end of the fourteenth century. Chapter Library, Prague.
122 Bells, triangle, recorder, jingles, trumpet, harp, shawm, fiddle, lute, organ, helicon, mandora, white zink, harp, trumscheit, psaltery, drums, bell chimes, rattle, clavichord, hurdy-gurdy. Otto von Passau, Codex from 1448. Library of the gymnasium Casimirianum, Coburg.
123 Jingles, fiddle, lute and psaltery harp.
124 Psaltery harp, one-hand flute with drum and psaltery; King Wenceslas IV Bible, end of the fourteenth century. State Library, Vienna.
125 Small drum, handbells and drum.
126 Shawm, trumpets, triangle, organ and fiddle; King Wenceslas IV Bible, end of the fourteenth century. State Library, Vienna.
127 Shawm and trumpet.
128 Bohemian wing *(ala bohemica)*; a Krumlov chrestomathy from the beginning of the fifteenth century. National Museum, Prague.
129 Lute: Krumlov chrestomathy of the beginning of the fifteenth century. National Museum, Prague.
130 Psaltery.
131 Mandora, drums and Bohemian wing *(ala bohemica)*; Litoměřice Bible, 1414. Archives, Třeboň.
132 Shepherd's horn, drum, lute and psaltery from the Bible of Queen Christina of Sweden, c. 1420. Vatican Library.
133 Psaltery types of the Bohemian wing; a Latin Bible from the first half of the fifteenth century. Chapter Library, Prague.
134 Small drums, fiddle, horn, triangle, lute and bagpipes; Olomouc Bible, 1417. University Library, Olomouc.
135 Pommers and trumpets (one trumpet S-shaped); illumination in the Richenthal Chronicle (the Leningrad Manuscript) 1464. University Library, Prague.
136 One-hand flute with small drum, portative, organ, dulcimer, tenor pommer, lute, recorder, trumpet, dulcimer; fifteenth century manuscript. City Library, Grenoble.
137 Double flute and lute on a carved ivory comb; fifteenth century French work. National Museum, Prague.
138 Lute on a Venetian enamelled goblet from the end of the fifteenth century. National Museum, Prague.
139 Small drum, bladder pipe and organ; Lobkovice breviary, 1494. University Library, Prague.
140 Rebec and lute.
141 Clavicytherium, or dulcimer with raised stringboard; detail from a wooden altar dating from the end of the fifteenth century. Parish church of Kefermarkt, Upper Austria.
142—143 Trumpets and wind-cap shawms; Litoměřice breviary, 1520.
144 Harp and lute; Litoměřice breviary, 1520.
145—146 Black (curved) zink, bass pommer. Harp

and *viola da braccio*. Mladá Boleslav gradual, 1570 to 1572. District Museum, Mladá Boleslav.

147—149 Alto pommer, grand bass wind-cap shawm and alto cromorne, sixteenth century. National Museum, Prague.

150 Tartoelts (dragon shawms) sixteenth century. Museum of Art, Vienna.

151 Recorder; Jan Kupecký (1667 to 1740). National Museum, Budapest.

152—153 Alto and bass recorders made by P. I. Bressan, seventeenth century. National Museum, Prague.

154—157 Hunting oboe by Fridrich, seventeenth century; and English horns (cors anglais) made in Bohemia, seventeenth to nineteenth century. National Museum, Prague.

158 Transverse flute; Jan Kupecký (1667 to 1740).

159—161 Oliphant belonging to the Polish King Jan Sobieski, 1683, and details. National Museum, Prague.

162—165 Czech basset-horns of the eighteenth and nineteenth centuries and detail of the first basset horn. National Museum, Prague.

166 Trumpet made by the Nüremberg instrument maker Antonius Schnitzer, 1598. Museum of Art, Vienna, from the collection of the Friends of Music in Vienna.

167 *Trompeta clarina* from the Lobkovice collection, made by Michael Leichamschneider, Vienna 1716, silver gilded, and inlaid with semi-precious stones.

168 Gilded silver *trompeta clarina* belonging to the King of Saxony Augustus III; eighteenth century. National Museum, Prague.

169—170 *Trompeta clarina* made by the Prague instrument maker Bauer, eighteenth century, and the pommel of this trumpet showing wrought metal ornamentation. National Museum, Prague.

171 Organ, flute, violin and 'cello; painting on a Czech goblet from the middle of the eighteenth century. Museum of Industrial Arts, Prague.

172 Harp and French horns; painting on a Czech goblet from the middle of the eighteenth century. Museum of Industrial Arts, Prague.

173—174 Bassoon and French horn; eighteenth century Viennese porcelain. Museum of Industrial Arts, Prague.

175 Recorder, black (curved) zink, lute, viola, *viola da gamba* and trumpet; wood carving from the royal throne of the Castle of Prague, second half of the seventeenth century. City Museum, Prague.

176 Soprano recorders and bagpipes; Brussels gobelin designed by Jacobus Jordaens, 1644. Hluboká Castle.

177 Lute, violin and black (curved) zink; Italian engraving of the year 1784. National Museum, Prague.

178 Organ of 1575. Smečno (Slaný district). Holy Trinity Church.

179 Portable Czech organ (positive), eighteenth century. National Museum, Prague.

180 Michael Engler organ, 1745. St Maurice Church, Olomouc.

181 Baroque organ made by the Brno organmakers Adam Sieber and Antonín Richter; Holy Hill, near Olomouc.

182 Small portable Czech organ (portative), eighteenth century. National Museum, Prague.

183 Lute; Jan Kupecký (1667—1740).

184 Double-pedal harp made by Erard Frères, Paris, mid-nineteenth century. National Museum, Prague.

185 Pedal harp with hook action; coloured engraving from the end of the eighteenth century. National Museum, Prague.

186—187 Lute made by Max Unverdorben of Venice in the sixteenth century, and one by Thomas Edlinger of Prague at the end of the seventeenth century.

188—189 The rosettes of both lutes. National Museum, Prague.

190 Lute; unknown painter of the seventeenth century. National Museum, Prague.

191 Flute, violin and chitarrone (George Frederick Handel as a young musician in Hamburg); eighteenth century French engraving. National Museum, Prague.

192—193 Theorbo and detail of the triple pegbox made by the Olomouc maker of lutes and violins Martin Bruner in 1764. National Museum, Prague.

194—195 Chitarrone and detail of rosette; made by the Prague lute maker Martin Schott, 1680. National Museum, Prague.

196—197 Czech guitar battente and one made by the Prague lute maker Andreas Ott at the end of the seventeenth century. National Museum, Prague.

198—199 Guitar and detail of rosette made by

the Viennese lute maker Matthias Fux in 1692. National Museum, Prague.

200 Back of a guitar made by G. Sellas.

201—202 Guitars made by Georgius Sellas of Venice in the first half of the seventeenth century and by Thomas Andreas Hulinzký in 1754. National Museum, Prague.

203 Cistra made by Girolamo de Virchi in Brescia, 1754, for Archduke Ferdinand of Tyrol. Museum of Art, Vienna.

204—205 Italian guitars of the seventeenth and eighteenth centuries. National Museum, Prague.

206—207 Cistras made by Maximilian Zacher, Breslau, 1751, and Johannes Michael Willer, Prague, 1799. National Museum, Prague.

208—209 Milanese mandoline made by Francesco Plesbler, Milan, 1773, and Neapolitan mandoline made by Johann Jobst Franck, Dresden, 1789. National Museum, Prague.

210 The oldest double virginals, the work of Hans Ruckers of Antwerp, 1581. Metropolitan Museum of Art, New York.

211 Lutes, shawms and flutes. Detail of the painting of the lid of Hans Ruckers' double virginals, 1581. Metropolitan Museum of Art, New York.

212 Seventeenth century dulcimer from H. Boddington's collection, London.

213 Dulcimer (tympanum); French engraving of the seventeenth century.

214 Grand clavichord made by Francesco Neri of Rimini (Italy) in the seventeenth century. City Museum, Prague.

215 Clavicytherium made by Marinus Kaiser for the Emperor Leopold I in the second half of the seventeenth century. Museum of Art, Vienna.

216 Harpsichord with keyboard of mother-of-pearl and tortoise-shell. Seventeenth century.

217 The eighteenth century Czech piano on which Wolfgang Amadeus Mozart played in January 1786 in the Ladies' College in Prague. National Museum, Prague.

218 Joseph Haydn's two-manual harpsichord, made by Burkat Shudi and John Broadwood, London, 1775. Museum of Art, Vienna (from the collection of the Friends of Music).

219 Eighteenth century harpsichord. National Museum, Prague.

220 Czech giraffe piano from the first half of the nineteenth century. National Museum, Prague.

221 Pyramid piano with a clock, made by Leopold Sauer, Prague, at the beginning of the nineteenth century. City Museum, Prague.

222 Table piano made by Leopold Sauer, Prague, at the beginning of the nineteenth century. City Museum, Prague.

223 Flute, lute and drone; Johannes Steen (1626—1679). National Gallery, Prague.

224 Trumscheit *(tromba marina)* engraving from F. Bonanni's book *Cabinetto armonico*. Rome, 1722. National Museum, Prague.

225—227 Trumscheits of the seventeenth and eighteenth centuries. National Museum, Prague.

228 *Lira da braccio*; Johannes Andrea, Verona, 1511. Museum of Art, Vienna.

229 Tenor, alto and descant, *viola da gamba* and lute; painting dated 1641 on part of a wooden ceiling in the former Pauline Monastery in Prague. City Museum, Prague.

230 Tenor *viola da gamba*; Johannes Verkolje (1650—1693).

231—232 Tenor *viola da gamba*, detail of the neck and pegboard; Johannes Udalricus Eberle, Prague, 1740. National Museum, Prague.

233—234 Tenor quinton and detail of the neck and pegboard; Thomas Andreas Hulinzký, Prague 1754. National Museum, Prague.

235—236 *Viola di bordone* (barytone) and detail of the neck and pegboard; eighteenth century. National Museum, Prague.

237 Lutes and violin; unknown Italian painter of the seventeenth century. National Museum, Prague.

238 Trumpets, kettle-drum, violin, shawm, lute and *viola da gamba*; unknown Flemish painter of the middle of the seventeenth century. National Museum, Prague.

239—240 *Viola d'amore* and English violetta (really an alto *viola d'amore* with double the number of sympathetic strings) made by Johannes Udalricus Eberle, Prague 1758 and 1727. National Museum, Prague.

241 Necks of Czech *violas d'amore*, eighteenth century. National Museum, Prague.

242 *Viola d'amore*. Thomas Andreas Hulinzký, Prague 1769. National Museum, Prague.

243 Jan Kubelík's violin, called the Emperor, made by Antonio Stradivari in 1715.

# INTRODUCTION

*There is no branch of musical knowledge which can illustrate the objects of its research so effectively as the study of musical instruments. Scores themselves are an independent branch of the engraver's art, and portraits of great musicians are subjects for the painter's brush; but musical instruments, those material tokens of immaterial music, cry out to be presented in pictures, to evoke by their very appearance the impression of the sound they make. Although no other branch has been so unkindly neglected and passed over by writers on music as has the history of musical instruments, this book does not set out to solve those problems still occupying scholars and musicologists. It is no more than an attempt to outline that fascinating march of events from prehistoric times to our own day which has led from the prototype to the highly developed instrument. Whereas the majority of those few works so far written about musical instruments have often lacked illustrations of the subject matter, this book presents the development of musical instruments in pictures, without extensive written text. By means of illustrations it aims at completing the mental picture formed by those who love the art of tones and the musical instruments which transform those tones into audible reality.*

PREHISTORIC TIMES · PRIMITIVE PEOPLES · AMERICA
CHINA AND JAPAN · FURTHER INDIA AND THE INDIAN
ARCHIPELAGO · INDIA · INSTRUMENTS OF THE PERSO-
ARABIC CULTURE

# PREHISTORIC TIMES

The first tone, announcing the beginning of musical history, was heard long, long ages ago. Prehistoric man drew it from a musical instrument which may have been a stringed or a wind instrument, or an idiophone. This first instrument has not been preserved; it disappeared not long after it was laid with prehistoric man in his grave, or when the first player laid it aside. Historians of music therefore base their theory of the rise of musical instruments on the study of the various types of instruments preserved among primitive peoples whose musical culture even today has remained on the level of prehistoric man.

Musical instruments are as old as man himself; they existed before ever tonality was known, or the reproduction of a melody. These early musical instruments produced a sound of a certain quality with no regard to pitch, and yet even at this stage of development, when the instruments were an end in themselves, considerable qualitative and quantitative differences were achieved.

Those prehistoric musical instruments which are preserved in museum collections date from long before the historic era, being of material which defied the destructive hand of time — bone and stone. They are signal whistles made of reindeer bone, from the palaeolithic era, intended not for music but to serve the needs of the hunt. On the other hand the bone whistle found in the Innigkofen settlement in Hohenzollern and the whistle with five tone holes found in a neolithic site on Bornholm were certainly already instruments for musical reproduction. Even at this early stage of development both the types of flute appeared, the *grooved whistle*, the prototype of the cross flute, and the *whistle flute*, the prototype of the recorder. The stone age also knew rattling instruments, of which the most important was the *scraper*. The palaeolithic bone scraper found in the Pekárna cave in Moravia has saw-like teeth over which a plectrum was rubbed. That as early as the Stone Age man liked making a rattling noise is proved by the clay *rattles* which have been found. These clay figures of various shapes, with little stones inside to rattle, were used in dances, rites, and as children's toys. They have been found in Greece and in Silesia in settlements dating from the Hallstatt era and particularly numerous examples have been found dating from the later La Tène era. An antique *gong* made of grey-green jade was discovered near Valencia in Venezuela — it proves that man very early in his history began to distinguish different kinds of stone by the quality of the sound they emit. Many of these instruments became extinct in the course of later development and are classified among musical instruments as an exception. As well as knowing these very primitive instruments prehistoric man was acquainted with membrane instruments, some of which showed a considerable degree of development. The Bernburg goblet-shaped *clay drums* belong to the neolithic era, and so do the pottery spirals shaped like binocles, found in the southern part of the Soviet Union.

During the Bronze Age prehistoric culture reached a high level; in addition to ridge and reed wind instruments the prototypes of mouthpiece instruments appear for the first time. In the early Bronze Age considerable advance in the working of metals made possible the creation of a bronze *horn* modelled on the horns of animals. The most highly developed instrument, however, both from the point of view of workmanship and of sound, was the *lur.* The discovery of these instruments in Scandinavian peatbogs in the nineteenth century aroused eager discussion among musical scholars. Their tube is slightly conical and bent into an unusual shape, ending with a completely flat, disc-like bell. The lurs, which as far as their technical execution is concerned belong to the world's curiosities, developed in northern Europe out of ordinary animal horn. The art of their production was cultivated by the prehistoric inhabitants of Scandinavia at the end of Bronze Age. In 1946 *a horn with holes* belonging to the early Iron Age was found in a peatbog in Konsterud in Sweden; this shepherd's instrument was probably used to drive wild beasts away from the flocks, and for communication over long distances.

## PRIMITIVE PEOPLES

Just as folk music has preserved for us almost all the instruments of the Middle Ages, so we find many musical instruments of the shape used in prehistoric times and at the same level of development among the primitive peoples outside Europe. Instruments of those countries which are furthest removed from the edges of the central Asiatic focus of culture, particularly the instruments of Africa and Australia, give us a glimpse into the musical culture of the Stone Age. In these lands music is magic, with the power of exorcising evil spirits and curing sickness. And so musical instruments too are sacred objects guarded so jealously by the shamans that even to touch them means punishment by death.

Perhaps the only race who do not possess any musical instruments at all are the Vedda of Ceylon, who accompany their songs by slapping their naked bodies with their hands. *Clappers* are a form of extension of the arm, seen in the most primitive form in the stamper used by natives of the Andaman Islands—a board placed over a pit. The double wooden clapper of the Papuans of New Guinea is a further development which has also a magic significance. The big *signal drum* of the Papuans is a hollow tree-trunk with a slit in the middle; the sound is produced by striking the trunk alongside this slit. A number of wooden bars and boards each tuned differently produced the *xylophone*, an instrument widely used in Further India, Melanesia, Polynesia and Africa. The Angolan *marimba* or wooden harmonica is related to the xylophone; it consists of sixteen wooden bars resting on two iron hoops bent into a half-circle, and struck with hammers.

All native tribes possess wind instruments in the form of reed and bone pipes. When a number of pipes are bound together the *pan-pipes* are created: these, together with the xylophone, can be considered the most highly developed of the primitive instruments. Often the pan-pipes are double, with one row of open pipes and one covered; the tones of these two rows of pipes bear the same relation to each other as the basic note to the octave. If the pipe has tone holes we get a pipe capable of producing many tones with the intervals and scales typical of various native tribes. The Polynesian *nose flutes* are remarkable; like the more highly developed *bazaree* of east Asia they are blown through the nostril, probably in order to leave the mouth free to make the humming sounds which are so popular. Wind instruments equipped with a single or a double reed probably developed at a higher stage of cultural development. As well as pipes, *horns*, often of bass size, are used. These are blown from the side as for example the *apunga* horn in the Congo.

The most primitive of the stringed instruments is the *musical bow*. Fundamentally it is the hunter's bow, made to emit a tone by plucking the taut string; at one end of the bow the mouth acts as a resonator and directs the sound. At a later stage of development, among the Kaffirs, for instance, a gourd is added which the player holds against his body or (as among the Hottentots) to his ear. The Bushmen's *gora* is a similar instrument: an ostrich feather is attached to one end, and this is put into the mouth and vibrated by sucking. This is an intermediate step to European instruments, to the *Jew's-harp* and the *mouth organ*. But stringed instruments could also come into existence in the same way as the Javanese *slendang*, where a slender strip is split from the cane and braced with two bridges like a string. A special group is formed by instruments with wooden and (later) metal tongues: either the player sounded them one by one between his teeth, as in the mouth organs of India and Oceania, or a number of them were fixed on a resonator (a coconut, gourd, or wooden box) and sounded by the fingers, as in the case of the *zanza* in the Cameroons.

Among the Negroes of West Africa, the Papuans of New Guinea, and other native tribes, *drums* of various shapes and sizes are used for much more than purely musical purposes, serving primarily for communication over great distances. *Scrapers* and *rattles* made from gourds and other material are commonly used, and have also been adopted by South American orchestras. Negro songs, with highly stylised manner, are accompanied by *clappers* and by *mirlitons*, which are fixed indirectly to the musical instruments. They are pipes with a membrane attached, into which the player sings, rather like singing through a thin paper on a comb, which gives the human voice a nasal timbre.

Some primitive instruments arose through the degeneration of the instruments of cultured peoples—the Negro harp *nanga*, for instance, grew out of the ancient Egyptian harp, and the pipes of the Kubuks in Sumatra came from the dwarf pipes of Javanese culture. Some instruments, like some melodies, travelled tremendous distances and bear witness to a common culture once enjoyed by very distant lands. Clappers travelled a long way, before becoming a mere toy for children. The clay pipe *cor* made by Khirghiz children is one such instrument; it resembles the old Chinese *hsuan* or *hiuen*, used at the time of the Confucian cult. This instrument in its turn is related to the clay pipe of the Babylonian excavations. It therefore originated in the Near East, although it is found as far afield as Borneo.

# AMERICA

We know nothing definite about the music of old American cultures. Some scholars incline to the belief that musical instruments were brought into America from China in the neolithic era. The striking similarity between some of the instruments, the lack of stringed instruments, the similarity of the pan-pipes, etc., would seem to support this view. It is strange that the Mexican civilisation, which created such wonderful examples of the builder's, sculptor's and miniature painter's art, lagged behind in instrumental music. On the other hand in South America, where they had not even acquired an alphabet, musical culture reached a relatively high standard, as can be seen from the pictures on vases and from the musical instruments excavated. But both in the most northerly and in the most southerly regions of this double continent musical culture remained at the stage of development of the early Stone Age.

America did not know stringed instruments at all. The only instrument of Central America capable of playing a tune was a small beaked flute called in Mexican *tlapitzalli*. The limited number of fingerholes (from three to five) meant that only a very simple melody could be reproduced. On the other hand the flutes of South America with their greater number of fingerholes and the pan-pipes with their row of reed pipes are proof of a more advanced musical culture. Pan-pipes of green talc were found in Peru, with a row of eight pipes; this seems to be the oldest example of this instrument in existence. The Mojo tribe in Bolivia made pan-pipes of remarkable size in which the fingerholes were drilled according to the sacred combination 23+3. The North American Indians use to this day a strange form of whistle pipe without fingerholes which is depicted in the ancient Mayan codices. It has something like a bent flue, tied on above the two holes, directing the wind from the first hole against the edge of the second. Archaeologists in Mexico have excavated large numbers of clay whistles shaped like animals and flowers, which we can consider forerunners of the ocarina. Double earthenware vessels have been found in Peru; they were filled with water, and when the player blew into one of them the water was driven into the second, compressing the air and driving it out through a whistle head. The remaining wind instruments are similar both in Central and South America. They comprise shell trumpets, the *acocotl* trumpet, and a kind of trumpet used by the Incas of Peru, made from a sea shell, called *pututo*.

South American drums were cylindrical and shallow; the skins were those of animals or captured enemies. The Aztecs of Mexico had a dull-sounding war drum, the *huehuetl*, which had neither bracing cords nor sticks. As well as skin drums slit drums were used in Central America, the *teponaztli*, made in the shape of some animal and carefully carved. But the majority of the ancient instruments of America were idiophones: bars of wood and metal used in Venezuela and Ecuador, various rattles made of shell, bladders or unglazed earthenware, necklets of rattling seeds, scrapers of bone and wood; then there were jingles of clay or metal filled with pebbles, and small conical bells with no clappers. The Peruvians used strange bells made of wood and equipped with clappers, similar to the bells still used today in Burma and the western regions of the Malay peninsula. Today America uses mainly instruments which originally came from Europe and to some extent from Africa.

## CHINA AND JAPAN

Scholars have commonly held that the character of Chinese music as a whole was determined solely by the pentatonic scale, but this opinion has now been refuted by the book *Go Yuy* of the fifth century B.C., which speaks of twelve half tones in music. In addition to the pentatonic scale, from which sprang many lovely examples of Chinese national art, Chinese musicians from ancient times up to the present have used all the tones of a twelve tone scale. This is also proved by the descriptions of ancient instruments and by the folk music of today.

The origin of China's musical instruments is to be found far back in the past. Recent archaeological excavations on the site of the former capital of the Shan dynasty (16th to 11th centuries B.C.) in the province of Hunan revealed musical instruments made of stone and a kind of ocarina of earthenware. Naturally enough the majority of the ancient Chinese instruments perished, for they were made of bamboo and other less durable materials. Confucius (551—479 B.C.) and his pupils played a significant role in the development of Chinese music. In his works mention is to be found of over a hundred different musical instruments; one of these, with twenty-three strings, has been found by archaeologists and is clearly the forerunner of the stringed instruments *chen* and *is* played today. In the musical part of the book *Li-ti* (first century B.C.) cosmic significance is attributed to music: "Music is the measure for heaven and earth, the principle of balance and harmony: human emotions cannot escape from its influence." Ancient Chinese writers speak of the number of strings on musical instruments being decreased, and write that when songs were accompanied by instruments melodic tones were omitted so as not to arouse the dangerous depths of the soul. During the period of the Chi'ng and Han dynasties, and particularly under the T'ang dynasty (618—906) music and musical instruments from India and Central Asia began to penetrate into China. Thus the Chinese acquired and perfected the lute-shaped stringed instrument *p'i-p'a*, which is still their national instrument. Before the T'ang dynasty came to the throne the seven-stringed *tsing* became very popular; it developed from a primitive stringed instrument depicted on ancient bas-reliefs from the Han epoch. The *tsing* has a faint, sweet sound; some of the greatest Chinese poets and writers took pleasure in it. There are many works dealing with the technique of playing this instrument, and a great number of small pieces composed for it have been preserved.

After the Ming and Tsin dynasties the Chinese theatre began to flourish, and new musical instruments made their appearance at the same time. Old instruments were altered and improved. Stringed instruments were paid greatest attention, but the quality of the other instruments, particularly percussion instruments, was also improved. We may mention the flute *ti* among the wind instruments, among the plucked stringed instruments the *san-sien*, and the only bowed instrument known in China, *erh-hu*, with a long bamboo neck and a barrel-shaped body with a soundboard of snake-skin. There is an astoundingly larger number of different musical instruments in China, a proof of the exceptional interest taken in music by the Chinese people. As early as the eighteenth century, the French missionary Amiot attempted to classify them in eight groups according to the material used: skin, stone, metal, clay, silk, wood, bamboo and gourd instruments. Sonorous percussion instruments are the most numerous; among them are the wooden trough, *chu*, which is struck with a hammer, and the wooden tiger, *yü*, which is stroked with a bamboo rod to produce the tones. The idiophones of stone (petrophones) and metal (metalophones) are very numerous. *Yün-luo* consists of ten gongs hanging in three rows on a portable frame; the *pien-chung* chimes are made up of two rows of eight gongs each, like the petrophone *pian-tsing*. Various different recorder flutes known as *siao* and cross flutes called *ti-tsu* are common among the wind instruments. The small mouth-organ *feng-sheng* has twenty-four bamboo pipes and a common windchest made from a gourd. The *suo-na*, a slightly conical oboe, has a brass bell and seven fingerholes.

In the China of today Chinese instruments are played in free combination with European instruments, which are becoming more and more frequent in musical practice. This significant moment in the musical culture of China promises further development of a flourishing tradition.

In Japan, too, music was held to have cosmic significance. When a performer on the table zither *koto* had completed the third and last stage of his education he was granted the special privilege of tuning the lowest string of his instrument to the octave. The attention paid to the technique of touching the strings and drawing the notes from the instrument points to the influence of the Chinese tradition. The music of ancient Japan is only played by one of the four castes of musicians in Japan, the noblest of all, *gakunin*, from whose ranks came the members of the Mikado's orchestra known as *gagak*. The *genin* caste performs secular music, the *incabushi* are farmers, and the *geishas* are the lowest of all. Each of these castes has its own scales and its own musical instruments. Noble Japanese play the *koto*, an instrument of the zither type originating in China, with two strings loosely strung. The middle-class woman plays the thirteen-string *koto* while her husband plays a *shaku hachi* with five fingerholes; the pitch is regulated by the lower lip. The geisha uses a large plectrum to play her three-stringed *shamisen*, the body of which is covered with cat or dog skin. Every bride's dowry in Japan includes a *koto* or a *shamisen*. Other Japanese instruments are the three-stringed *biwa* and the four-stringed guitar *gekkin*, a variant of the Chinese *shuang-ch'in*. There are many instruments of the pipe type, one of which is a type of cross flute called *yokobue*.

# FURTHER INDIA AND THE INDIAN ARCHIPELAGO

The music of Further India and Indonesia has always attracted the interest of European listeners. If nowhere else, then certainly in Java the European feels the power of that "magic" all oriental peoples attribute to their music. There musical instruments are treated with that respect which sometimes borders on worship. They are not objects in daily use, but beings radiating spiritual strength and endowed with names like "the comforter", "moving to laughter", "rain of perfume" and the like.

Two scales are known in the islands of Java and Bali; the older of these divides the octave into five equal parts and is called *gamelan salendro*. The more recent, known as *gamelan pelog*, divides the octave into seven parts of two different intervals. In Siam and Burma the octave is divided into seven equal parts, each being somewhat smaller than our whole tone. These systems have influenced the instruments in the famous *gamelan* orchestra which rules the Mongol-Malayan world from Korea to the Sunda Islands. It is mainly composed of melodic percussion instruments. The *saron* is a slightly bent stand with bronze slabs; there are seven of these slabs in the *pelog* system and six in the *salendro* and the *kelenton* of Sumatra. They are made in four sizes an octave apart. The *gambong* consists of sixteen, eighteen or twenty flat, slightly rounded wooden slabs with a range of three and a half to four octaves, resembling the Japanese *mokkin*. In the *gender* there are twelve metal slabs suspended from a cord of cotton. The *bonnan* is made up of two rows of gongs, ten in the *salendro* system and fourteen in *pelog*. There are at least seven different types of gong in Java: *gon*, *kempul*, *bende*, *beri*, *kenon*, *kempyan* and *ketuk*. In addition there are other percussion instruments such as *drums*, *plate rattles* and so on. Among the wind instruments the *flutes* and *oboes* are worth mentioning; in the *salendro* system they have more fingerholes than in *pelog*. The *tjempelung* zither, which is struck with a stick, is a relative of the Chinese *shê*; it has from ten to fifteen strings. The only stringed instrument, the *rebab*, played with a flageolet technique, has a shallow heart-shaped body and a turned neck; it is probably of Arabic origin. The leader of the *gamelan* conducts the whole orchestra with this instrument in his hand.

H. J. Moser aptly described the pleasing sound of such a performance: "Listening to this orchestra, whose complicated 'score' begins softly, growing to a crescendo of joy and dying away like a slumbering stream, we hear above the central tones of the *gamelan* chimes, which are softer in Java and on Bali, a fairy-tale golden sound, the tiny trickle of sound made by the warbling flute over the pedal-point of the deeper lutes, kettle-drums, drum chimes and xylophones. Sweet, almost childish girls' voices lament, rising and falling or playfully twittering, often ending in artistic tremolos; slightly nasal male voices answer them, the gurgling of the *gamelan* brook changes into a cascade of sound; from time to time, deliberately rarely, the deepest bass gong rings out between the brief, commanding motifs. The most important thing, just as with the gipsies, is the way the players treat the fundamental melody, as if scoring it according to the position, technique and the rhythmic figural possibilities inherent in each instrument—what the Greeks used to call heterophony."

# INDIA

The musical tradition of India developed and was shaped long before the Christian era, but under quite different conditions and subject to quite different influences from those which obtained in Europe. And just as Indian painting is mostly two-dimensional and Indian literature mostly lyric, so Indian music is purely melodic. Ancient Indian texts distinguish altogether nine *ragas*, or flavours determining the quality and character of a musical composition; they are: love, heroism, ugliness, anger, merriment, horror, pity, calm and wonder. The tradition of playing together on stringed, wind and percussion instruments has much in common with Perso-Arabic music, particularly in the north, where the impact of Persian culture in the wake of the Muslims in the tenth century brought about a refinement of music and the perfection of musical theory. Just as in the sphere of Perso-Arabic culture, many stories were current in India relating the remarkable virtuosity of performers on musical instruments and the generosity they met with at the Princes' courts.

North and south differ both in their system of tones and in the character of their music. Instrumental music is more highly developed in the north; the south remained relatively free from the influence of Islam, and therefore secular elements did not assume such importance as in the north. Harmony is not known in Indian music, which developed entirely along the lines of a single melody for one voice, accompanied by strumming on a stringed instrument reminiscent of the European hurdy-gurdy and bagpipes. Even so the treasury of Indian instruments is rich in the extreme. Indian painters long ago bore eloquent witness to this, particularly in garden wedding scenes, where whole swarms of long-necked lutes accompanied by eight-stringed harps and gay rows of wind and percussion instruments gave the impression of something far away and gentle in tone. And this is indeed the impression we get when listening to Indian music; it is perhaps partly due to the soft echo the performers draw from their instruments, equipped with strings which sound sympathetically as well as with bowed strings.

The fundamental unit is not the orchestra, which is rare in Indian music, but small ensembles made up usually of a few string and percussion instruments, or occasionally wind instruments, to accompany a singer.

Every instrument in India has several variants. One of the most widely played stringed instruments in northern India is the *sitar*, which is made in almost all the bigger towns. In Bengal a kind of *sitar* known as the *surbahar* is played, plucked by the fingers as well as a plectrum. The well-known *tamburi* is used throughout India to accompany both songs and instrumental music. In Nearer India the *vína* is particularly liked because of its ancient provenance; it is an instrument of the guitar type with seven wire strings. The "crocodile zither" of Further India, which is really a pipe zither, has three strings and eleven bridges. The *dilruba*, which could be translated as the "stealer of hearts", with its four wire strings and fifteen sympathetic strings, is a kind of knee-violin, often played together with its relative the *sarangi*, a four-stringed *bajader* instrument equipped with eleven sympathetic strings in Thakur and fourteen in Day. Closely related to this instrument are the two-stringed *ravanastron* of the mendicant friars and the stringed *sarinda*. The wind instruments include various flutes and whistles and a kind of recorder with seven finger-holes; there is also a double *tumeri*, used by snake charmers, with a gourd wind-chamber. The *bansari* is one of the numerous variants of the flute. As well as the shell trumpet known as the *sankha* there are many different trombones, trumpets, percussion instruments, drum and tuned clappers played in India.

## INSTRUMENTS OF THE PERSO-ARABIC CULTURE

The cradle of the Perso-Arabic culture, which came into being under Perso-Greek influence, lies in Mesopotamia. In 822 the famous Persian musician Zirjab moved from Bagdad to Andalusia, and so oriental music found its way to southern Europe. After the fall of Moorish Spain the Arabs were pushed back into their present home in Tunisia and Algeria, where they have retained their musical culture relatively untouched up to the present time. The Moors are said to have lost Granada and therefore Spain because they were mad about music and did not bother about the enemy's attack. One of the songs handed down from generation to generation in North West Africa and commonly referred to as Andalusian lists what is needed to make up a festive occasion: *tar*, *ūd*, *rabab*, a goblet of wine, a friend, and the absence of a hated observer.

The European, although he admires the beauty of the works of art of the countries of the East, their carpets, their hand-wrought metals, their architecture, their feeling for colour and line, cannot understand their music. Perso-Arabic music subjects musical instruments to strict rules and creates systems out of the tonal relations between the instruments; the older theory divides the octave into seventeen short intervals, the more modern school into twenty-four. This means that the Oriental is singing and playing in quarter-tones, which sound false to the European ear. In the domain of the Koran vocal music is supreme, as we see from the round songs of the dervishes, accompanied by hand-clappers, and the hourly calling of the muezzin from the minarets of the mosques. Even so the number of musical instruments is quite surprising. These instruments, which in the Middle Ages played such an important role in the formation of European instruments, are inseparably linked with every phenomenon of oriental life. Ambros mentions eighteen kinds of bells, jingles and rattles; there are as many as thirty-two variants of the lute, twenty-eight of the recorder, and twenty-two kinds of oboe. The Oriental finds the strongest impulse towards musical expression of his emotions in nature: percussion instruments imitate the rhythm of camels on the march and the gallop of horses; the stringed and wind instruments with their trills and their coloratura passages wind round this rhythm like audible arabesques.

The most important and the most widely-spread instrument is the *ūd* (*al-'ūd*), which came to Europe in the twelfth century during the Crusades, and from whose name arose the words *lûte*, *laute*, *loutna*, *lute*. It has four pairs of strings; the *ūd* developed by Zirjab had five pairs. A strummed instrument which resembles the lute, recalling ancient Egyptian instruments, is the *tunbūr*; it has a long and four to eight strings. A monochord instrument used by the theoreticians of old, whose name *g nūn* can still be heard in the Greek word "canon" (rule), was something like our zither. The Bedouins also play stringed instruments: the *kam nja* and the *rabāb*, which are held on the knee; during the Middle Ages they found their way among European instruments in the form of the *rebec*. The *murabba* is a cross between the drum and the violin; it has the neck of a violin, one string, and a four-sided body with skin stretched over both sides. Of the wind instruments the double reed *zamr* is remarkable for its shrill sound. The most widespread flute is the *nāy*, made of bamboo cane with seven fingerholes. In the double flute *arghūl* a longer pipe without fingerholes is always joined to a shorter pipe which has fingerholes like those of bagpipes. The *habbaba*, a beaked flute, is very popular, as is the *nafir* trumpet and—as throughout the East—a large number of percussion instruments. A singer does not always require an instrumental accompaniment, but he cannot do without a rhythmical percussion instrument. These are kettle-drums of various sizes, *tabl*, the tambourine *tār*, the enamelled kettle-drum *nagara*, covered with skin and beaten with two drumsticks and finally the *darabukka*, a small hand drum used by dancing girls; it is shaped like a pitcher with tanned leather over the opening.

THE SUMERIANS AND BABYLONIANS • EGYPT •

THE GREEKS AND ROMANS

# THE SUMERIANS AND BABYLONIANS

We shall never know what music was like at the dawn of the history of the ancient peoples. The most noteworthy musical relic—and perhaps the most ancient depiction of musical instruments in existence—is a fragment of a lapis lazuli vase found during excavation of a south Babylonian temple in Bismya. It dates from the third or maybe even the fourth millennium B.C. when the Sumerians still ruled the region round the Tigris and the Euphrates. The first of the musicians is shown playing a *harp* which resembles the arched harp used in Burma and Africa; the next has a similar instrument with a triangular soundbox and long tassels like Assyrian harps later on. The most surprising thing about these instruments is their efficient construction, pointing to long development. From the number of the strings—seven on the first instrument and five on the second—we can conclude that a five-note scale was already in use at this time. As well as these lyre-like harps, which were held slanting and pressed against the body, *frame drums*, always played by women, were also used during court ceremonies. Sometimes these drums reached tremendous size, as much as five feet; there are still drums to be found hanging in Japanese and Chinese temples with their skins nailed in the same way as the Sumerian-Babylonian drums. A musical instrument in the real sense of the word was the eleven-string *lyre* with a bull on the edge of the body. That is how it is depicted in a relief from the Sumerian royal palace in Tello. It is worth noting that the Georgians in the Caucasus not so very long ago still played a harp with two horses and a bull carved in a circle. Another instrument was the *lute* with a small body and a long narrow neck, seen in the hand of a shepherd with his dog on a clay fragment from the middle or the end of the third millennium.

In the meagre accounts of music in ancient Babylon we are surprised by the poem on Ishtar's journey to hell, with its remarkable similarity to the later Greek myth of Orpheus. We have no information about music or instruments under the Middle Kingdom. Not until the first millennium, when Syrian and Hittite influences became apparent, do we find musical instruments on reliefs once more: a short *trumpet*, a small *lyre*, a *lute* with two strings and a long neck, a double *oboe* and *cymbals*. Assyrian music reached its highest point in the centuries preceding our era. Musicians occupied a privileged position and were placed above the officials, immediately below the gods and the king. The voices of the gods were compared to the sounds of musical instruments. Ishtar had a voice like a sweet flute, while the god of the winds, Ramman, was like an oboe. In the Chaldee Empire, which followed the rule of the Assyrians, the number of musical instruments was so great that the well-known passage in the Book of Daniel, calling upon the people to worship the golden image, enumerates a whole collection of instruments.

# EGYPT

The earliest reports about Egypt go as far back as the beginning or even the end of the fourth millennium before Christ; reliefs dating from the fourth dynasty depict musical instruments which have already reached a high stage of development. Musicians are often shown playing in groups, with *long flutes* and *arched harps*, while singers beat time by clapping their hands. The old Kingdom was also acquainted with *frame drums* and wind instruments of the *clarinet* type. The paintings in a tomb near Beni Hassan prove that at the beginning of the second millennium Syrian nomads brought the *lyre* to Egypt. About the year 1500 B.C., the kings of the eighteenth dynasty conquered Asia Minor, and the slaves who wended their way to the Egyptian court, taking their musical instruments with them, considerably influenced the instruments of Egypt. Of the original Egyptian instruments the *harp* was the chief one to survive; the flute was surperseded by its shriller counterpart, the Syrian *double clarinet*, which still lives among the Egyptian *fellahin* today in the slightly different form of the *argul*. As well as the arched harp we get the Asiatic *angular harp*, lutes and trumpets. The renown of the ancient Egyptian harp was too deep-rooted for it to disappear altogether, and so at least the number of strings was increased and the body made bigger. These new wind and stringed instruments were joined by *bent flutes* during the period of the Serap cult; these flutes also probably came from Asia, for the Greeks considered them a Phrygian invention. Finally we find *hand drums* shaped like barrels, used to accentuate the rhythm.

In the temple music of Egypt *clappers* and *rattles* were used as well as harps; but the most important instrument was the *sistrum*, a kind of rattle which served a purpose similar to that of the Catholic sacrament bell. This instrument, which belonged to the cult of Isis, then continues right through ancient times, extending its influence to all the lands round the Mediterranean sea and leaving traces not only in Abyssinia but as far away as the Caucasus. Egyptian music played outside the temples remained Syrian in character right to the end of its independent existence and not even the penetration of Greek and Roman culture during the last three centuries B.C. could change this Asiatic influence.

During Roman times Alexandria was the centre of Egyptian musical culture, where the Egyptian and Syrian traditions were joined by that of Greece. An Egyptian terracotta figure of a musician wearing a Syrian cap and playing pan-pipes is preserved in the Museum in Berlin. There is a bag attached to the instrument, with a pipe leading from it to the mouth of a boy, who is blowing up the bag. This arrangement is a transition stage between the bagpipes and the organ with a bag known in Asia Minor. A real revolution in the development of the organ occurred in the third century B.C. when the engineer Ktesibios perfected wind-action and set up the first *hydraulis* in Alexandria.

# THE GREEKS AND ROMANS

While the great arts of the Greek people were architecture and sculpture, which served European art as a model even as late as the Carlovingian period, Greek music was exclusively imported. Therefore the musical instruments of the ancient world are only a part of the cultural heritage of those great peoples of Asia who have kept alive the tradition of these instruments right up to the present day. But although no instrument had its origin on Greek soil, Greek music itself was admired both for its standing and for the degree to which it was cultivated, for music played a part in every phase of Greek life. Music was an important element in the education of the young, in the ceremonies of the cults, in military life and in the private life of individuals and in social gatherings. Philosophers meditated on its ethical significance and historians studied its past.

In spite of all this studious attention, more physiological and ethical than aesthetical, the *harp* held by the Phaeacian singer Demodokos and the seven-stringed *cithara* played by Achilles in his tent show the Greeks' liking for joyful and inspiring music. The cithara belongs to the noblest type of instruments of the lyre family, and played an outstanding role in Greek music. There were originally seven gut strings stretched over the rectangular flat soundbox, from which two stretched out, joined by a cross-bar; later on the number of strings was raised to eleven. The origin of the cithara must be sought in the instruments of the lyre type played in Egypt and Syria; the first historical mention of this instrument is in an ode by Terpandros, 675 B.C. Paintings on vases show two distinct types of this instrument: one was held close to the body with the help of a telamon belt for carrying. The later type was held upright, as depicted in the classical representations of Apollo, Orpheus, Amphion; the strings were struck with a plectrum. The second most characteristic stringed instrument of Greece, the *lyre*, which gave its name to the lyric writers of the island of Lesbos, came from Thrace. The body was formed by a tortoise shell with a piece of skin as a soundboard, and two animal's horns jutted out, joined by a cross-bar. It was easier to make and to play a lyre than a cithara, and so the former was the instrument used in the home, for teaching and for amusement. *Magadis* was the name given to two different types of instrument, one stringed and one wind instrument. The stringed *magadis* was of Lydian origin, and was already known to Anacreon; it had a triangular soundbox with twenty strings, giving the ten fundamental notes and their respective octaves; the fundamental notes were struck by the left hand, the octaves by the right, without using a plectrum. This type of *magadis* was formerly considered to be the *pektis* invented by Sappho, but more recent authorities consider it merely related.

The wind *magadis* was perhaps a variety of the *aulos*; documents have been preserved testifying to both types of *magadis* being played together. The most important wind instrument was the *aulos*. Legend has it that the mythical singer Olympus brought this instrument from Phrygia to Greece. The first virtuoso was Sakadas from Argos, who in 586 B.C. won the prize at the Delphic Games for an instrumental nome on Apollo's fight with the dragon Python.

Because of its shrill tone this instrument was considered barbaric and theorists excluded it from use in education as harmful to the soul. Originally three fingerholes were enough to produce the tones of the tetrachord; later an increased number of holes made it possible to play octaves and twelfths. When playing the *aulos* at concerts musicians wore broad collars across their mouths, known as *phorbeia* (halters), to prevent the air from escaping and at the same time to hide grimaces made when blowing hard. A double pipe was usually played, the Greek name of which is in the plural, *auloi*. The pipes were fitted with a double reed and were of slightly different length; this doubling increased the volume of the sound and could be used for heterophony. The right pipe played the melody and the left accompanied it on a higher note. They were never made of metal, but in Athens and Pompeii *auloi* have been preserved which have a kind of stop arrangement which made a wider range of tones possible. Since *auloi* were used in the orgiastic cult in Hellenistic Rome the Church condemned them and in the fifth century A.D. they disappeared within the bounds of Christendom.

The *syrinx*, or pan-pipes, consisting of a row of reed pipes of various lengths, was an instrument played by the people, as was the *keras*, an animal's horn. The metal military trumpet was called *salpinx*. Among the many rattling and percussion instruments were the *tympanon*, a hand drum, and a kind of clapper on the foot, known as *scabellum*; it was a loose wooden sole on the sandal of the leader of the chorus, and served to beat time more emphatically. The *cymbal* recalls the one-handed flute with a drum; it was a bowl beaten against another metal disc with the help of a flexible metal stick, while the other hand played a wind instrument.

When the Romans conquered Greece half-way through the second century B.C. they became the immediate successors to the culture of Alexandria. The Romans no longer believed in the educational powers of music and therefore paid much less attention to it than the Greeks. The musical ethicism of Plato was succeeded by the formalism of Epicurus, which was set out by Cicero. He declared that music could not be of real service to man, since it only brought him childish enjoyment which is worthless since it does not point the way to spiritual happiness. It is from this angle that we must judge all that Rome could do to further the development of musical instruments. The music of imperial Rome, already bearing the signs of decadence, was ruled by Greek musicians and Greek musical instruments, already falling victim to the cult megalomania. Martianus Capella, for instance, writes that lyres were as big as litters, while orchestras had reached such a size that Seneca saw more performers than listeners in the theatre.

The music of the Romans differs from that of the Greeks by the preponderance of instrumental music. Wherever music was played in Rome we find in the forefront the *tibia*, a single reed pipe probably of Etruscan origin. The *tibia* was doubled like the *aulos*; the right pipe was shorter, with a higher tone, and the left longer, with a lower tone. Later on, under the influence of Greek music, the *tibia* was superseded by the *aulos*. The most important group of instruments were the brasses, which played an important part in the highly developed military life of Rome, and it was precisely in military music that the Romans surpassed the music of Greece. The chief signal instrument of the infantry was the *tuba*, a straight trumpet with a conical bore and a funnel-shaped bell; it was the counterpart of the Greek *salpinx.* The cavalry had a hooked trumpet called the *littus*; the *buccina* was a signal horn made almost in a circle. A Celtic invention, a trumpet with the tube turned up at right-angles and ending in a fantastic dragon's head, was known as the *karnyx.* It is interesting to note that this form was revived at the beginning of the nineteenth century in France in the bass horn, which developed from the bass serpent. Most of these instruments served to accompany merry marching in triumphal parades.

Stringed instruments were much rarer among the Romans. They learned to play the cithara from the Greeks. We learn from Dionysus Halikarnas that in ancient liturgical rites a seven-stringed lyre known as the *barbita* was played, as well as the *tibia.* The only instrument which the Romans helped to perfect was the *hydraulis*, the organ, in which (unlike the pneumatic organ) the pressure of air was regulated by a column of water in the windchest. The *hydraulis* soon became indispensable in Roman musical life and by the time of the fall of the Roman Empire it was the most important instrument. It appeared at the court of Emperor Nero and in the circus as well, where it accompanied the fights of the gladiators along with the other wind instruments, as can be seen on the mosaic in a Roman villa in Tripolis. While the *hydraulis* was slowly falling into oblivion in the west, in the east of the Roman Empire its further development was secure. The last mention of the *hydraulis* comes from Leo Magister in his poem praising the baths of Byzantium. And then its place was taken for good by the pneumatic organ.

THE MIDDLE AGES • THE RENAISSANCE • BAROQUE

ROMANTICISM • THE MODERN ORCHESTRA

# THE MIDDLE AGES

From the very start, Christianity had taken its stand in favour of vocal music and sharply opposed to instrumental music. This meant bringing the natural development of musical instruments to a complete standstill, and in many cases the instruments degenerated to mere signals. For centuries the organ was held to be an instrument of luxury from the court of the emperors of the Eastern Roman Empire, and the devil's voice was said to sound in the pipes of the organ. And when at last the organ found its way into the churches it was used to accompany vocal and not instrumental music. The instruments of antiquity were seen only in the hands of light women and clowns. On the other hand all the instruments of the Old Testament (and especially the harp of David) were regarded with exceptional respect, even if nobody had ever seen them. The illuminations in a Cambridge manuscript contrast those instruments permitted by the Church and those condemned; they even contrast God's musicians and the Devil's music-makers, who like Satan's sacristans were compared to wild beasts. Among the instruments permitted we find the *harp*, *organ*, *zink* or *cornet* and *chimes*, while the *fiddle*, *horn*, *drum* and *rattle* were used to accompany the bear-dances and tumblers.

Nevertheless a number of instruments were actually used in musical practice, as we can see from mediaeval painting and sculpture where the social function of these instruments is also portrayed. Many of them were used to accompany folk songs and dances, secular songs, and polyphonic vocal music. Hardly any musical instruments have actually survived, however. The oldest exhibits in the big museums of musical instruments date mainly from the sixteenth century. Thus there is a gap of ten or eleven centuries in our knowledge of the development of musical instruments, from the discoveries of instruments from the antique world to these late mediaeval relics. In the history of music, too, the time of the migration of the peoples is one of the least clear. The illuminated manuscripts which are almost the only source we have for information on musical instruments are not older than the ninth century: that is to say, they come after a great important stage of development in European musical instruments had already been completed. This stage covered the first absorption of types of instruments brought from the east: the first revival of antique instruments like the *aulos*, *cithara*, *hydraulis* etc., even if only schematic and lifeless. The only relic of the time of the migration of the peoples is the Avaric *double pipe* excavated near Jánoshida in Hungary in 1933; it is a clear proof of the influence of the Orient on European instruments in the early Middle Ages. Even if the supposition that this pipe (which is really nothing but a double clarinet) is of Slav origin should prove to be correct, it still remains clear witness to the fact that many of the mediaeval illustrations showing a double pipe considered up to the present to be a double flute or antiquated *aulos* in fact portrayed a type of double clarinet introduced from the Orient.

It can be said that no instrument of mediaeval Europe was native, but that they were all imported from Asia. The migration did not take place during any one clearly defined period, but gradually, at various intervals of time and by various routes, of which the most important led through Byzantium and North Africa. Up to the ninth century the illustrations we know are influenced by classical culture, and so the instruments shown are like echoes of those of Greece and Rome, as we can see in the Bible of Charles the Bald. Not even the Utrecht psalter, which is the first serious record of instruments, succeeded in freeing itself entirely from the influence of classical antiquity; the organ it depicts is still really a hydraulic organ, and even the *crot* is not very far removed from the *cithara*. Only the fiddle showed signs of the first timid steps towards the dramatic development which was to culminate in Stradivarius. Among the wind instruments of the early Middle Ages, besides the large military *horns* and the elegantly carved *oliphants* of ivory, we find small *horns with fingerholes*, the earliest form of the family of *zinks* which became so widely known later. Of the flutes the *pan-pipes* were in existence, along with the double pipe we have already mentioned.

The age of chivalry, with its troubadours and minnesingers, testifies to flourishing instrumental music. The Provençal jongleur of the thirteenth century was required to possess the following accomplishments: "Player, you must be acquainted with nine instruments, the fiddle, the bagpipes, the pipe, the harp, the hurdy-gurdy, the jig, the ten string (decachordum) the psaltery and the crot. If you learn them all well, you can meet all demands. Let the lyre also sound and the bells tinkle." The Zbraslav chronicle contains interesting information about Czech instruments; their wealth and variety is depicted in the verses written by the chronicler Petr Žitavský describing the coronation of King Wenceslas II in Prague in 1297. The mediaeval theorist Johannes de Grocheo wrote that stringed instruments occupied first place, and their preponderance is also clear from the list in a Latin-Czech dictionary of the sixties of the fourteenth century, which quotes almost all the instruments of the time.

In the fourteenth century an event occurred which assumed tremendous importance for the further development of instrumental music. Wandering musicians, the descendants of those clowns to whom Byzantium had denied human rights, were no longer counted among the groups of wandering fire and knife swallowers and were allowed to form their own musicians' guilds. Among the new responsibilities of these musicians was that of playing a chorale when the hours were called and when a fire alarm was proclaimed from the church steeples. On these occasions they played *zinks* and *trombones*, but were not allowed to play the *trumpet*, the privilege of the knights. And so from the utilitarian music of the town-criers and horn-blowers there grew the music which was to influence even our own time.

## THE RENAISSANCE

The instrumental style which was coming more and more to the fore developed instrumental principles along quite different lines from those encouraged by vocal music. Whereas in the early Middle Ages instrumental technique had to be considered as merely taking over vocal forms, and musical instruments served primarily as aids to vocal performance, instrumental style later forced both vocal music and the intruments themselves to adapt themselves to its requirements, until it reached its peak in the sixteenth century, when Giovanni Gabrieli in Venice wrote which instruments were to play each part in his scores. The generally accepted view that instruments did not always develop directly but were discovered and invented over and over again is also true of the Renaissance, and all the more so because instrumental music, which was becoming more and more important, was calling out for instruments. The growing interest in colour, in contrast and blend of timbres, had a far-reaching influence on the construction of musical instruments, the great variety of which has never been equalled before or since. The visitor to museum collections of instruments comes to the interesting conclusion that the Renaissance knew more different kinds of musical instruments than our own day. This wealth as well as the ever-increasing importance of musical instruments is reflected in contemporary theoretical works which give us some idea of what the instruments looked like at that time. And here it is very noticeable that compared with the earlier preponderance of stringed instruments, the Renaissance provided a riot of varied wind instruments. Most of them were wooden instruments, unlike earlier periods, when wind instruments for the most part were brass winds (trumpets, trombones) and then horns (horns with fingerholes, oliphants) and only a few instruments of the flute and reed type (flutes, shawms).

The desire to achieve deeper tones and solve the technical problem of playing by arranging the channel in as small a space as possible led to the development of wooden wind instruments of unusual design, such as the *sorduns*, in which the channel bent two or even three times in the body, and the *rankets*, which had a cylindrical body inside which there were nine channels. The *tartoelts* were a variety of ranket, made of bronze cast in the shape of a dragon, painted red and gold; the dragon's mouth with its movable tongues formed the bell and the twisted, sharply narrowing tail supported the bent tube with the mouthpiece. The ever-growing emphasis on the need for deep tones led to the construction of extraordinarily large instruments; the *double bass pommer* reached a length of 100 inches. Next to *recorders* the most popular instruments were the *zinks*, which were something in between the wood-wind instruments (with which they shared the same material and construction—wood and a system of fingerholes) and the brasses (to which they belonged by reason of a common way of producing their tones—through a mouthpiece). The mouthpiece was held firmly between the lips; this was the way instruments were held in ancient times, before mouthpieces had been devised and when the tube itself was simply thrust into the mouth. The zinks became so widely known because the strict guild rules permitted the playing of trumpets only by certain privileged musicians. But as soon as the trumpet became more widely used and the dignity of the town pipe-bands degenerated, the glory of the zinks faded too, after lasting until the thirties of the nineteenth century.

Among the stringed instruments, the *lute* was generally known as early as the thirteenth and fourteenth centuries, but the playing and making of lutes reached its highest glory in the sixteenth century. Like all the instruments of the Renaissance, the lute developed into a whole family covering all the tone ranges, from the little octave lute to the archlute. About 1500 the *viola da gamba* made its appearance as the bass form of the old descant *fiddle*, and soon became the greatest family of seven members ranging from the descant *viola da gamba* to the double bass. Towards the end of the sixteenth century the *viola da braccio* gave rise to the highest of the stringed instruments, the *violin*, but its real fame was yet to come. The composers of the sixteenth century served to extend the renown of the violin and to perfect this most important instrument of all time when they realised its lovely sound and its particular suitability for orchestral performance. Thanks to them masterly instruments were born as early as the sixteenth century in the workshops of Duiffopruggar in Lyons and Gaspar da Salo in Brescia, in the course of fifty to sixty years.

During the Renaissance we see for the first time stringed instruments equipped with a keyboard; the most important is the *clavichord*, which developed out of the mediaeval monochord, or *manicordium*, to which its name was distorted. In due time this instrument was given more than one string; thus it was no longer a one-stringed instrument, and changed its name from monochord to helicon. In the fourteenth century the organ keyboard was taken over for this many-stringed instrument; the keys of the clavichord are the direct descendant of the bridges of the monochord. As soon as they were shaped like rods and made of metal, they were given the shape of little tongues which not only struck the strings but also stopped them. In the course of time this double function of the tangents, as they were called, changed in the case of the "free" clavichord, as the number of keys grew much larger than in the old "bound" clavichord, into a single function, that of sounding the strings alone. The *harpsichord* grew up about the same time as the clavichord, or slightly later; in the harpsichord the tangent mechanism was replaced by ravens' quills or leather tongues which plucked the strings. And as the lute had been given drone strings to increase the volume of its tone, so about 1600 the instrument maker Johannes Rueckers of Antwerp provided the harpsichord with double gut and wire strings. The harpsichord began to die out at the end of the eighteenth century, but it is always being brought to life again just when it has died a natural death.

The chronicler P. Benoit, writing of the emissaries sent by Ladislav Pohrobek (Posthumous) to the court of the French King Charles VII to ask for the hand of Princess Madeleine, in 1457, says that there were big *kettledrums* in their following. This, the most important membrane instrument in the European orchestra, came from the Middle East during the Crusades and right up to the time of the eighteenth century was always carried with the trumpets. Drums of other kinds had also been known from the earliest times, and later on two types became constant: the *military drum*, with a high wooden frame and a deep thundering sound, and the small *tabor drum* with a narrow frame and taut spun strings fitted beneath the skin, which gave the clear note of this drum a rattling timbre. The *tambourine* was also introduced to Europe by means of the Arabs. During the centuries which followed it never changed its original shape—a narrow frame fitted with rattling discs and covered with skin on one side only.

# BAROQUE

When towards the end of the sixteenth century the number of members of a family of instruments reached the eccentric figure of five or even seven a radical change took place in music, round about the year 1600. The polyphonic style began to lose importance and a new style, monody, took its place; in the descant the bass, known as the *basso continuo* or thorough bass, became the most important element. In contrast to the principle by which Renaissance music used the numerous members of each family of instruments to create a homogeneous group of the same timbre, in agreement with polyphonic practice, the thorough bass style introduced a leading melody in one of the parts.

When we consider the short time the new style required to come to the fore by changing the old instruments, we realise that the baroque orchestra developed almost unobserved from the vast reserves of Renaissance instruments.

During the course of the seventeenth century the string orchestra led by the violins became the basic grouping in Italy; it was always accompanied by the instruments required to form the thorough bass—in ecclesiastical music the *organ*, in secular music the *harpsichord*; in order to attain greater volume either several harpsichords were used, or a single instrument was supplemented by a harp, lutes (particularly the *theorbo* and *chitarrone*) and *gambas*. The wind instruments were not contrasted with the stringed instruments in the orchestra, but played obbligato passages as solo instruments. Up to this time the range of the wind instruments did not exceed the notes produced by the fingerholes, but monody called for a wider range in order to express sudden and violent contrasts. Many instruments were found unsuitable for the new style of music, not only because of their small compass but also because they had not the dynamic flexibility required. The first to go were the wind instruments fitted with a wind cap, for they were incapable of dynamic, flexible interpretation and could not be "overblown" into a higher octave. The mysterious *schryari* went too, and so did the *wind-cap shawms* (Ger.: *Rauschpfeife*); they had a dull, colourless sound because of the breadth of the reed tube, and so were not suitable for compositions which were growing more and more exacting. *Cromornes* existed up to the middle of the eighteenth century in France, because they changed into a new type of instrument with a body in two parts, covered in black leather, and with a bassoon crook. Under the name *tournebout* they played an important role in France in the second half of the seventeenth century, when five of them were played in the Grande Ecurie.

Of the remaining instruments the *pommers*, those awkward monsters, gave way more and more to the *bassoon*, until in the eighteenth century writers on music do not even know them. *Sorduns*, which could barely produce more than a mezzopiano note even when blown very hard, grew out of date towards the end of the seventeenth century, and were no longer played. The throaty organ stop mentioned by Praetorius kept their name alive a little while longer. The *rankets*, built on the same principle, died out during the second half of the seventeenth century. Only three of the wood-wind instruments survived; the *shawm* which developed along a complicated road into the *oboe*; the *bassoon*; and finally the *transverse flute*.

The flutes in the scores of Scarlatti, Bach and Handel are still recorders, not transverse flutes. The latter was one of those rare wind instruments which only existed in three sizes during the Renaissance. Now it became the most distinctive solo instrument of the eighteenth century.

The recorder held its own until the middle of the eighteenth century when it was superseded by the transverse flute: thereafter it degenerated on the one hand into the most primitive form of folk instrument (the *chakan* and *fuyara*) and on the other hand to a mere signal instrument (signal whistles).

Of the brasses the trumpets and trombones were taken over unchanged for the most part. The only newcomer was the "glorious pompous horn", as Mattheson in his book "Das neueröffnete Orchester" calls the instrument which developed from the hunting horn by lengthening the reed tube and decreasing the breadth of the body.

The desire to enhance the individual character of each musical instrument and to provide opportunities for solo playing, a development which was also made possible by the perfection of the art of instrument making, had already led, a century earlier, to a differentiation between chamber and orchestral effect. New instrumental forms were constantly appearing and becoming stabilised, calling for changes in the construction of individual instruments as well as in the composition of the orchestra. The stringed instruments were supplemented by the wind instruments, divided into wood-winds and brasses, which completely ousted the plucked instruments. Whereas up to this time the wind instruments had been considered most important, the new age chose to give the stringed instruments the leading role. It suffices to mention, in illustration, that out of twenty-two instruments quoted in a list of the seventeenth century, eighteen are stringed instruments, two plucked and one wind. Johann Sebastian Bach, who used to lend instruments to music-lovers for a few months at a time in return for a fee, left seventeen instruments at his death; it is interesting to note that there was not a single wind instrument among them. The importance of the strings was also apparent in the creation of new types. From the *viola da gamba* and the *lira da gamba* the *viola bastarda* was born; at the beginning of the seventeenth century this instrument was given sympathetic strings, only to discard them again in the second half of the century. A combination of sympathetic strings with a plucking technique was tried in the *viola di bordone*, or *barytone*, as it was called. The happiest solution to the problems of constructing sympathetically vibrating strings resulted in the transformation of the *viola da braccio* into the *viola d'amore* which became one of the most popular stringed instruments of the eighteenth century. The *violoncello* began to come into its own towards the end of the seventeenth century by the side of the *viola da gamba* when Antonio Stradivarius established its classic shape. Until then the *viola da gamba* had been an instrument both for domestic music-making and for solo performance, and even in the history of improvisation it had played an important role.

Side by side with the accepted types of stringed instruments developed various related types which had not enough vitality to survive for long. Thanks to J. S. Bach a five-stringed *viola pomposa* was constructed in Germany—*quintons*, a kind of five-stringed gamba, were invented in France. The *basso di camera* had the same number of strings, or one more; half way through the eighteenth century a *descant viola* called the *pardessus de viole* was invented. But the most important addition must be considered the piano. This invention was really inspired by the dynamic advantages of the *dulcimer* and the brilliant playing of the virtuoso Pantaleon Hebenstreit on a dulcimer he had perfected himself and called the *pantaleon*. It happened in 1709, when the Paduan Bartolomeo Cristofori, keeper of the collections of musical instruments in Florence, replaced the old tangents by mechanical hammers with wooden butts covered with leather. The first real maker of hammer pianos was the Freiburg instrument maker Gottfried Silbermann; his instrument was called a *fortepiano*, for it was possible to play both *piano* and *forte* on it. From Silbermann the line of development then goes straight to John Broadwood, who constructed the present English action in England in 1780. Silbermann's pupil Georg Andreas Stein no longer fastened the hammers to a special rail but to each of the key levers, thus returning in fact to the keys and mechanism of the clavichord and harpsichord. When his son-in-law, Andreas Streicher, perfected this mechanism and applied it to the instruments made in his Vienna workshop, the system became known as the Viennese action.

## ROMANTICISM

While music had a universal character in the eighteenth century, the nineteenth century was the era of national movements in music. After the French Revolution the aristocratic little salons of the nobility were replaced by the concert halls of the rising bourgeoisie. The era of the travelling virtuoso began, often figures wrapped in legend. The Genoan Niccolo Paganini performed such acrobatics with his violin that people thought he was a charlatan. Franz Liszt, who displayed unheard-of audacity and strength of attack at the keyboard, provoked his audiences to storms of admiration such as can hardly be imagined nowadays. The demands made on musical instruments both from a technical point of view and that of sound were constantly increasing. And so violins made by Antonio Stradivarius and Guarneri del Gesù, with their clear tones, were preferred to those made by Jacob Stainer, with highly arched soundbox and a weak flute-like timbre. The mechanism of the hammer piano, which still sounded dull and rather weak, was always being improved. In 1823 Erard exhibited his double escapement in Paris. At the same time Streicher constructed a hammer mechanism which struck the strings from above; this gave rise to the mechanism of the *pianina* constructed by the Englishman Robert Wornum in 1826. Czech instrument makers also have their share of the credit for improvements in the mechanism of the piano as early as the beginning of the nineteenth century. The names of the Prague makers of Empire grand pianos and *upright pianos* such as Jakub Weimes, Leopold Sauer, Michal Weiss, Martin Kratochvíl of Jindřichův Hradec, and Antonín Hief of Hradec Králové are among the finest of the time. The urge to achieve ever better and more powerful sound effects is also apparent in the endless additions made to the instruments of the orchestra, culminating in the orchestra of Hector Berlioz.

The advance of industry brought with it the improvement of manufacturing technique in the making of musical instruments as well. Factory production gradually pushed the small workshops out. The increasing popularity of brass instruments led to the formation of popular bands often modelled on military bands in composition and technique. It was Carl Maria von Weber who revealed the true beauty and romantic value of wind instruments, in his *Freischütz*; Berlioz added to them and provided a constant third player for the wood-winds: the *piccolo* for the flutes, the *English horn* for the oboes, the *bass clarinet* for the clarinets and the *double bassoon* for the bassoons. About 1850 Adolf Sax created the *saxophone* and the *tuba* in Paris, for Wagner's *Ring des Nibelungen*. This constant effort to achieve new sound effects is somewhat reminiscent of the sixteenth century, but now the aim is not polyphonic contrast and clarity, but greater emotional effect. This demand for expressive, emotional music provided the growing orchestra with new instruments and multiplied them in various registers. Clarinets were made in eight sizes and saxophones in five. In order to meet the demands of the composer, who now fixed the orchestration of his work down to the smallest detail, the wind instruments in particular had to undergo fundamental changes. The *trumpet*, for instance, previously simple or inventive, was fitted with stops like the wood-winds by Weidinger of Vienna in 1801; twelve years later Blühmel and Stölzel invented the modern *valve trumpet*, which became the main descant instrument among the brasses. The *French horn* underwent a similar development. The key mechanism of the wood-wind instruments was improved and the number of keys considerably increased. After many attempts French instrument makers produced a system of stops for the oboe, about 1840, using ring-keys. Boehm's system was introduced for flutes and clarinets. Even the harp, which Berlioz took over as an almost permanent member of the orchestra, became chromatic after having been diatonic for thousands of years, and the kettle-drum, where tuning had always been a matter of great difficulty, was made easily tunable by means of pedals.

The sentimental dreaming of the ordinary man called for the opportunity to express his feelings freely even during the common round of life: and so pianos were built combined with cupboards, desks and sewing tables. Then the ordinary man wanted to have a musical instrument with him even when he went for a walk; ingenious violins, flutes, clarinets and guitars shaped like walking-sticks are no rarity in any museum collection. This was the age with the greatest number of idiophones, which acted on the nerves of the listeners by means of their combinations of harmonics. As well as the *nail violin* or the *nail harmonica* invented by Johann Wilde in the eighteenth century, the *glass harmonica* was very popular; Mozart himself wrote for this instrument, and Jan Ladislav Dusík was a virtuoso performer on it. At the beginning of the nineteenth century an absolute fever to create instruments of this kind broke out, seeking for supernatural and ethereal tones. Chladny's *euphone*, Buschmann's *terpodion*, Träger's *nail piano* and Martin Kratochvíl's *coelison* are witnesses to it.

To play a musical instrument calls for a certain degree of skill and musical education not granted to everyone. And so every age felt the strong urge to make performance mechanical and to invent a musical instrument which could be played without any knowledge of music. We have proof that the Byzantines already had mechanical musical instruments, as well as the Arabs of the Middle Ages. It was the romantic period, however, which saw the full bloom of this fashion; musical boxes were hidden even in articles of daily use. There was hardly a home without a picture, clock, tea-table, tobacco box or goblet fitted with a mechanical musical instrument. Towards the end of the nineteenth century new types of musical boxes were being made, with removable metal cylinders which made it possible to play any number of pieces. These mechanical instruments played the role of the gramophone later on, and were made in innumerable types; we may mention at least the *ariston*, the *polyphone*, the *heraphone*, the *maliphone*, the *euphonion*, the *synphonion*, the *halycon* and *the manopan*. Makers of mechanical instruments in Bohemia in the nineteenth century enjoyed the highest reputation. At the international exhibition of musical instruments in Paris in 1855 František Řebíček won the first prize for his musical box. From 1870 his son Gustav managed his workshop; by that time Prague musical boxes were world-famous. Among the largest mechanical instruments are *orchestrions*, which can sometimes create the superficial impression that a complete orchestra is playing.

## THE MODERN ORCHESTRA

The revolutionary change which took place in music half way through the eighteenth century, centred round Mannheim, Paris and Vienna, was fundamentally a question of individualising the various groups of musical instruments. By creating a completely new dynamic scale it laid the foundations for the laws of balance in the modern orchestra. The first far-reaching consequences of the reforms initiated by the pre-classical masters were seen in Gluck, Haydn and Mozart. It can be said that in their hands the balance between stringed and wind instruments was settled for good, their individual role and place in the ensemble, the intensity of their colour and the possibilities of combination, and — most important — their individual existence. Towards the end of the eighteenth century the orchestra enjoyed its first and most classical great period, as if it were itself a musical instrument, or rather the most perfect of all instruments, demanding independent orchestral thought from the composer. The composers of operas and symphonies in the nineteenth century expanded the orchestra to enormous proportions. The number of strings was increased from the time of Spohr and Habeneck, and soon the wind instruments rose to the same level. The mammoth orchestra of Berlioz's Requiem had no equal throughout the nineteenth century. Wagner began to make his orchestra smaller. At first sight it looks as though our own century had taken over the instruments of the Romantic period unchanged. This is not quite true, however, though Richard Strauss's contribution is really implicit in Berlioz's theory of instrumentation. Strauss's smaller orchestra in his opera *Salome* consists of the following instruments: piccolo, four flutes, two oboes, English horn, heckelphone, five clarinets, bass clarinet, three bassoons, double bassoon, four trumpets, six French horns, four trombones, bass tuba, four kettledrums, small kettledrum, tom-tom, cymbals, large and small drum, tambourine, triangle, xylophone, castanets, chimes, two harps, celesta, thirty-two violins, ten to twelve violas, ten violoncellos, eight double basses. Off stage: harmonium and organ. Seven years later his *Ariadne on Naxos* (1912) has more solo parts, where instruments on which chords can be played predominate. The chamber division of the strings is of particular interest: two flutes, two oboes, two clarinets, two bassoons, two French horns, trumpet, trombone, celesta, harmonium, two harps, piano, six violins (three stands), four violas (two stands), four cellos (two stands), two double basses. The return of the piano to the orchestra and the orchestration for chamber playing with emphasis on the importance of wind instruments would all seem to point in a new direction. In fact, however, this is only a continuation of the tendency of the nineteenth century. The same is true of the percussion instruments; in Stravinsky's *L'histoire du Soldat* there are six percussion instruments to six melodic instruments. This too is a comprehensible development if we consider that for centuries harmony has predominated at the expense of rhythm. There would be nothing strange about it if the twentieth century turned to a thorough rhythm structure just as the seventeenth century long before had built up its music on the basis of the thorough bass.

The *heckelphone, dulcimer* and *saxophone* have become regular members of the modern orchestra. The composition of the orchestra and the use of certain instruments is of course an individual matter to be settled by the composition itself. The theory of orchestration can only provide a rough skeleton giving the possibilities of orchestral colouring. The inexhaustible wealth of sound of the orchestra can only be seen in practice. In conclusion it can be said that the development and improvement of musical instruments accompanied increased demands until it culminated in the maximum of sound effect represented by the modern orchestra. Constant effort by the human mind over many thousands of years was needed to achieve this. The final result is the modern orchestra, which provides incomparable sound impressions, the sources of which are musical instruments.

# FOLK INSTRUMENTS

# FOLK INSTRUMENTS

By folk instruments we mean those musical instruments, in the narrow sense of the word, which the peasantry make themselves by hand and which are or were played by country people for any length of time. There are very many such instruments, including no small number which may have come down from prehistoric times like *rattles*, *clappers* and the *Jew's harp*. The rattle is a very old instrument which came to Europe from Asia. The Roman Catholic church calls the faithful together from Maundy Thursday to Easter Eve by means of special instruments instead of the church bells; these instruments, one of which is the rattle, have all a sad, deep sound. The Jew's harp (distortion of the jaw's harp) is a primitive horse-shoe-shaped instrument formerly made of wood but later on exclusively of iron; a little steel tongue is fixed firmly by one end in the curve of the frame. The player holds the narrower end of the instrument between his teeth and produces tones by moving the free end of the steel tongue with his finger. The various positions of the tongue, lips and cheek muscles form a natural sound box which amplifies the overtones. Thus the Jew's harp can only play tunes which keep within the natural tone range. The *bukál*, also called *bukatch* or *bandaska* (German *Rommelpot*), is an instrument played by carol-singers in Bohemia; it is a pot, pitcher or other pot-bellied vessel with skin or bladder stretched over the opening in the manner of a drum, with a tuft of horse-hair sticking up in the middle. The player takes the instrument between his knees and rubs the horse-hair in an upward direction with the wet fingers first of one and then the other hand, singing at the same time the well-known song "Buku, buku, buku! panimámo zlatá, otevřte ruku, koledičku dejte."*

Side by side with instruments which were taken over by folk music at a later date (*harmonica*, *ocarina*, *mandoline*, *balalaika*, *clarinet*, etc.) almost all the instruments of the Middle Ages have been preserved. We find the recorder preserved with only slight changes in *pipes* and *fuyaras*, long pipes played by the Detvan shepherds; a row of recorders of different lengths carved out of a single piece of wood in the form of pan-pipes in Příkazy in Moravia; a kind of double flute in the Yugoslav and Bulgarian *double pipes*; and the one-hand flute in a Valach pipe with three fingerholes in Moravia. The shape of the angels' trumpets so often depicted in mediaeval miniatures has been preserved in the *Alpine horns* found in Switzerland and even earlier in Austria, Rumania, the Caucasus and other mountainous regions of Asia. The *bagpipes*, an ancient instrument already played in Babylon, remained a folk instrument up to the present day, with the exception of the short period during the eighteenth century when the French concert bagpipes known as the *musette* were popular. The bagpipes came to Europe from Asia about the first century A.D. Not only in Scotland, where bagpipes are still played in military bands, but throughout Europe they were very popular; now they are played more as a folk-lore curiosity, for example in the Domažlice and Strakonice regions in Bohemia.

Very much the same can be said of the *hurdy-gurdy*, a popular instrument in the Middle

* "Beech-tree, beech-tree, beech-tree! goodwife kind, open your hand and give us a wassail."

Ages. Being a mechanical instrument it held the seeds of artistic degeneration; although the hurdy-gurdy has its place in musical history as an instrument for which serious composers wrote music, it was held in such low esteem that even such a careful historian as Praetorius has no more than its picture in his book. Even he considered it beneath his dignity to give any description of the instrument of beggars. Only in the eighteenth century was it revived for a few decades in France, where like the bagpipes it became popular among the aristocrats as an idyllic shepherds' instrument. After this short interlude the hurdy-gurdy disappeared from serious music once more, to remain exclusively a folk instrument. It is played by means of a wheel which rubs against the strings when the right hand turns the crank to which it is attached, while the left hand stops the strings by means of a special system of keys on the upper part of the instrument. The hurdy-gurdy is shaped like a crude guitar with a deep case. One of the three strings plays the melody while the other two drone an accompaniment at a fifth or an octave. In Bohemia during the nineteenth century the hurdy-gurdy was played by wandering musicians, and later by beggars. It died out in Slovakia during the nineteenth century. Today it is found only rarely, in certain regions of north-east Europe and in some parts of Rumania. Like the hurdy-gurdy and the bagpipes the *dulcimer* was a folk instrument which became fashionable and was played by dilettantes in France and elsewhere, until it was gradually forgotten. It came to Europe from the Perso-Arabic sphere about the twelfth century. It was a very simple instrument, being really nothing more than a shallow box with about ten strings of different lengths stretched across it, fixed by nails at one end and at the other end twisted round pegs. The Slavs played it with wooden sticks while in Italy the strings were plucked with a plectrum. The dulcimer of today (*cimbalom*) is trapeze-shaped and has a large number of wire strings stretched across it. It is played particularly by gipsy bands which cleverly use the humming timbre of its tones, and by folk music bands in the countries of Central Europe. In Bohemia and Moravia the short lute *koboz* used to be widely known. It is still played in Hungary, Rumania, Poland, Latvia and the Ukraine by folk musicians. This instrument, which was once a kind of lute apparently of Arab origin, has nothing more in common with the short lute of today than the fact that both are stringed instruments. It is one of the citterns, with a shallow soundbox and a large number of wire strings, four of which are usually stretched over a fingerboard fitted with a metal bridge. In the Jihlava region of Bohemia we find *dyndy*, *niti*, or *payerky* which look absolutely the same as the mediaeval fiddle; they are carved from a single piece of sycamore and only the soundboard is of fir. The construction and the method of playing the bass *dyndy* known as *plashprment* reminds us of the mediaeval trumscheit. In the trumscheit the short free leg of the bridge produced a drumming sound, and the same effect is secured in the bass *dyndy* by a peg added to the pegbox and touching a piece of metal fixed to the soundboard with resin. Just as in the Middle Ages, this instrument is carried on a strap over the left shoulder; the bridge and the bow shaped like an archer's remind us of the bows and bridges seen in mediaeval illuminations.

Interest in and appreciation of the relics of folk art brought the primitive stringed instrument *kantele* to life again in Finland, where from ancient times it had been used to accompany folk musicians singing their runic songs. It may have been the Letts who brought this instrument to the Finns long ago; about seventy years ago it almost died out. The oldest *kantele* had five horse-hair strings, while newer instruments have a larger number of wire strings tuned to the diatonic scale of G major. The instrument is laid on a table or flat on the player's knee. One of the typical northern instruments is the *nyckelharpa* or *keyed harp*, which has however nothing to do with the harp. This instrument has only been preserved in Sweden; it is really a bow hurdy-gurdy with three to five strings, played in a horizontal position and carried hanging by a string. The Norwegian violin *hardangerfelen* is remarkable for having sympathetic strings as well as bowed strings, like the viola d'amore. The rich decoration of mother-of-pearl and ivory and the poker-worked designs point to a foreign origin for this instrument. The *hardanger* violin, which ousted most of the folk stringed instruments of Norway, was played "on all occasions, at weddings and funerals, where the violinist often sat by the coffin all day long tirelessly playing", wrote Bishop Pontoppidan of Bergen in 1750.

A typical area and one rich in folk instruments is the European part of the Soviet Union. Here there are instruments of all kinds, and the fact that there are often many and varied types of one and the same instrument provides unusually valuable material for research into national musical traditions. The most numerous are the plucked instruments; the commonest of these in Russia, White Russia and the Ukraine is the *balalaika*, played both as a solo instrument and in orchestras in five sizes: prima, secunda, alto, bass and double bass. It has three strings and the characteristic triangular body. It sprang from the *domra* at the beginning of the eighteenth century. The *domra* was known as early as the sixteenth century as an instrument with three strings, made in different registers. Four-stringed *domras* are now played in Russian folk bands in six sizes. The *bandura* is a Ukrainian plucked instrument; a state *bandura* orchestra has been formed in the Ukrainian SSR. At the beginning *gussly* meant every stringed instrument in Russian. Later on the name was reserved for a certain instrument with a trapeze-shaped soundbox and a large number of strings. The *gussly* is one of the very oldest Slav instruments, spoken of as early as the twelfth century. At the beginning of this century Privalov made four sizes (piccolo, prima, alto and bass). As well as this *gussly* a *keyboard gussly* is played, a sort of piano without keyboard and without hammers, and a "*shchipkovy*" gussly which has a special little soudbox standing on legs. Among the wind instruments we have the Ukrainian pipe known as *sopilka*, the Russian and White Russian *dudka*, the double *zhalejka* with a horn soundbox, and the *svirel*. The bagpipes known as *volynka* are known in many regions of the USSR. The most popular Russian instrument is a chromatic accordeon called *bayan* and a variant of this, *vyborny bayan*, which differs from it by not having ready-made chords, which must be played by the left hand.

The vast circle of the development of musical instruments ends with those of the peoples of the USSR living in the Caucasus and Central Asia, which in fact brings us back to where we started our historical survey: to the Asiatic cultural centre. A type of oriental violin we have already met with among the Arab instruments is the *kemancha* or *gydjak*; it has three or four strings and a rounded body made from a gourd with an ox bladder stretched over it. The *kobuz* is a two-stringed instrument played with a flageolet technique. The plucked instrument of the Transcaucasus is the *tar*, with a soundbox in the shape of a figure eight and an ox bladder on the soundboard; it is noteworthy that on the long neck there are many frets which form intervals of less than half a tone. The *dutar* is pear-shaped, with a thin wooden soundboard; it is played both by plucking and by striking with the wrist. Among the wind instruments we find the *duduk*, which is really the Transcaucasian cylindrical oboe, and the *zurna* or *surnay*, the conical oboe played by many of the peoples of Central Asia, Caucasus and Crimea. The *zurna* has a shrill timbre which makes it only suitable for playing out of doors, and the *duduk* takes its place indoors. The *koshnay* is a double Uzbek pipe with a single tongue and the *karnay* is a brass instrument two yards long with rattling pebbles in the bell, used for war-signals and ceremonials.

# TABLE OF INSTRUMENTS EMITTING SOUND

1. NOISE-MAKERS

rattles, clappers, whips, spurs, bird-calls, wind, thunder, rain and hail machines, etc.

2. TONE-MAKERS

hunting horns, post horns, signal horns (military and firemen's bugles, scout bugles, watchmen's bugles), whistles, motor horns, fanfare trumpets, sirens, tuning forks and tongues, etc.

3. MUSICAL INSTRUMENTS
4. MECHANICAL INSTRUMENTS
5. ELECTROPHONIC INSTRUMENTS

organs, pianos, guitars, harmonicas, double bass, etc.

6. ELECTRIC MUSICAL INSTRUMENTS

Theremin's etherophone, Bertrand's dinaphone, magrophone, Trautwein's trautonium

7. MUSIC MACHINES

phonograph, gramophone, wireless, magnetophone, selenophone, etc.

## MUSICAL INSTRUMENTS THROUGH THE AGES

### I. IDIOPHONES

- BARS
  - LYING
    - no resonator
      - xylophone
      - chimes
      - tubaphone
    - resonator
      - marimba
      - celesta
      - vibraphone
  - HANGING
    - triangle
    - orchestra bells
    - Javanese anklung
  - FIXED
    - no resonator
      - direct vibration
        - harmonium
        - harmonica
      - indirect vibration
        - terpodion
        - euphone
        - coelison
    - resonator
      - Jew's harp
      - Zanza
      - tongue organ pipes
      - nail violin
- PANELS
  - LYING
    - castanets
    - slit drum
  - HANGING
    - cymbals
    - gong
    - jingles
    - Chinese Pavilion
    - glass harmonica
    - tower bells
  - FIXED
    - musical saw
    - flexatone

### II. MEMBRANE INSTRUMENTS

- DIRECT VIBRATION
  - tuned
    - kettle drum
  - untuned
    - bass drum
    - side drum
    - tenor drum
    - tabor drum
    - tambourine
- INDIRECT VIBRATION
  - mirlitons

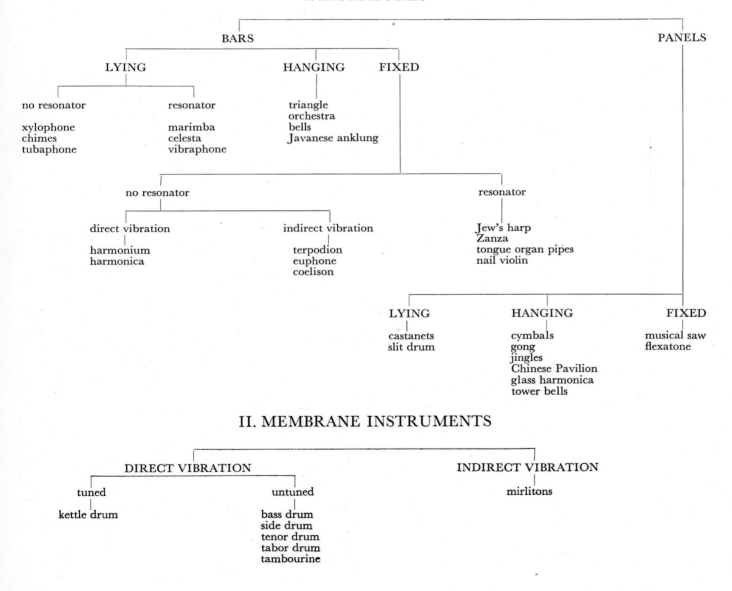

## III. STRING INSTRUMENTS

- PLUCKED WITH THE FINGERS
  - no fingerboard
    - harp
  - fingerboard
    - lute
    - guitar
- PLUCKED WITH A PLECTRUM
  - no fingerboard
    - lyre
    - psaltery
    - cetera
    - Bohemian wing (ala bohemica)
  - fingerboard
    - cistra
    - mandoline
    - zither
    - balalaika
    - banjo
  - keyboard
    - harpsichord
    - spinet
    - virginals
- BOWED
  - crot
  - fiddle
  - viol
  - gamba
  - violin
  - viola
  - 'cello
  - double bass
  - bowed zither
  - philomela
  - bowed melodion
- RUBBED
  - hurdy-gurdy
- STRUCK
  - no keyboard
    - dulcimer
    - tambourin de Béarn
  - keyboard
    - clavichord
    - piano

## IV. WIND INSTRUMENTS

- LIPS
  - RIDGE
    - no groove
      - pan-pipes
      - transverse flute
      - *näy* flute
    - groove
      - lip organ pipes
      - recorder
      - chakan
      - fuyara (played by Detva shepherds)
      - pipes (folk)
  - MOUTHPIECE
    - horn type
      - animal horns
      - horn with holes
      - zinks
      - oliphants
      - serpent
    - cornet type
      - lurs
      - buccina
      - bass horn
      - ophicleide
      - tuba
      - sousaphone
    - trumpet type
      - trumpets
      - bugle
      - trombone
      - Aida trumpet
    - French horn type
      - French horn
      - post horn
      - valve cornet
- REED
  - SINGLE REED
    - clarinet
    - basset-horn
    - tarogato
    - saxophone
    - bagpipes
  - DOUBLE REED
    - no windcap
      - aulos
      - shawm
      - pommer
      - sordun
      - ranket
      - oboe
      - English horn (cor anglais)
      - bassoon
      - heckelphone
      - sarrusophone
    - windcap
      - tumeré
      - bladder-pipe
      - windcap shawm
      - cromorne
      - schryari

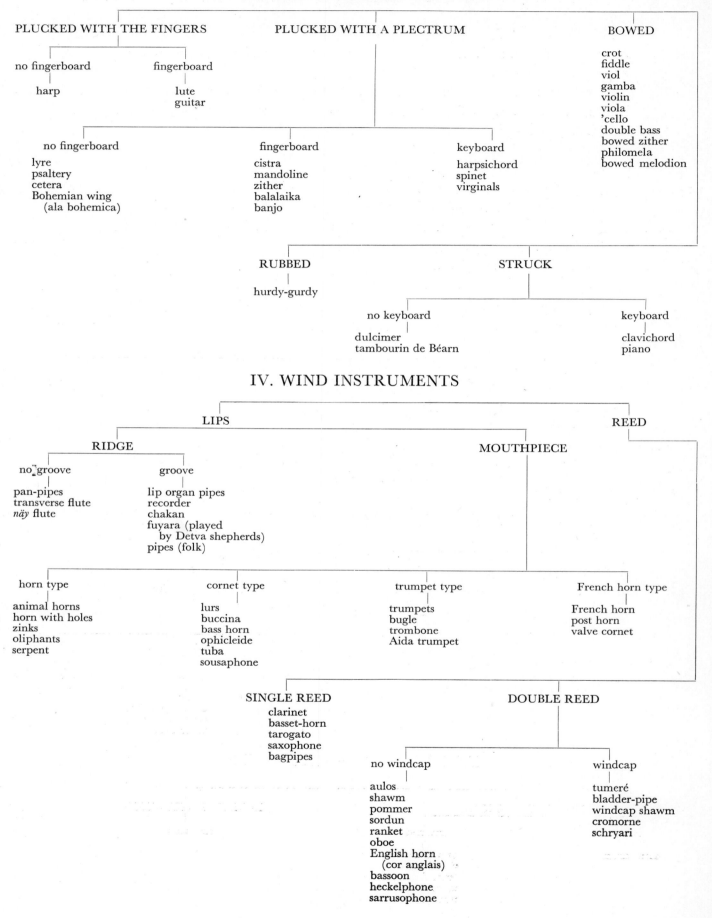

## V. MECHANICAL INSTRUMENTS

- IDIOPHONES
  - plucked
    - musical bones
    - polyphones
  - struck
    - chimes
- WIND
  - lip
    - bird organ
    - *(sérinette)*
    - flute clock
    - barrel-organs
  - tongue
    - harmoniphone
    - manopan
- STRINGS
  - rubbed
    - Aeolian harp
  - plucked
    - chordophone
    - (mechanical zither)
  - struck
    - musical clock
    - pianola
    - triophonola
- COMBINED
  - orchestrion

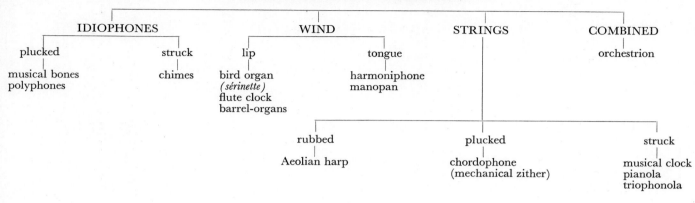

# HISTORICAL TABLE

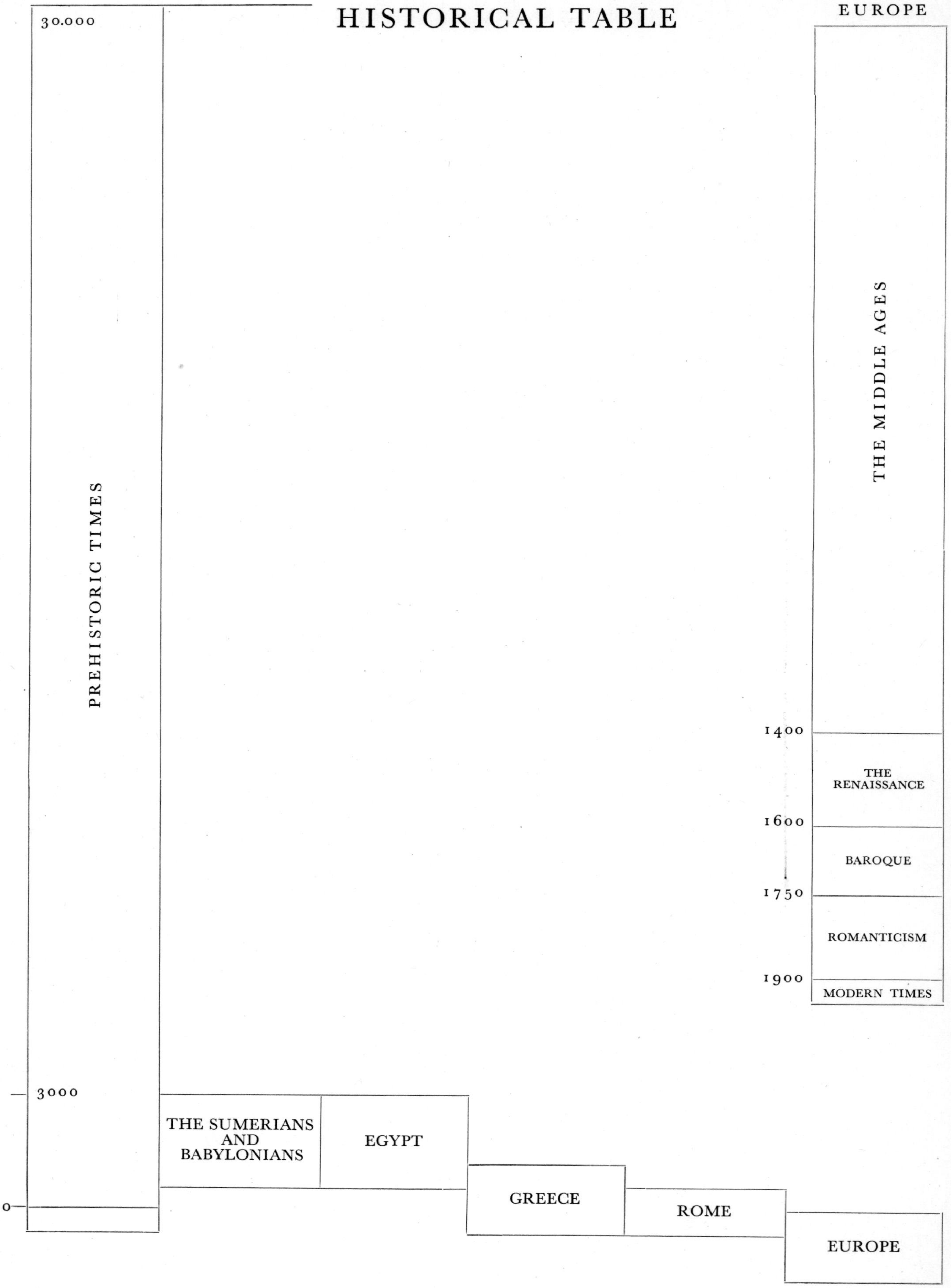
EUROPE
30.000
PREHISTORIC TIMES
THE MIDDLE AGES
1400
THE RENAISSANCE
1600
BAROQUE
1750
ROMANTICISM
1900
MODERN TIMES
3000
THE SUMERIANS AND BABYLONIANS
EGYPT
0
GREECE
ROME
EUROPE

# ILLUSTRATIONS

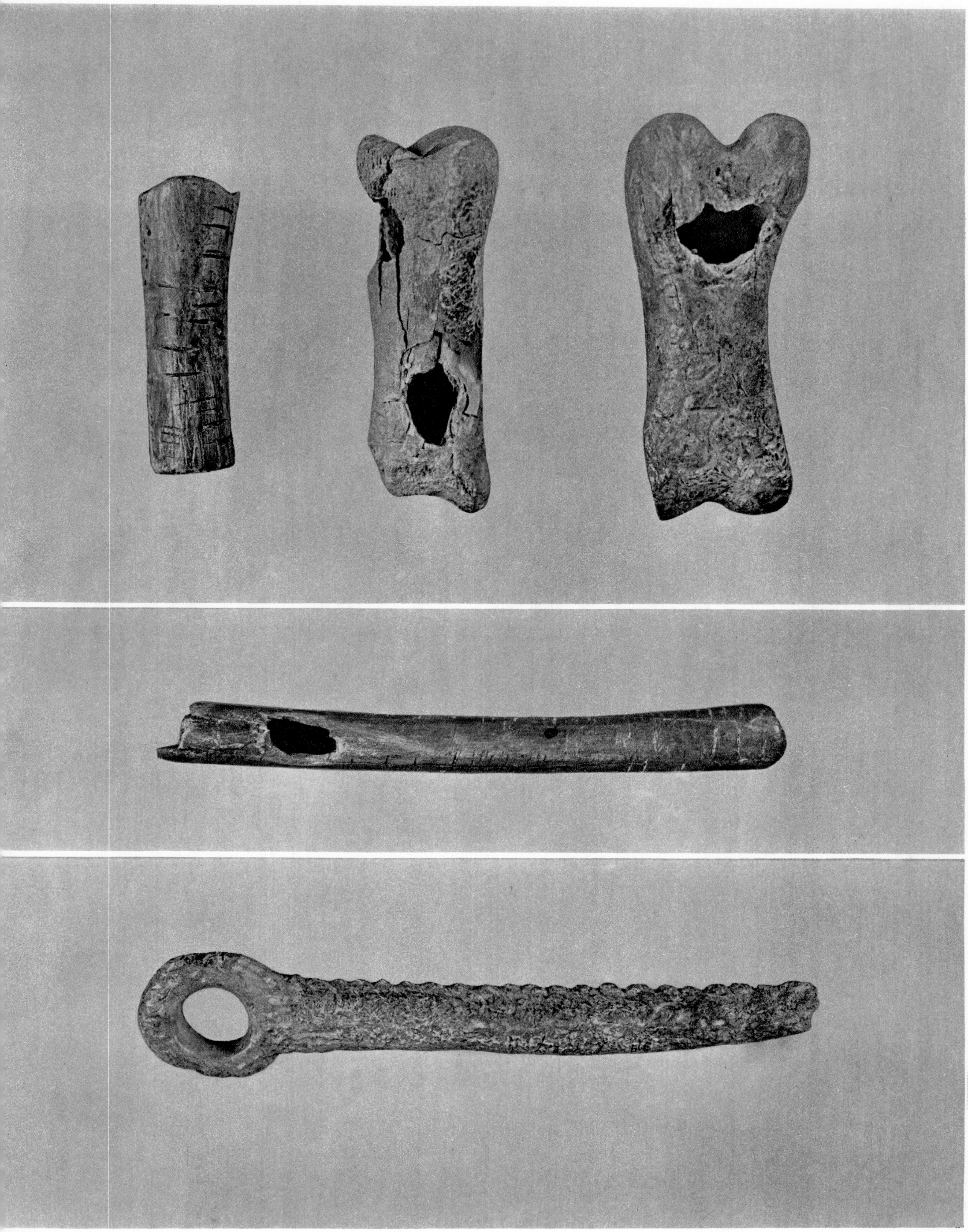

1—3 Signal whistles of reindeer bone from Dolní Věstonice and the Pekárna cave (Moravia).
4—5 Whistle and scraper from Pekárna cave; palaeolithic. Moravian Museum, Brno.

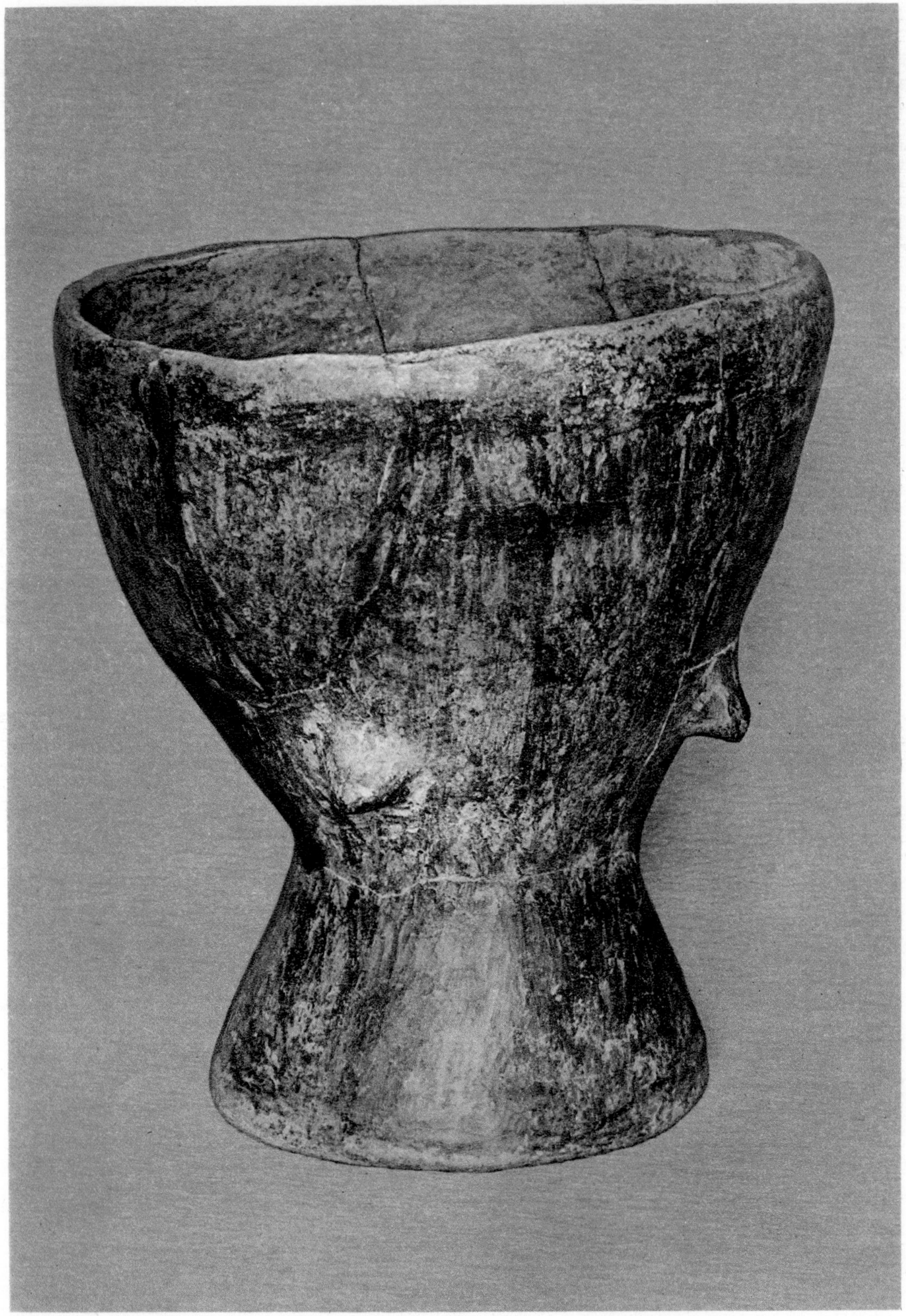

6—7 Clay drums from Kralupy and Brozany on the Ohře (Bohemia); c. 2000 B.C., Bernburg culture. National Museum, Prague.

8—9 Clay rattles from Silesia; eighth century B.C. Moravian Museum, Brno.

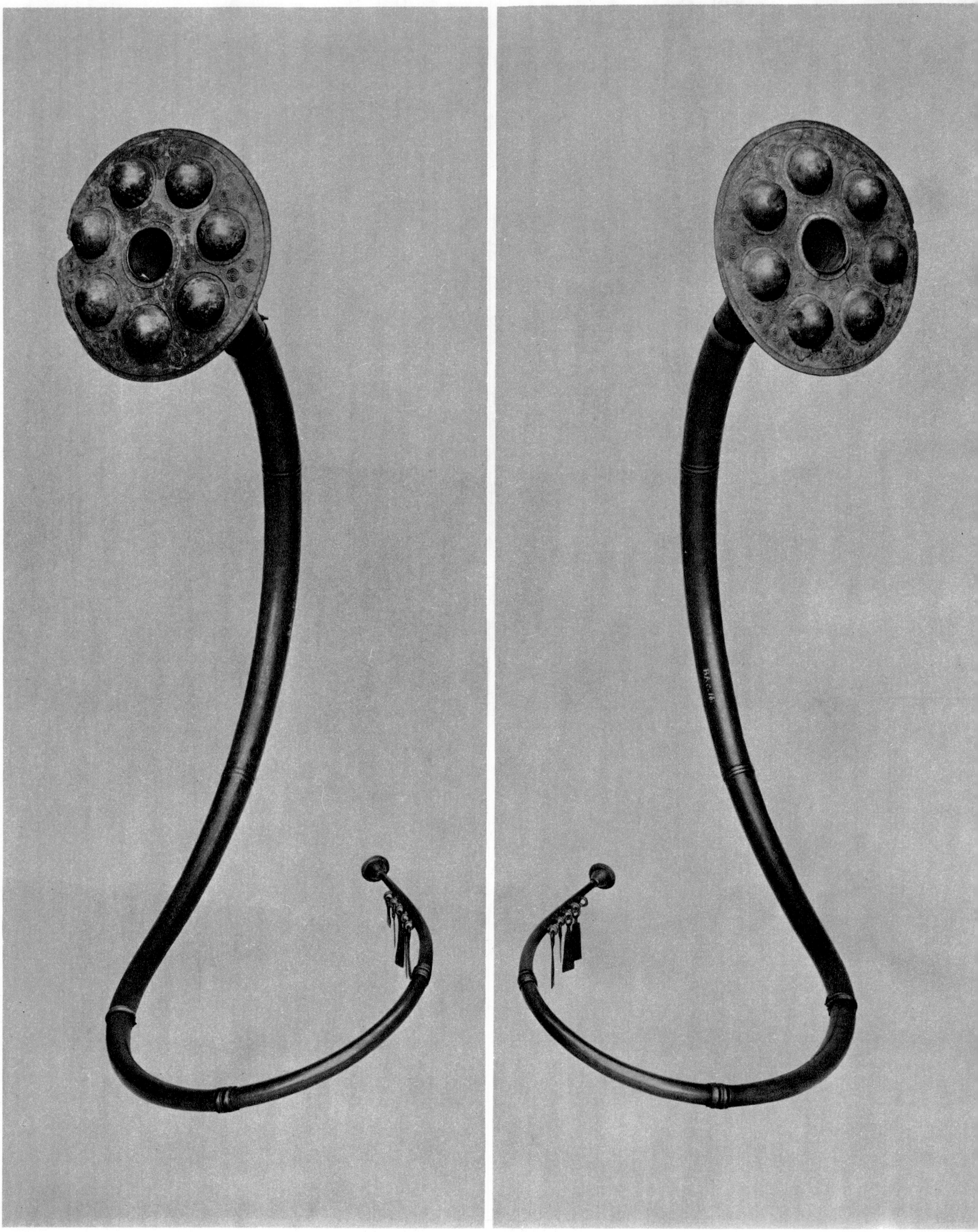

10—13 Lurs. Danish Bronze Age trumpets. National Museum, Copenhagen.

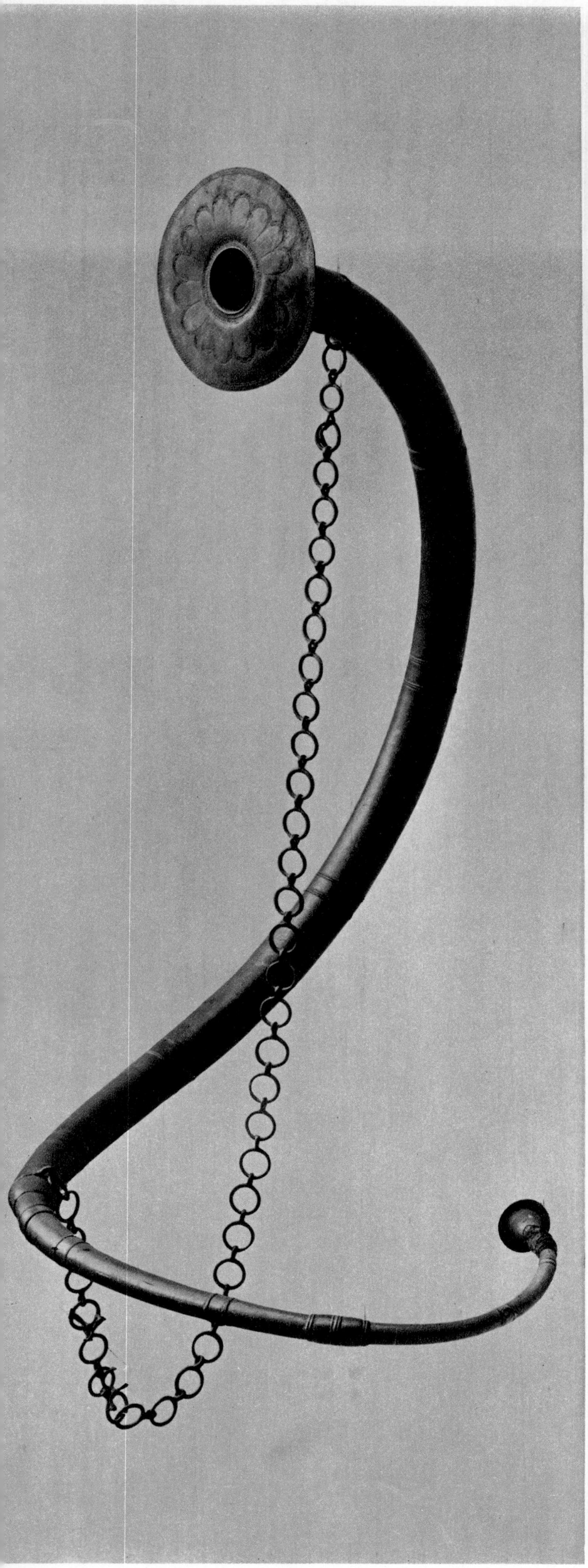
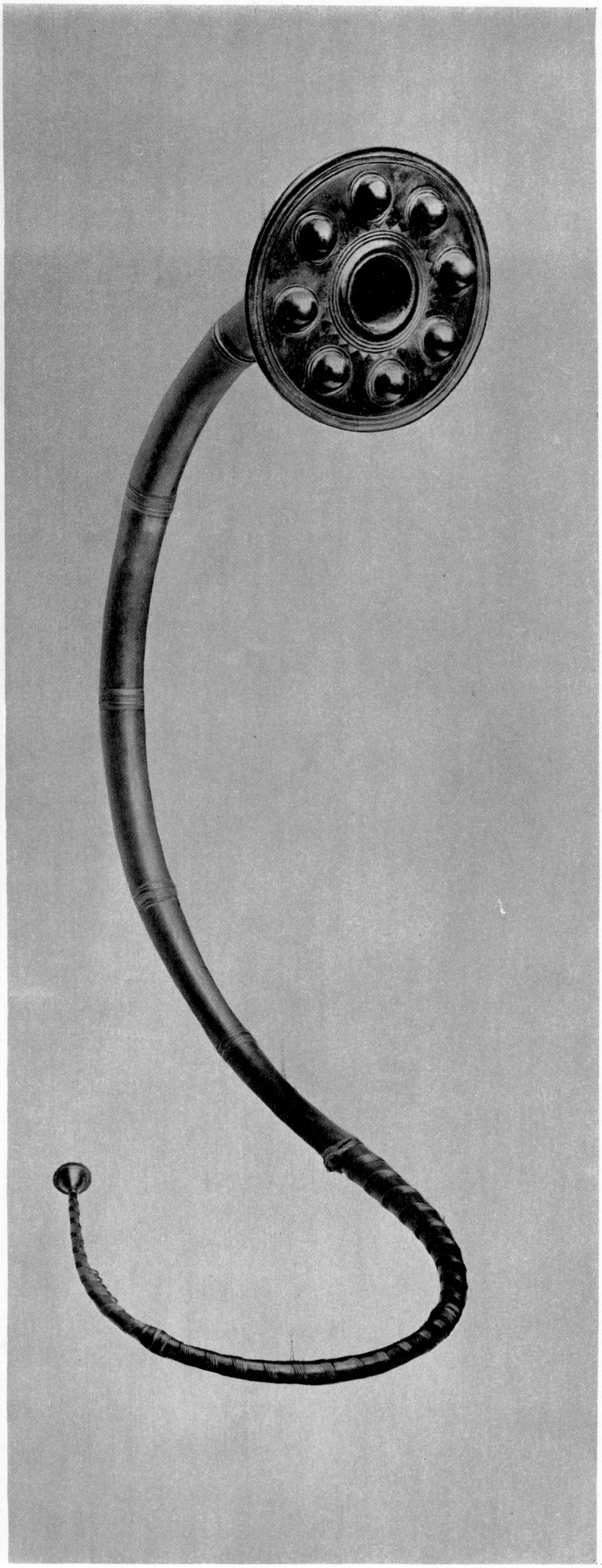

14. Celtic warriors' trumpet the *karnyx*; relief on a silver vessel of the later Iron Age. National Museum, Prague.

15. Celtic trumpeter from Hradiště near Stradonice; first century B.C. National Museum, Prague.

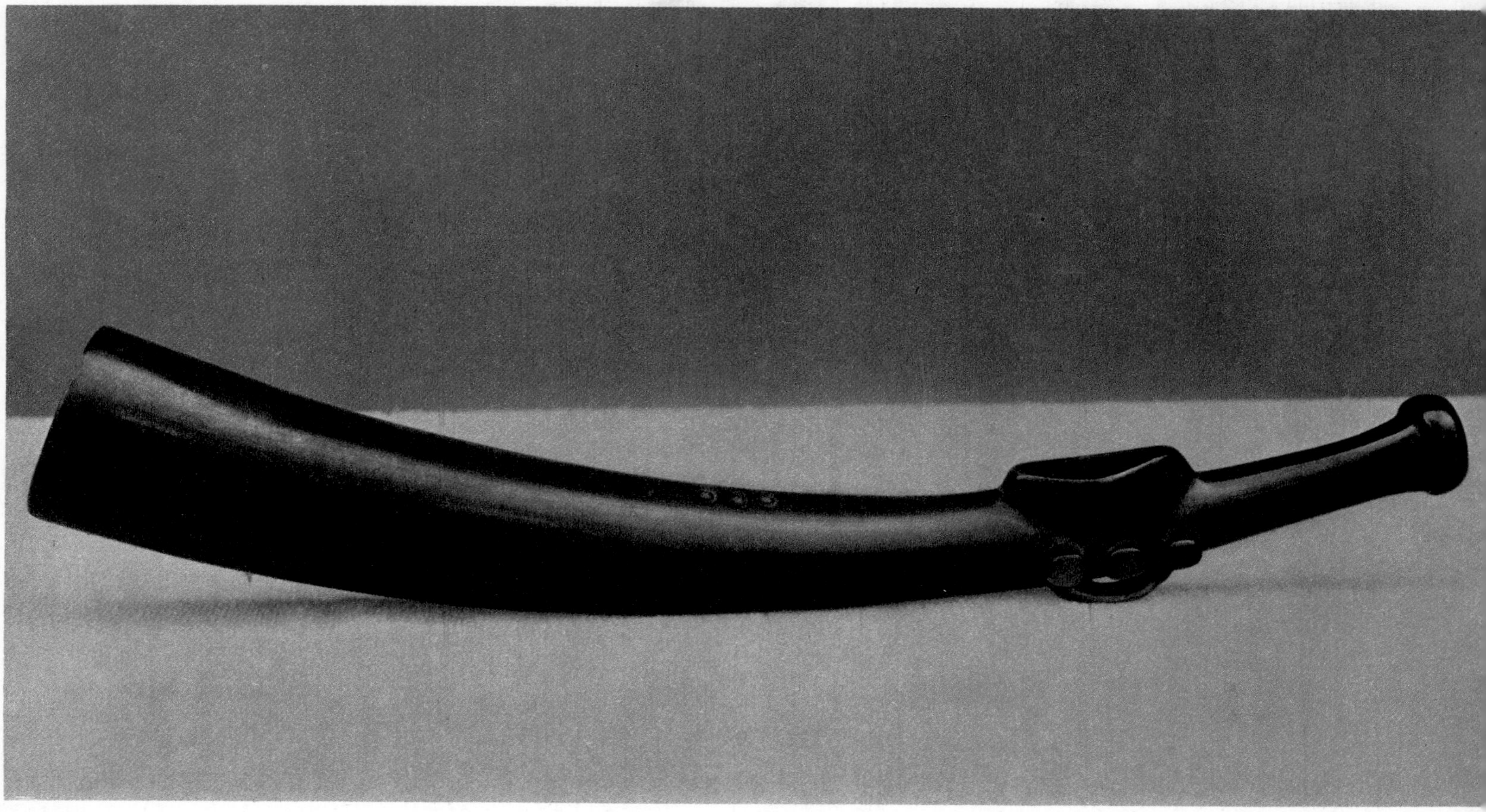

16—17 Horn made from an elephant's tusk, *apunga*, and a rattle of the Mangbet tribe in the Congo. National Museum, Prague.

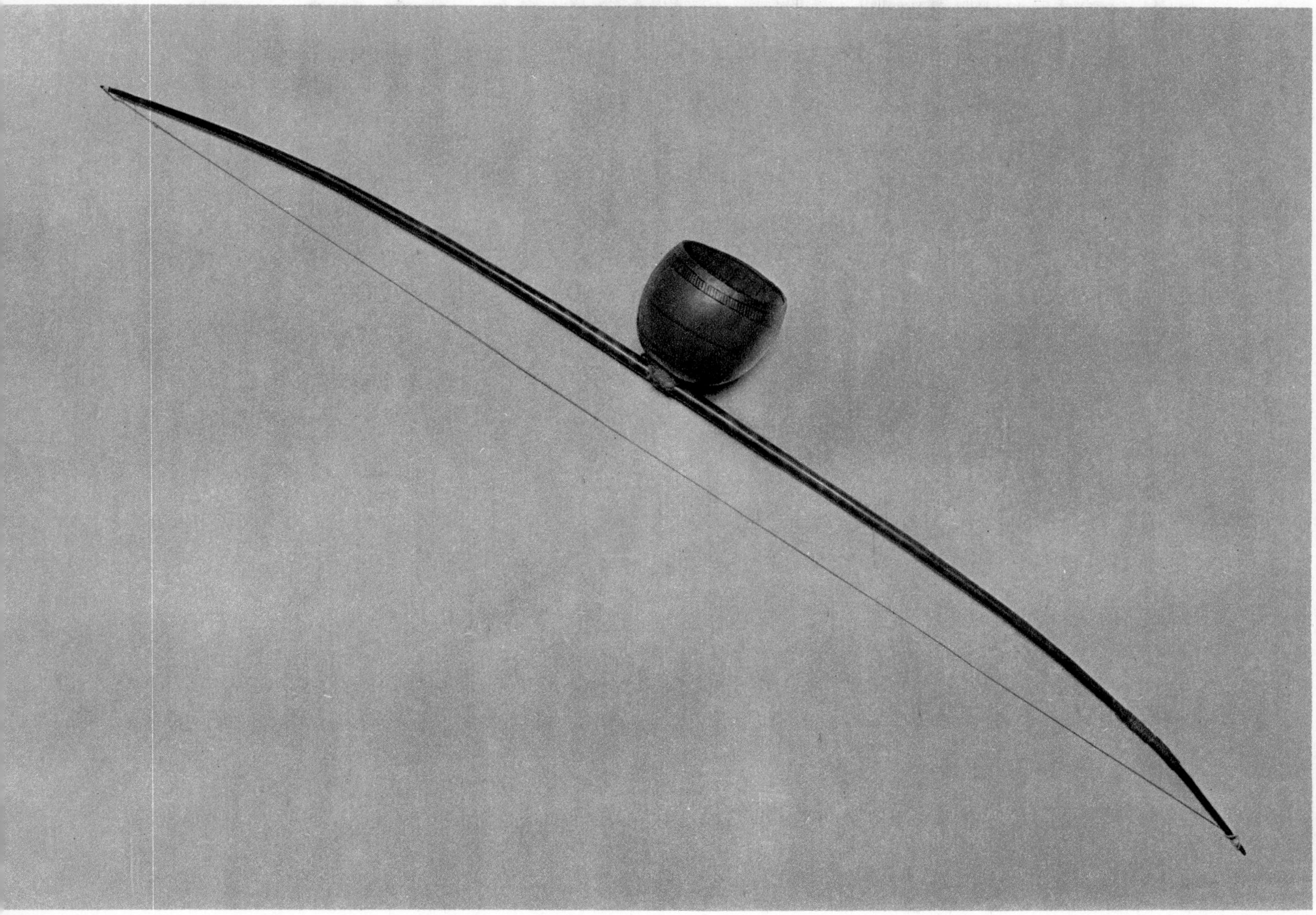

18—19 Musical bow from the Kilimanjaro region in East Africa and one from the Medje tribe in the Congo. National Museum, Prague.

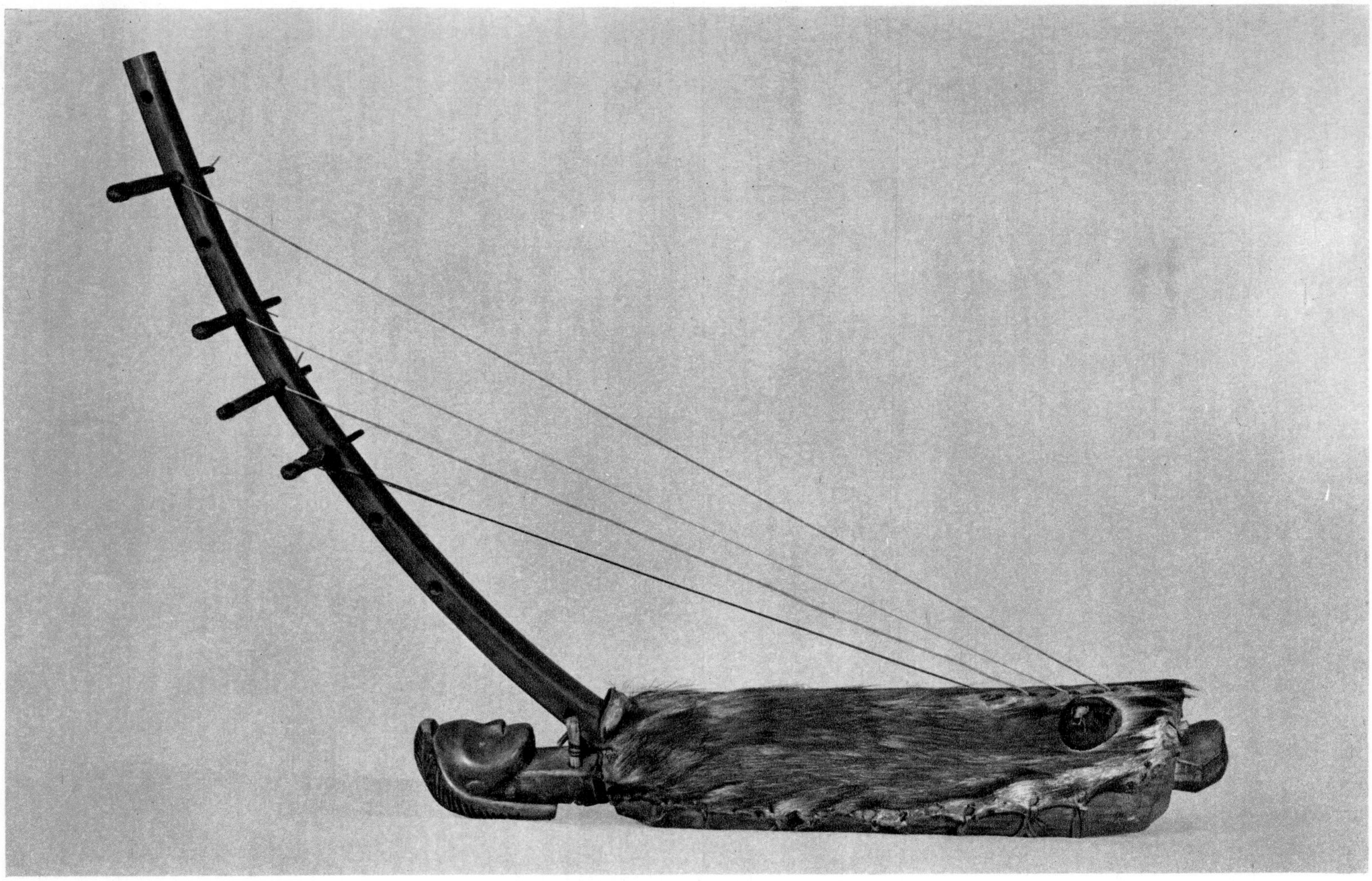

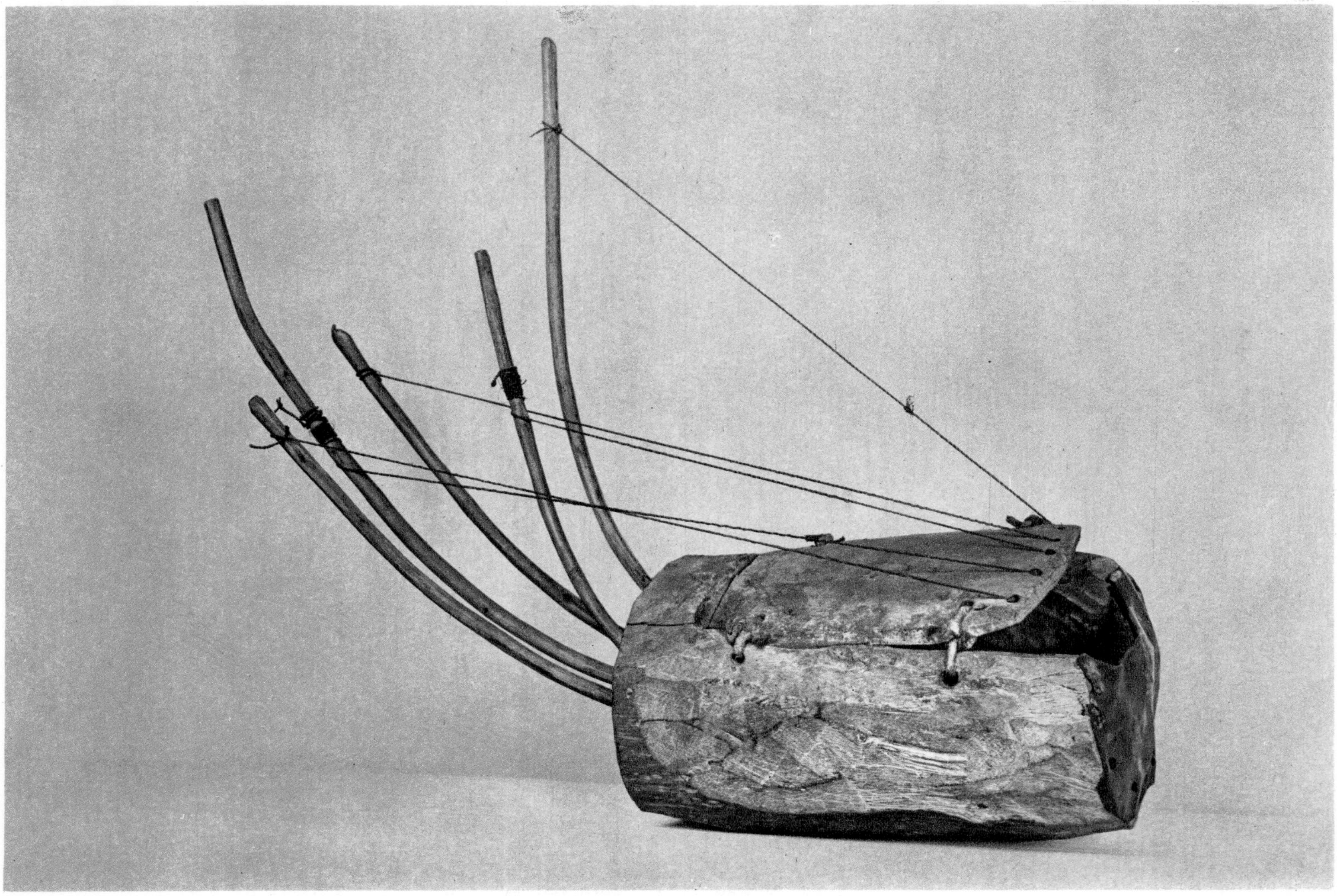

20—21 String instrument of the Bateke tribe in Central Africa, *vambi*, and the harp known as *nanga*, reminiscent of the ancient Egyptian arched harp (East Africa). National Museum, Prague.

22—23 Harp-lute type of instrument known as *kasso*, from Senegambia, and the Nubian *kissar*, resembling the ancient Greek lyre.
National Museum, Prague.

24 Dance accompanied by a drum; brass statue from Dahomey, West Africa. National Museum, Prague.

25 Slit drum from New Guinea. National Museum, Prague.

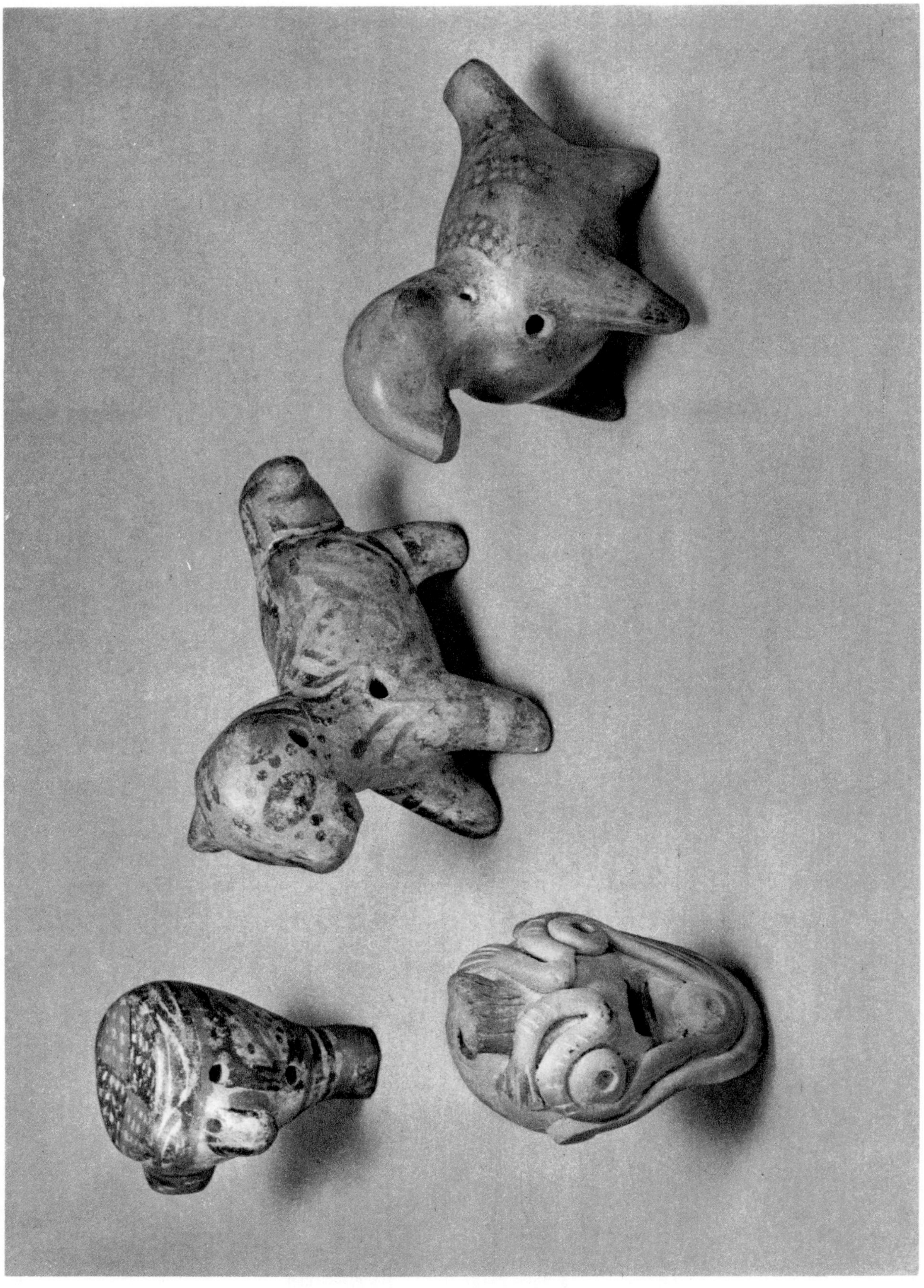

26—32 Earthenware pipes found during archaeological excavation in Mexico. National Museum, Prague.

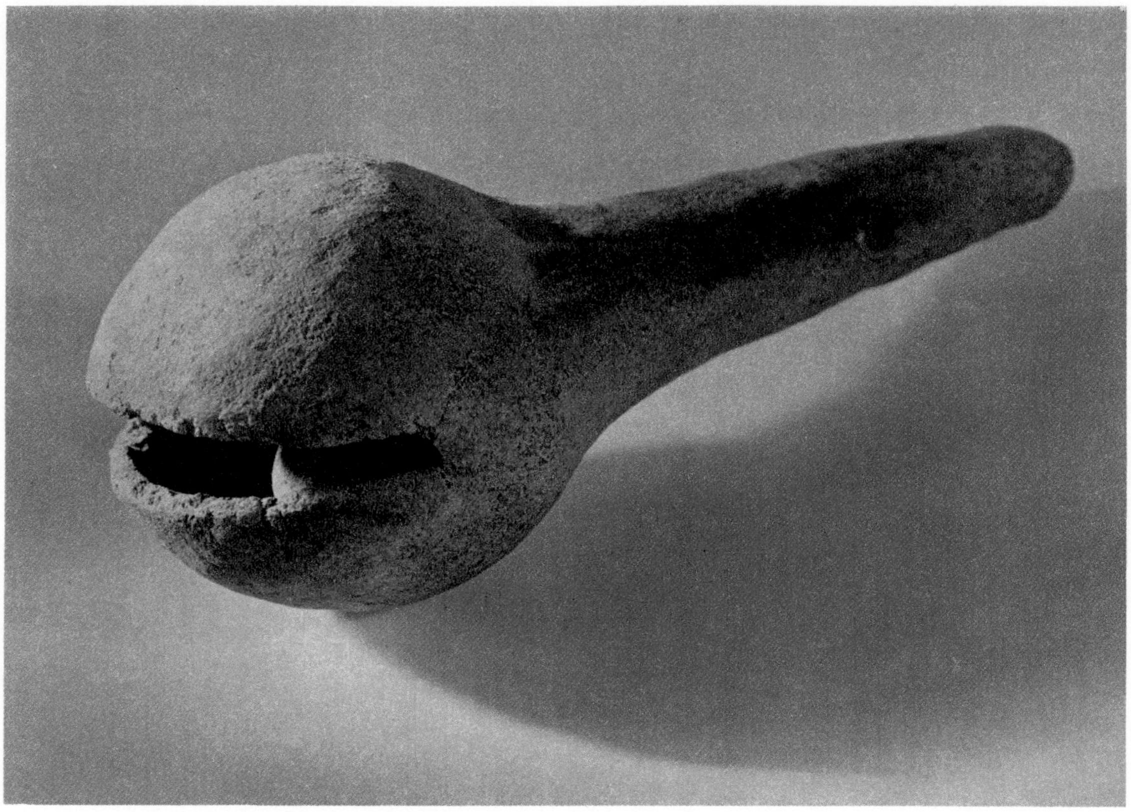

33—34 Mexican rattle and whistle of earthenware. N. Frýd's collection, Prague.

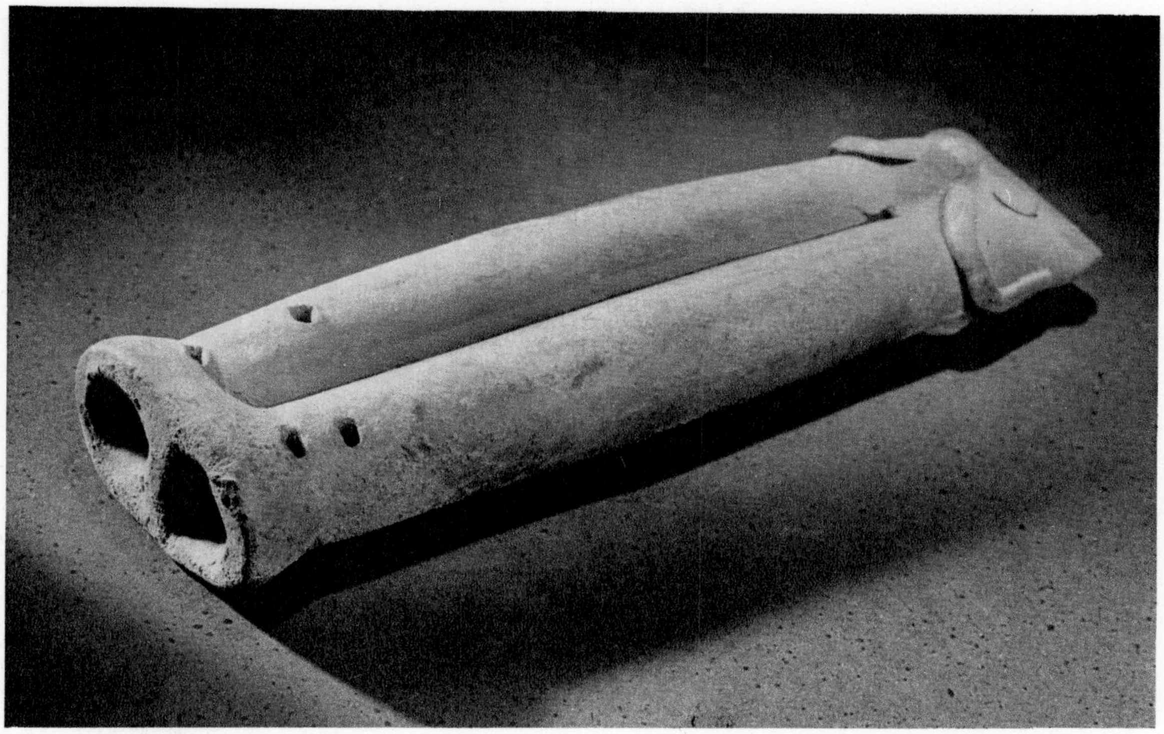

35—36 Mexican double pipe of earthenware, and detail of the mouthpiece. N. Frýd's collection, Prague.

37 Drummer; archaeological discovery from Mexico. Property of N. Frýd, Prague.

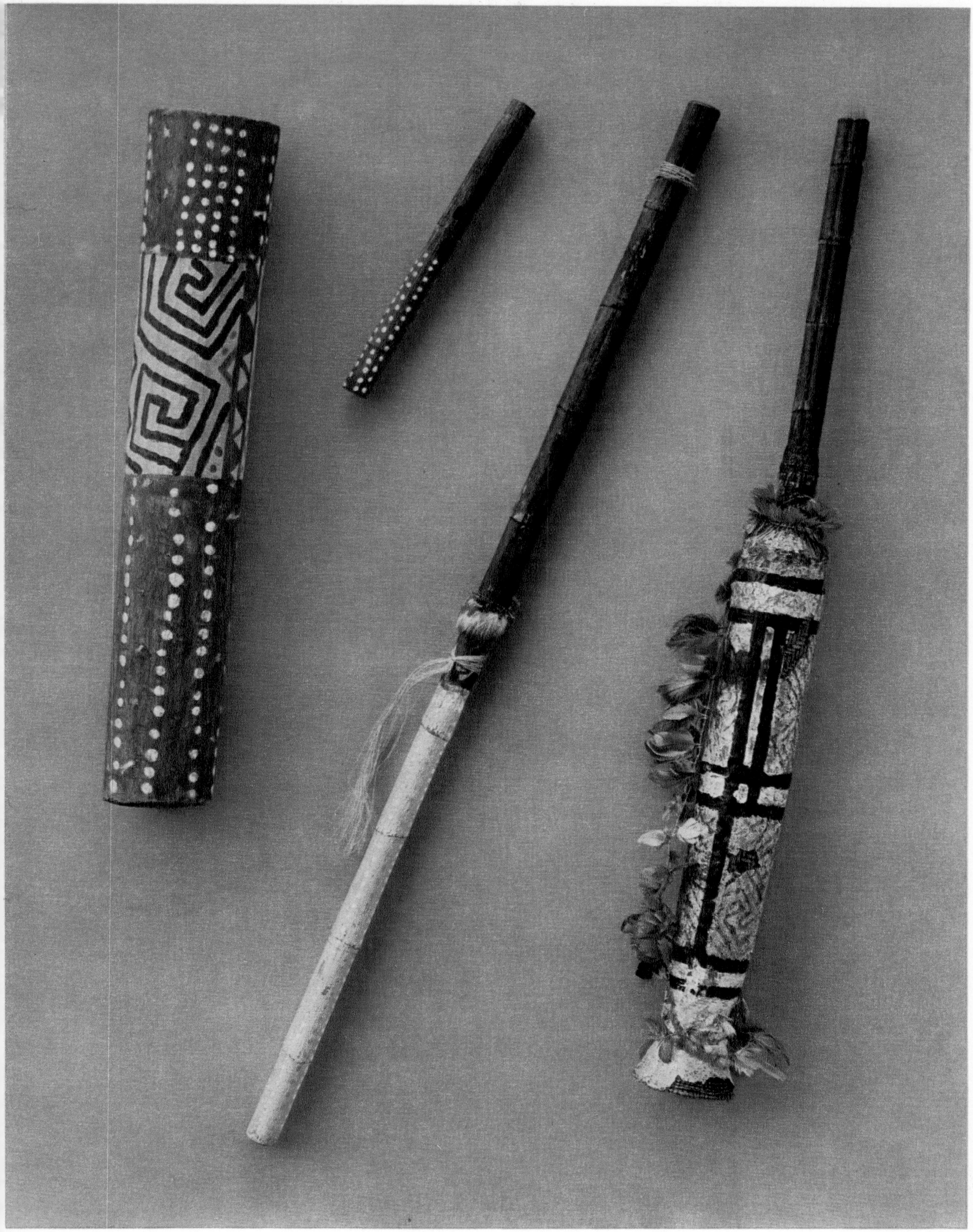

38—41 Drum and wind instruments of the tribe of Baniva Indians, Venezuela. National Museum, Prague.

42 The Chinese gong chimes *fang-siang*, the zither *cheng*, the Pan pipes *p'ai-siao*, the oboe *kuan*, the guitar *yuan*, *ti* flutes, *tien-pan* clappers and *chang-ku* drums.

43 The *chang-ku* drum. Wall painting from the Tung-huang caves in the Kan-su province, dating from the T'ang dynasty (618—907).
See also No. 42.

44 Chinese lute *p'i-p'a*, the oboe *kuan*, Pan pipes *p'ai-siao*, the harp *k'ung hao (schu-ch'in)*, the *tien-pan* clappers, the mouth organ *sheng*, the *ti* flute and the drum *puo-fu (ku)*. Wall paintings from the Tung-huang caves in Kan-su province, dating from the T'ang dynasty (618—907).

45 Chinese lute *p'i-p'a*, moon guitar *yue-chin* and table zither *tchin*; detail of a painting on silk of the Ming dynasty (1330—1644). National Museum, Prague.

46 Chinese gong of the Chan dynasty (200 B.C.—224 A.D.). National Museum, Prague.

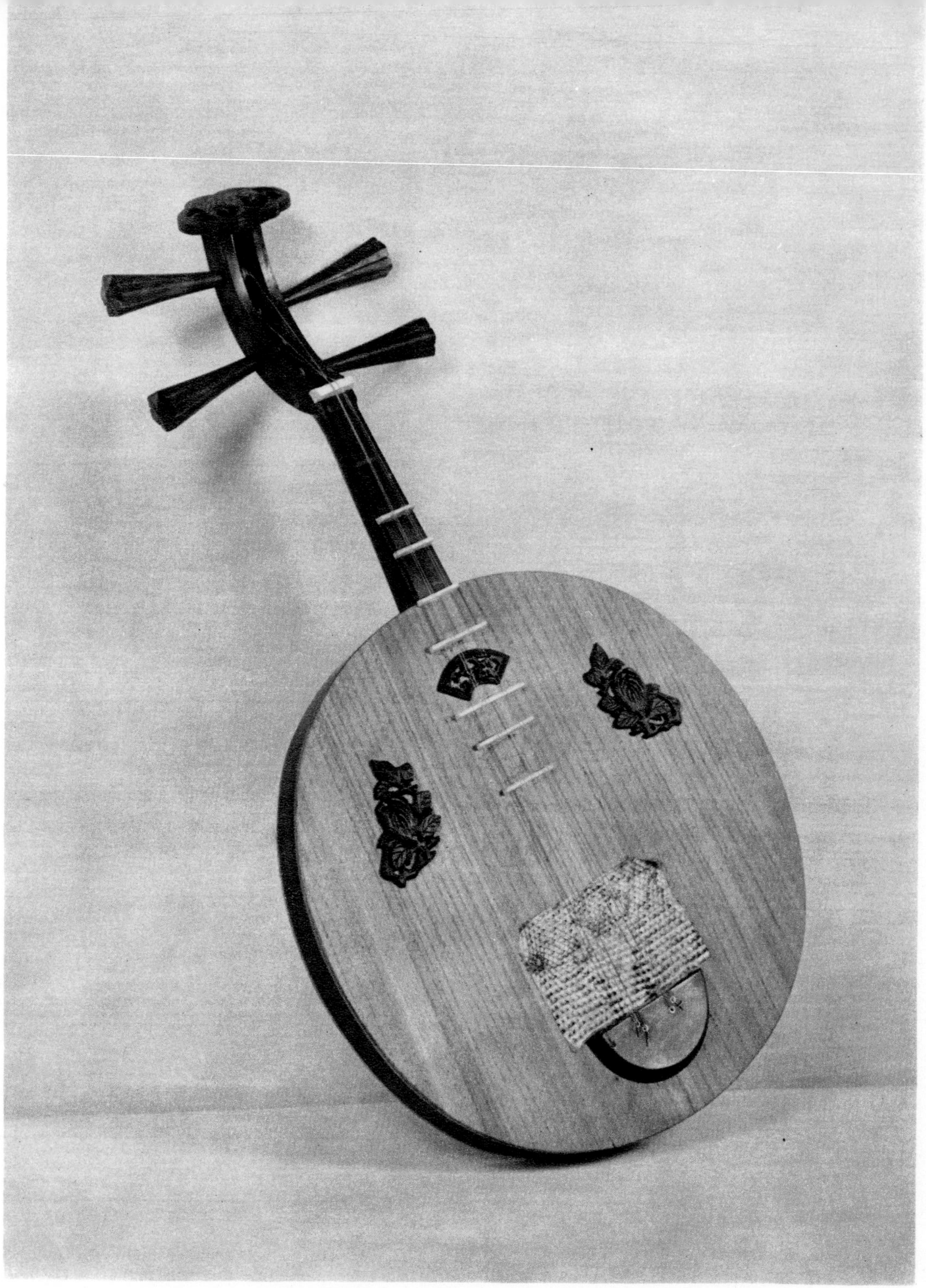

47—48 Chinese lute *p'-ip'a* and Japanese moon guitar *kokin*. National Museum, Prague.

49 Japanese transverse flute *yokobue*; coloured woodcut by Ishiyesai Yoshichua; nineteenth century. National Museum, Prague.

50 Japanese plucked instrument, the *shamisen*, with plectrum. Coloured woodcut by Hokuye; beginning of the nineteenth century. National Museum, Prague.

51 Japanese zither *koto*. Coloured woodcut by Kunichika; nineteenth century. National Museum, Prague.

52 Japanese gong chime, detail. National Museum, Prague.

53 Indian barrel drum *mrdanga*, the lute *sitar*, and tambourine. Austrian National Library, Vienna.

54 Bronze statue of the Indian god Krishna playing on a flute. National Museum, Prague.

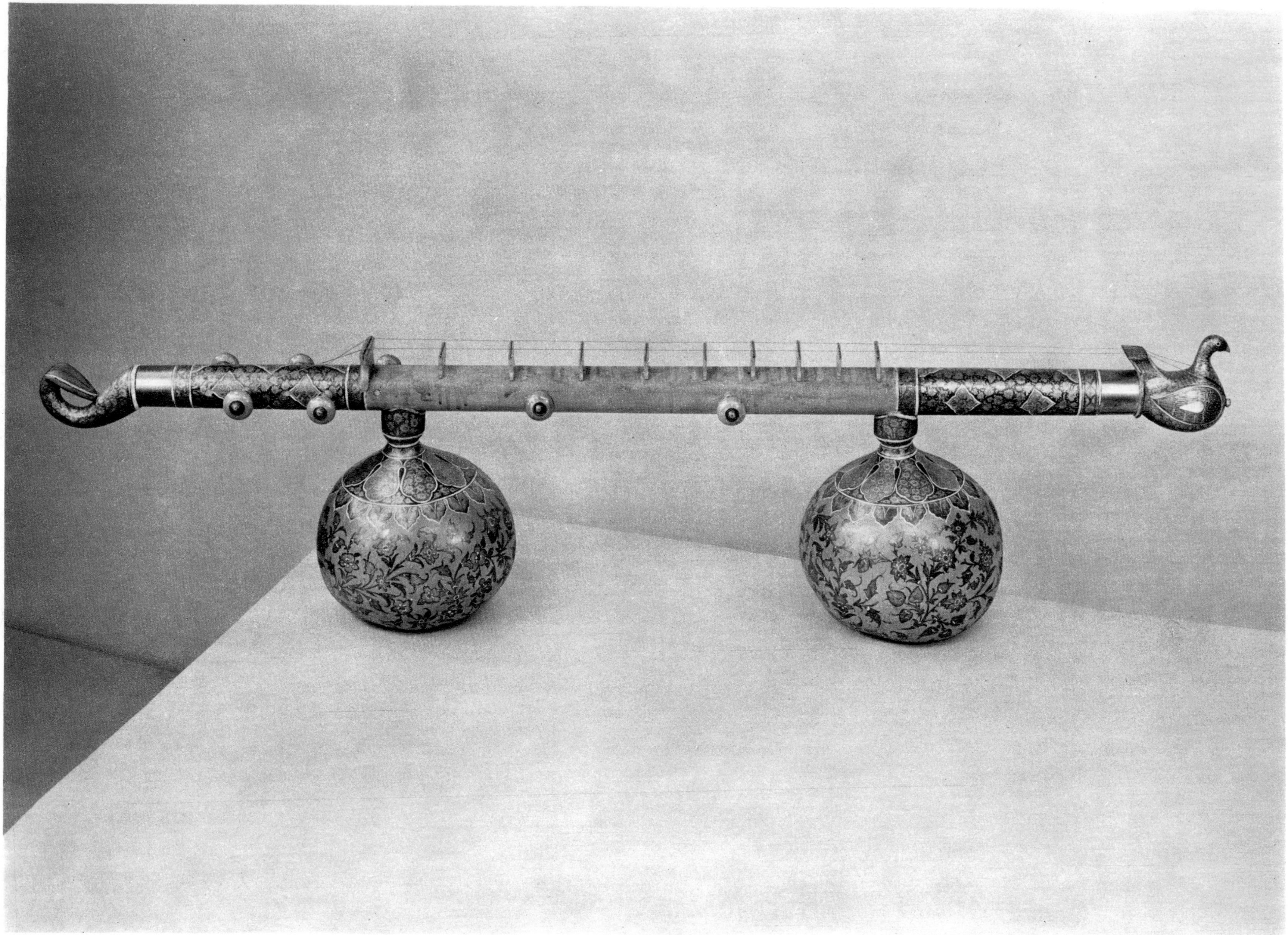

55 Indian stringed instrument *vina*, National Museum, Prague.

56 Indian bow instrument, *tayuc*. National Museum, Prague.

57 Gong from Cambodia. National Museum, Prague.

58 Turkish shawm, tambourine and kettledrum; seventeenth century miniature. Private collection, Hanover.

59 Persian dulcimer, *santir*, Moravian Museum, Brno.

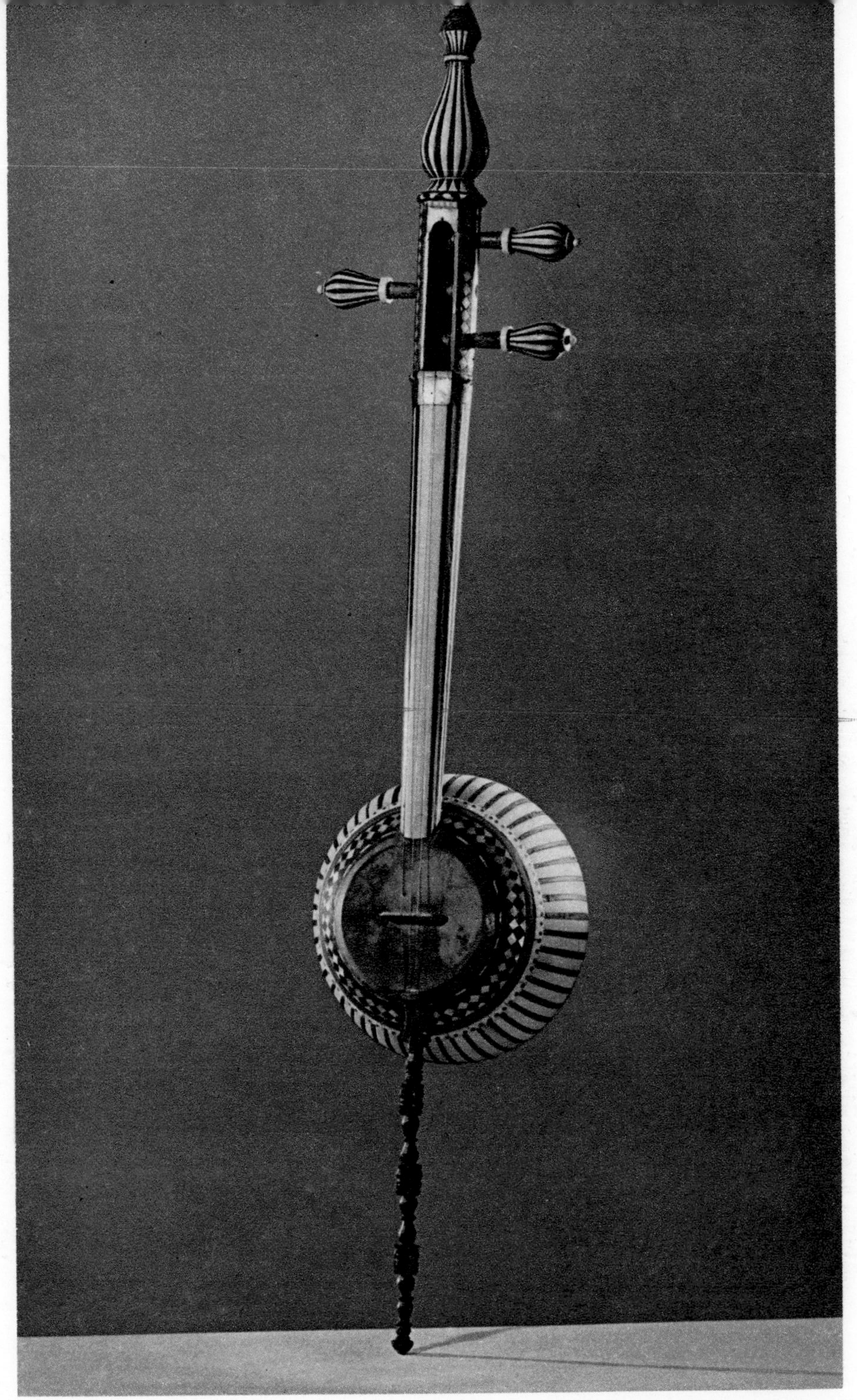

60—61 Persian spike-fiddle, *kamang'a*, and drum, *darabukka*. Moravian Museum, Brno.

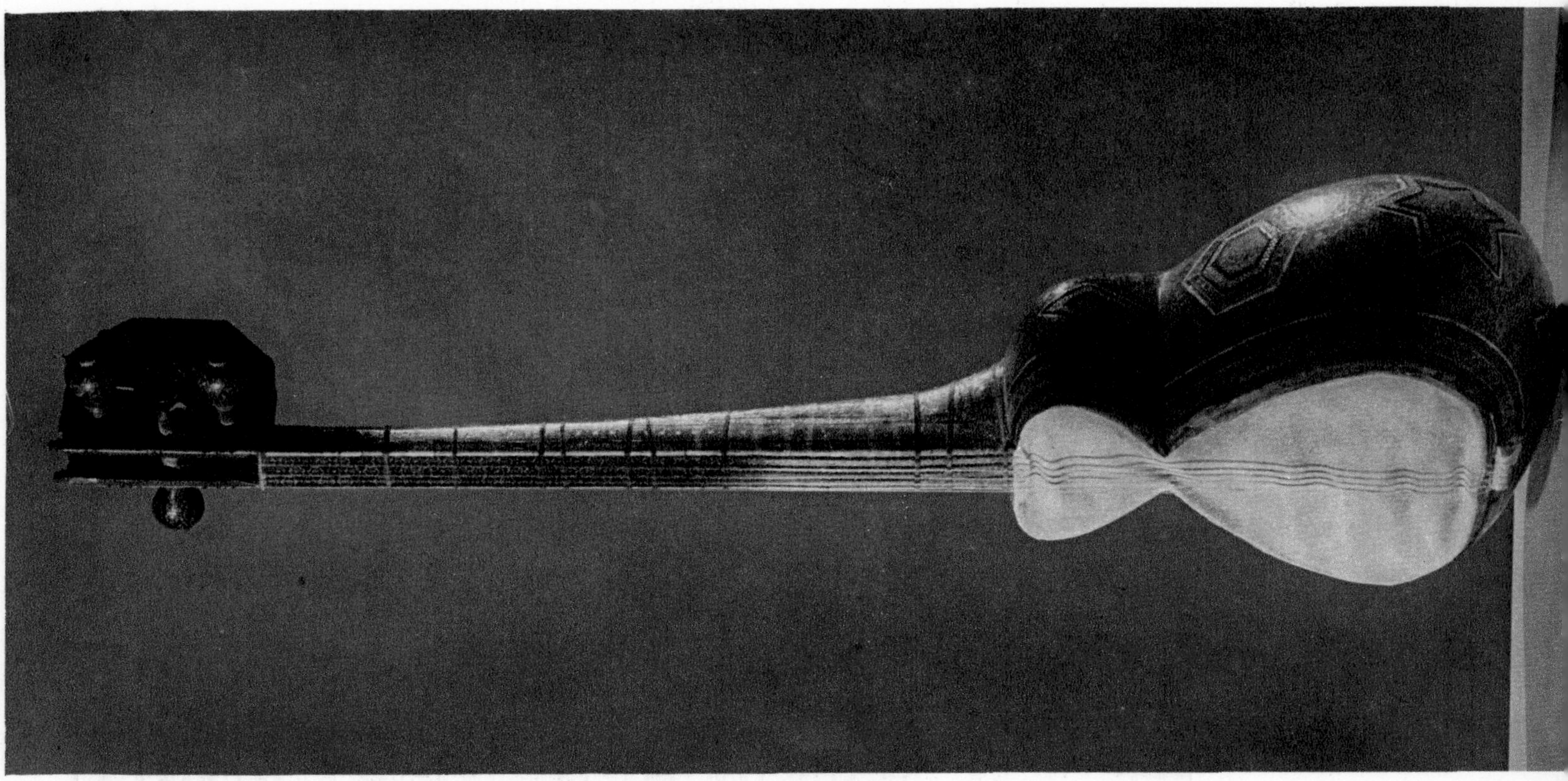

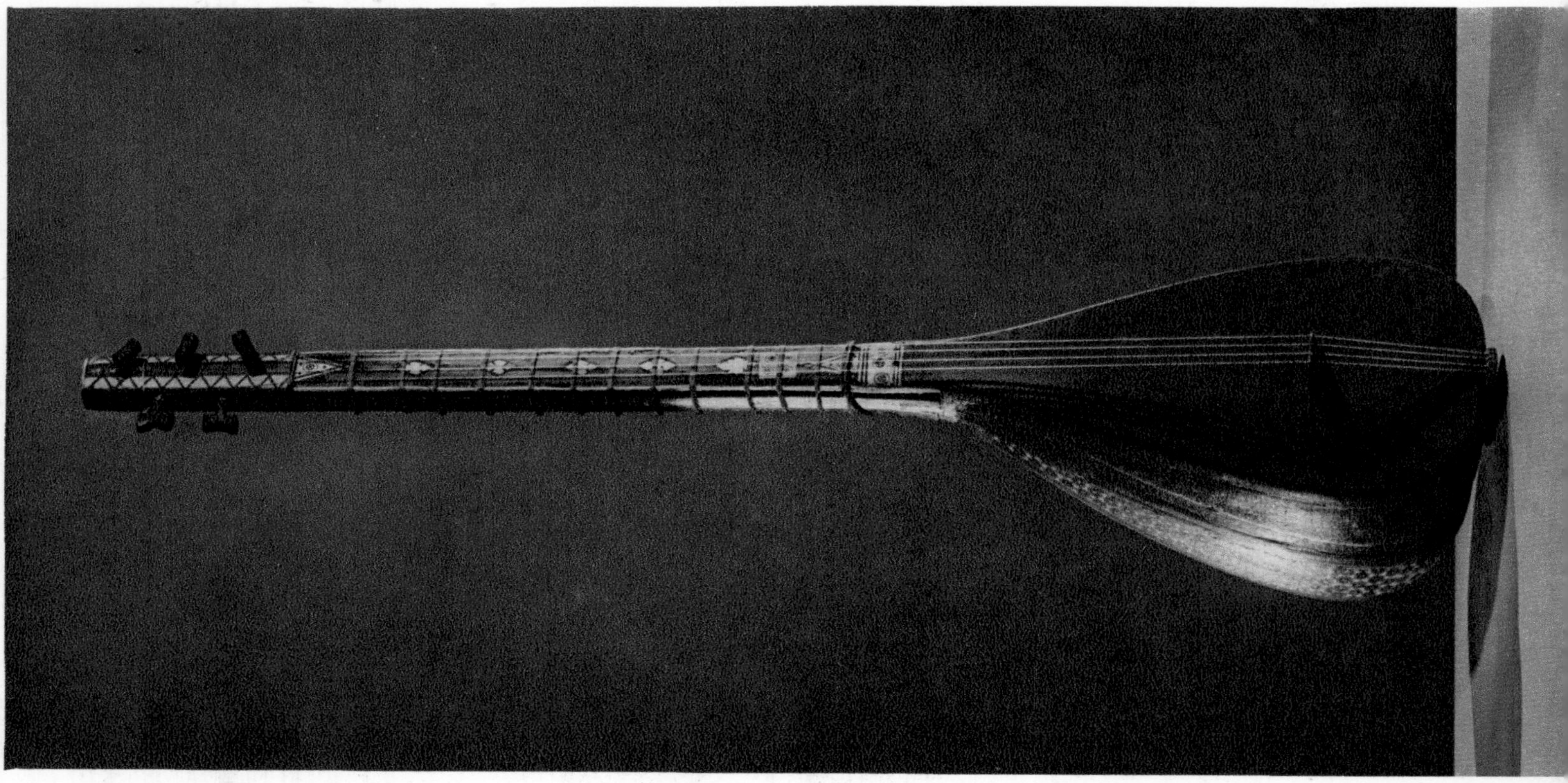

64 Sumerian drum from the middle of the third millennium B.C. Louvre Museum, Paris.

65 Sumerian lyre on a relief from the royal palace in Tello; c. 2400 B.C. Louvre Museum, Paris.

66 Assyrian harp, lyre and double flute on a relief from the royal palace in Nineveh; c. 700 B.C. Louvre Museum, Paris.

67 A Semitic lyre; painting on a tomb in Beni Hassan; c. 1920—1900 B.C.

68 Egyptian arched harp, lute, double oboe and lyre; tomb painting in Veset (Thebes) c. 1420—1411 B.C.

69 Egyptian lute carved on a wooden goblet; c. 1400 B.C. Egyptian Museum, Berlin.

70 An Egyptian lyre of the eighteenth dynasty.

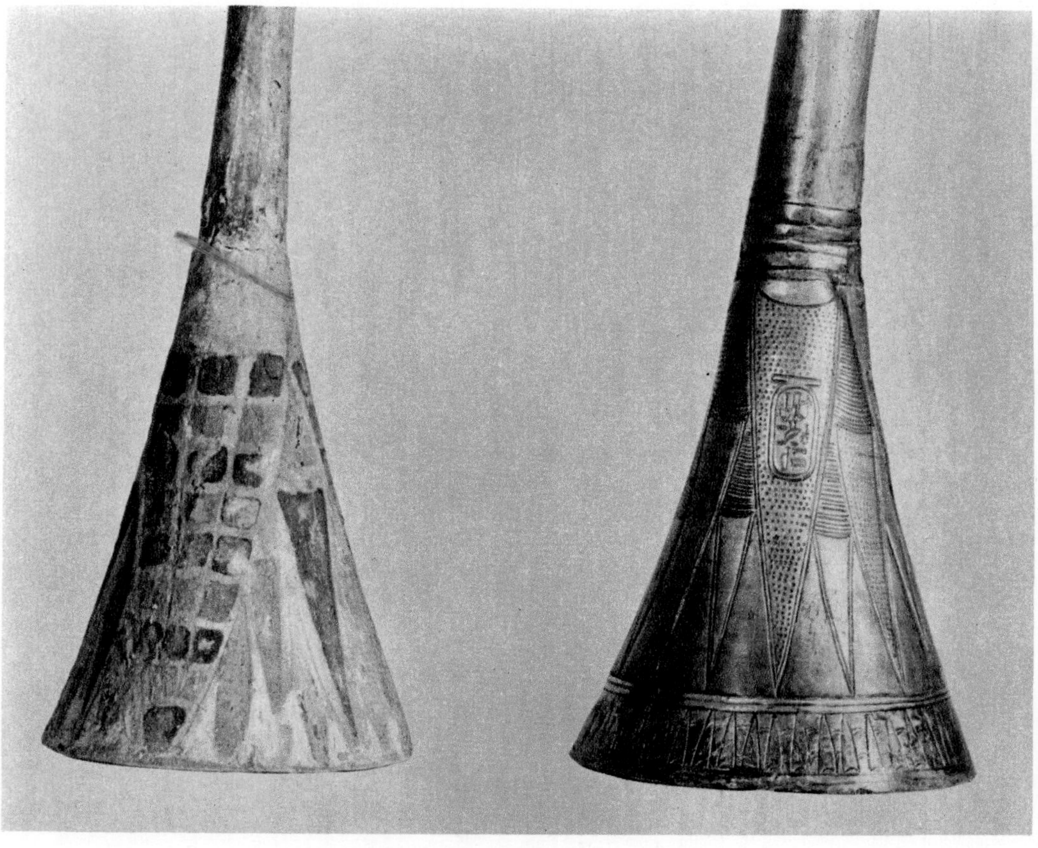

71 The bell of a silver trumpet, decorated with a frieze in the form of a lotus blossom, from the tomb of Tutankhamon (1320 B.C). Cairo Museum.

72 Egyptian angular harp from the time of the nineteenth dynasty. British Museum, London.

73 Sambyke harp, cithara and lyre; painting on a Greek vase from the end of the fifth century B.C. Collection of Classical Antiquities, Munich.

74 Tambourine; painting on a Greek vase; c. fifth century B.C. National Museum, Prague.

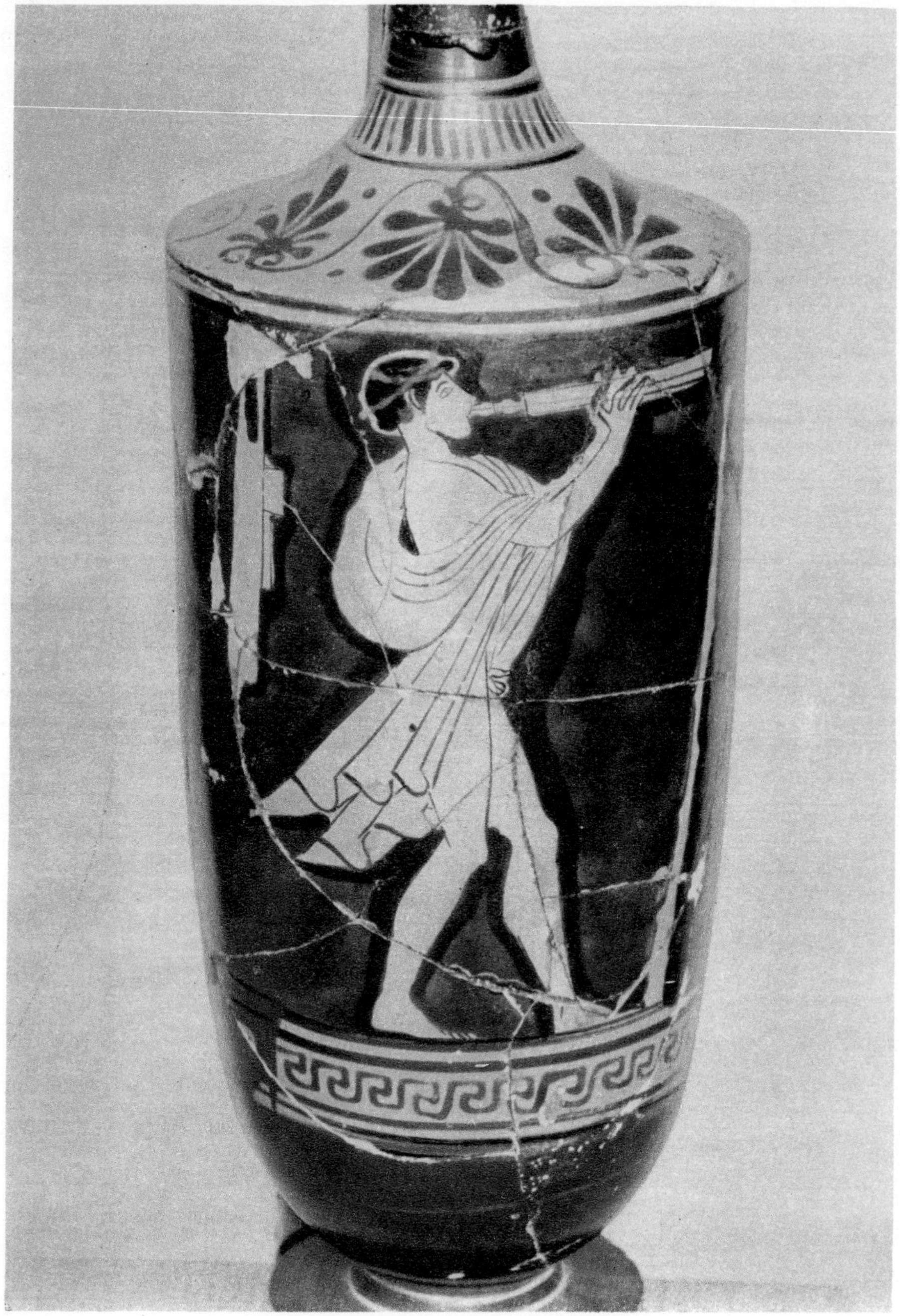

75 Aulos, painting on a Greek vase; c. fifth century B.C.
National Museum, Prague.

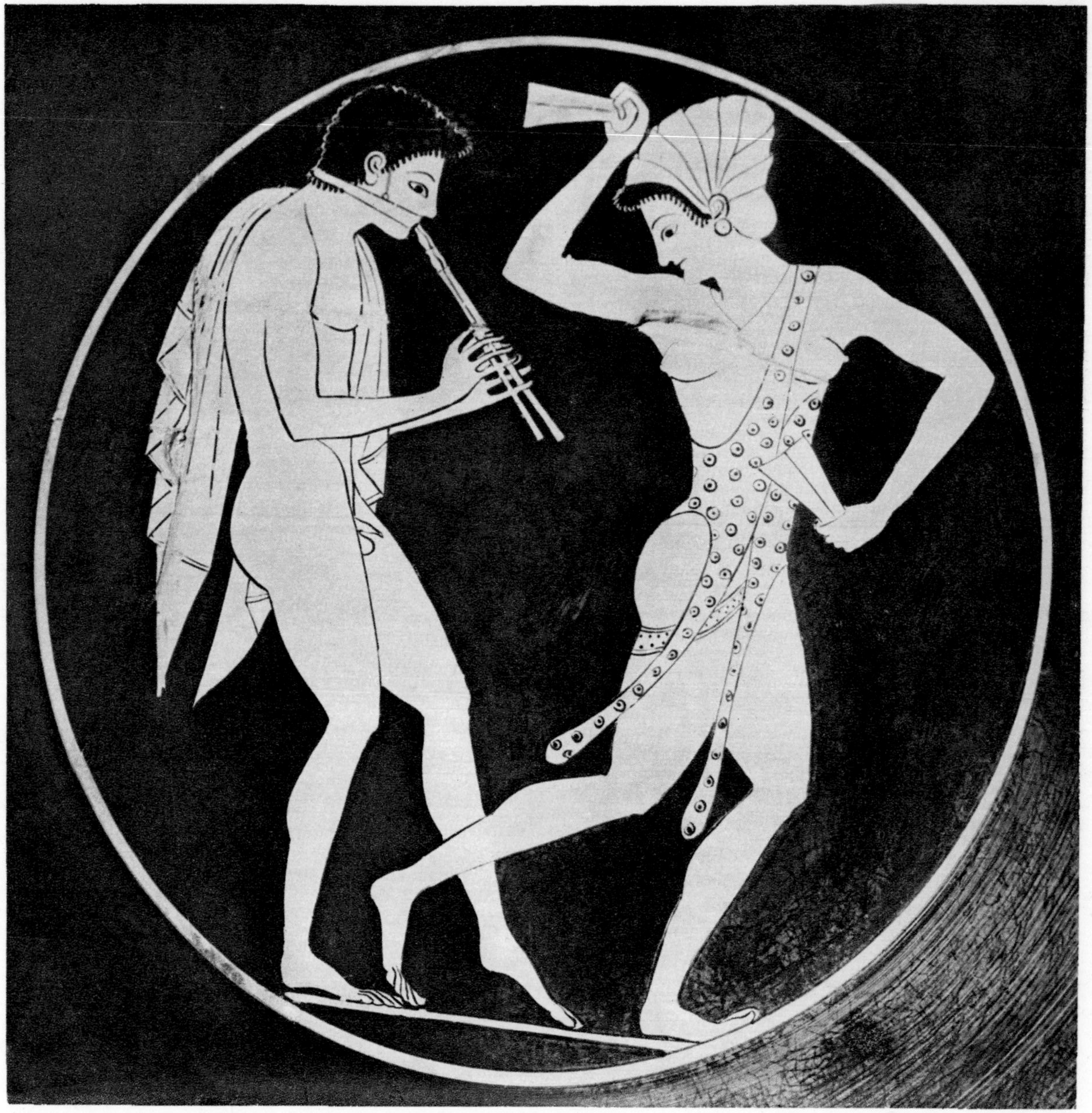

76 *Aulos* and clappers; from Epictete's painting on a goblet; c. fifth century B.C. British Museum, London.

77 Cithara on a coin from Umbria; third century B.C. 78 Lyre on the reverse of a tetradrachm; c. 200 B.C.
79 War horns on a denarius from 44 B.C.
80—81 *Kinnor* and straight trumpets, *chacocra*, on denarii; from the period of the second rising of the Jews 132—135 A.D.

82 Roman cymbals and *aulos*. Marble relief of the year 50 A. D. National Museum, Naples.

83 Roman *cornua* from a stone relief of the year 109. National Museum of Antiquities, Bucharest.

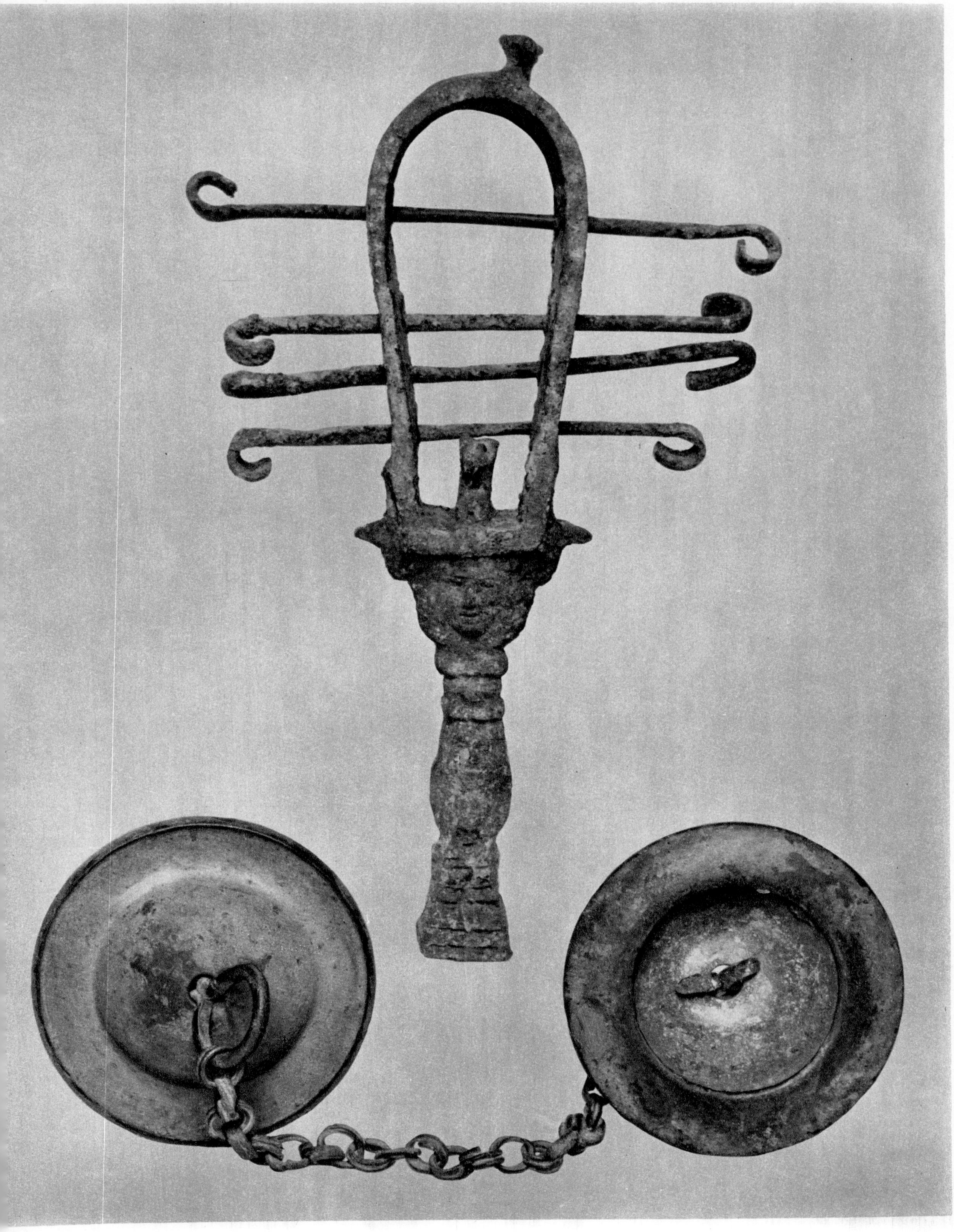

84—85 Roman cymbals and *sistrum* (rattle) from Pompeii. National Museum, Naples.

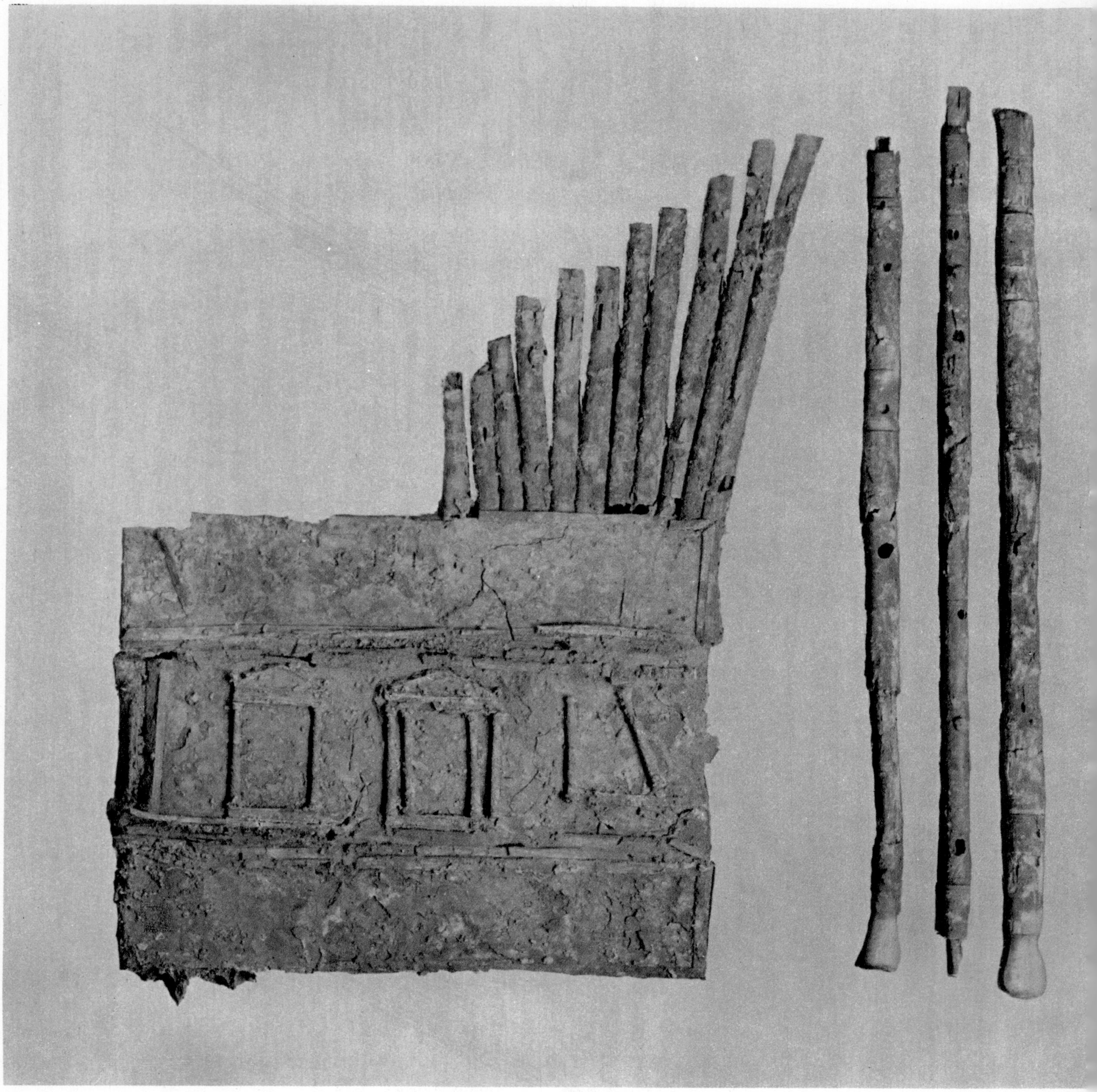

86 Roman organ known as *hydraulis*, from Pompeii. National Museum, Naples.

87 Horn, clappers, harp, lyre and *lituus*; Bible of Charles the Bald, ninth century. National Library, Paris.

88—89 The famous hunting horn sounded by Roland, nephew of Charlemagne. According to the legend the sound of this horn carried so far that from many miles away Charlemagne heard Roland sounding his horn for help as he lay wounded in the Pyrenees in the year 778. In his mortal anxiety Roland blew his

90—91 Hunting horn from an elephant's tusk, 9—10th century. Charles IV placed this oliphant together with Roland's horn in the castle of Karlštejn,

92 *Crot;* psalter from the middle of the thirteenth century. University Library, Prague.

93 Fiddle; *Mater verborum* of the thirteenth century. National Museum, Prague.

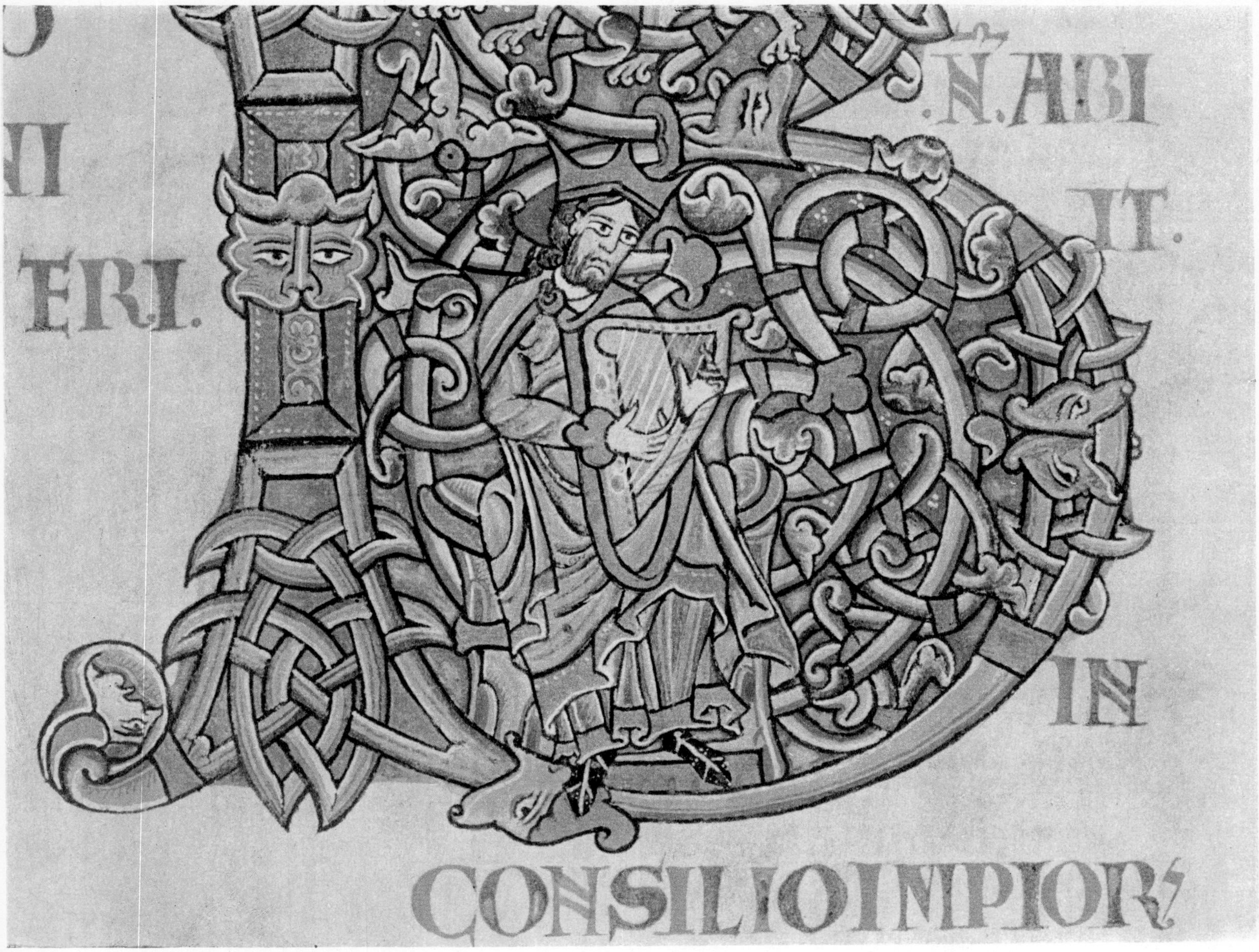


94 Harp; thirteenth century psalter. University Library, Prague.

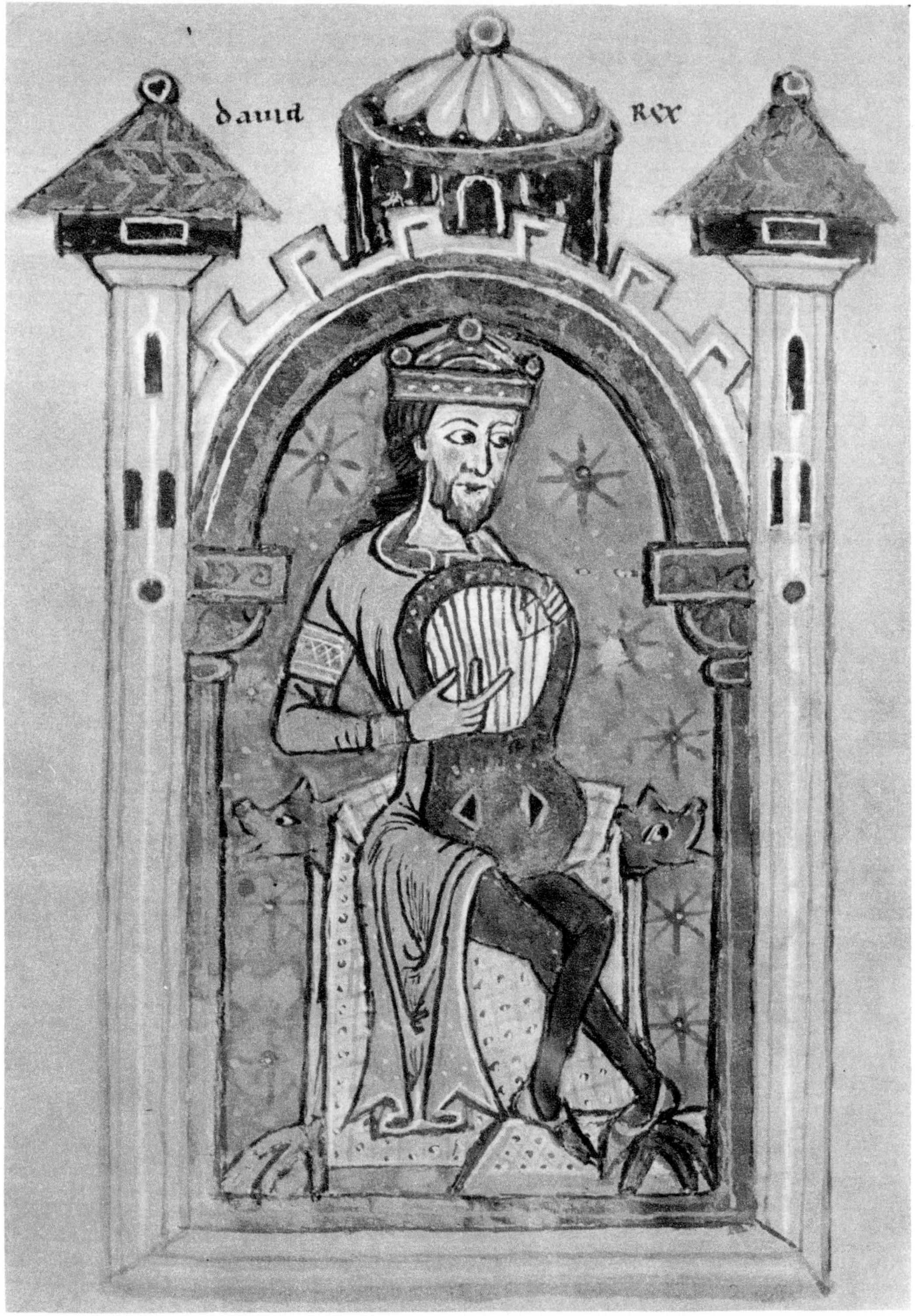


95 *Crot* from the Psalterium Juttae Tarsinae; thirteenth century. Zwettl Monastery Library, Austria.

96 Bell chimes; Lectionarum Arnoldi Misnensis, 1290—1300. Monastery Library, Osek.

97—98 Harp, Bohemian wing *(ala bohemica)*, fiddle and *cetera*. Passional of Abbess Kunhuta, 1319—1321. University Library, Prague.

99 Drum, flute, shawm, fiddle, psaltery and bagpipes; illumination in a collection of songs of Zurich, the Codex of the Manesse family, from the beginning of the fourteenth century. University Library, Heidelberg.

100 Shepherd's horns; Velislav's Bible, 1340. University Library, Prague.
101 Decachordum (ten-stringed), *crot*, horn and trumpets; Velislav's Bible, 1340. University Library, Prague.

102 Psaltery and fiddles; Velislav's Bible, 1340. University Library, Prague.

103 Psaltery harp, bell chimes and psaltery; Velislav's Bible, 1340. University Library, Prague.
104 Bohemian wing *(ala bohemica)*, *cetera*, fiddle and psaltery; Velislav's Bible, 1340. University Library, Prague.

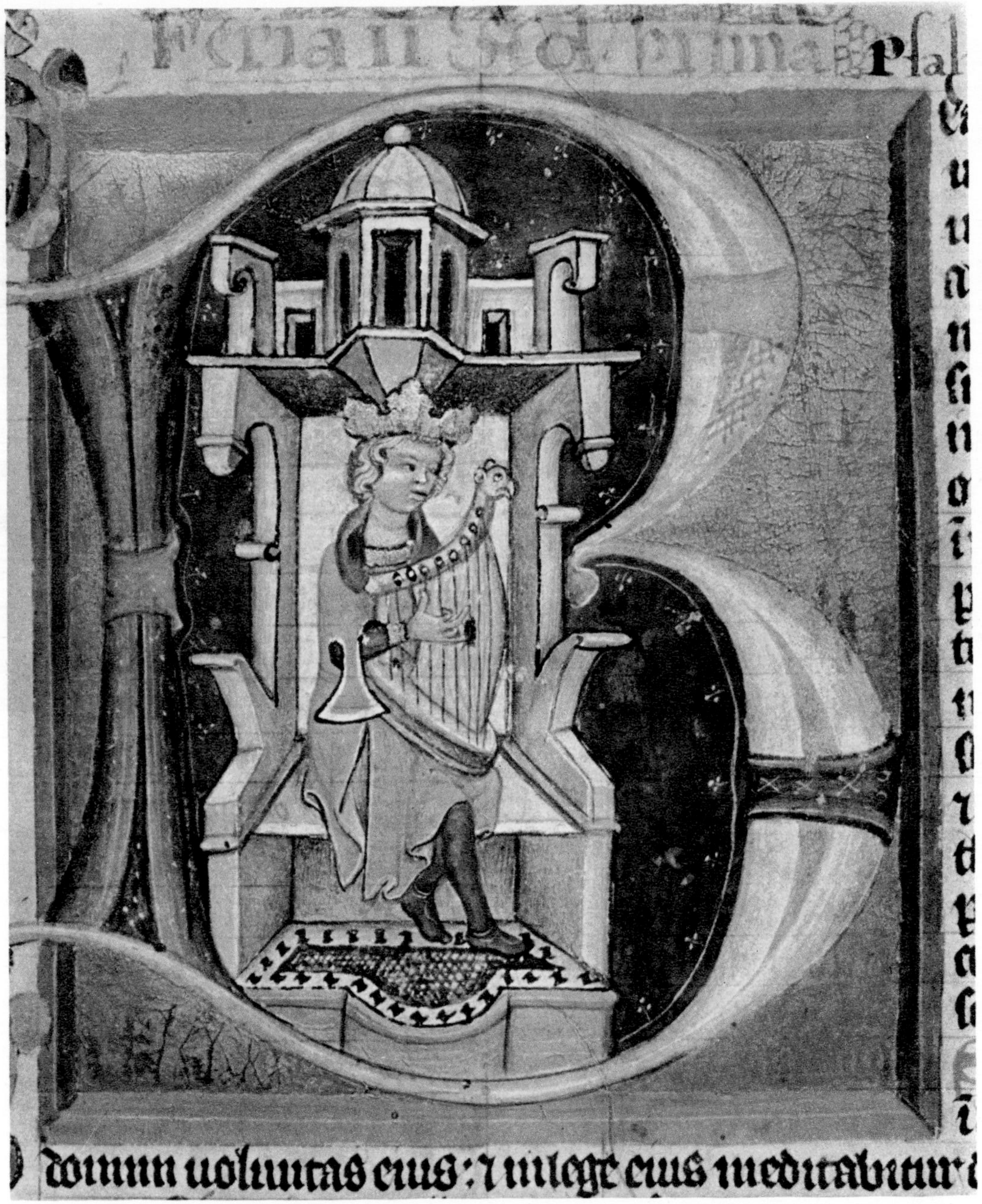

105 Psaltery harp; a breviary of 1343. Monastery Library, Rajhrad.

106 Organ; Bologna breviary of the middle of the fourteenth century.
University Library, Prague.

107 Psaltery; Roudnice psalter, fourteenth century. Chapter Library, Prague.

108—109 Lute and *lira da braccio*; detail of the frame of a Madonna by Thomas of Modena; fourteenth century. Karlštejn.

110—111 Beaked flute and shawm; wall painting, fourteenth century. Karlštejn.

112—113 Horn with fingerholes and bagpipes; wall painting, 14th century, Karlštejn.

114—115 Cromorne with bladder and shepherd's horn; fourteenth century wall painting. Karlštejn.

116 Bladder-pipe; fourteenth century wall painting. Karlštejn.

117 Handbells, mandora, fiddle and Bohemian wing *(ala bohemica)*; Thomas of Štítný, *Six Little Books on Christian Matters*, c. 1376, University Library, Prague.

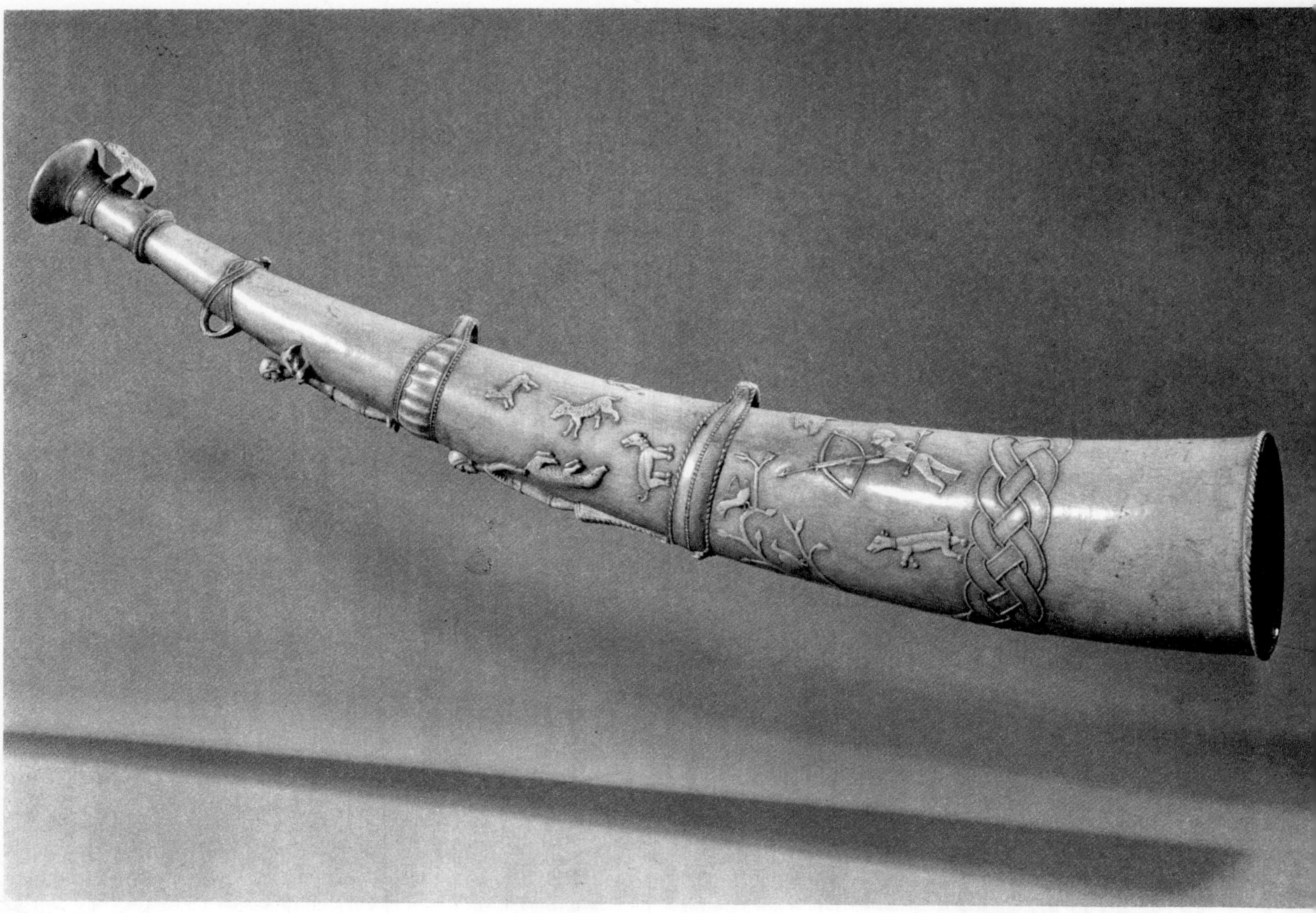

118—120 Fourteenth century oliphant, and details. National Museum, Prague.

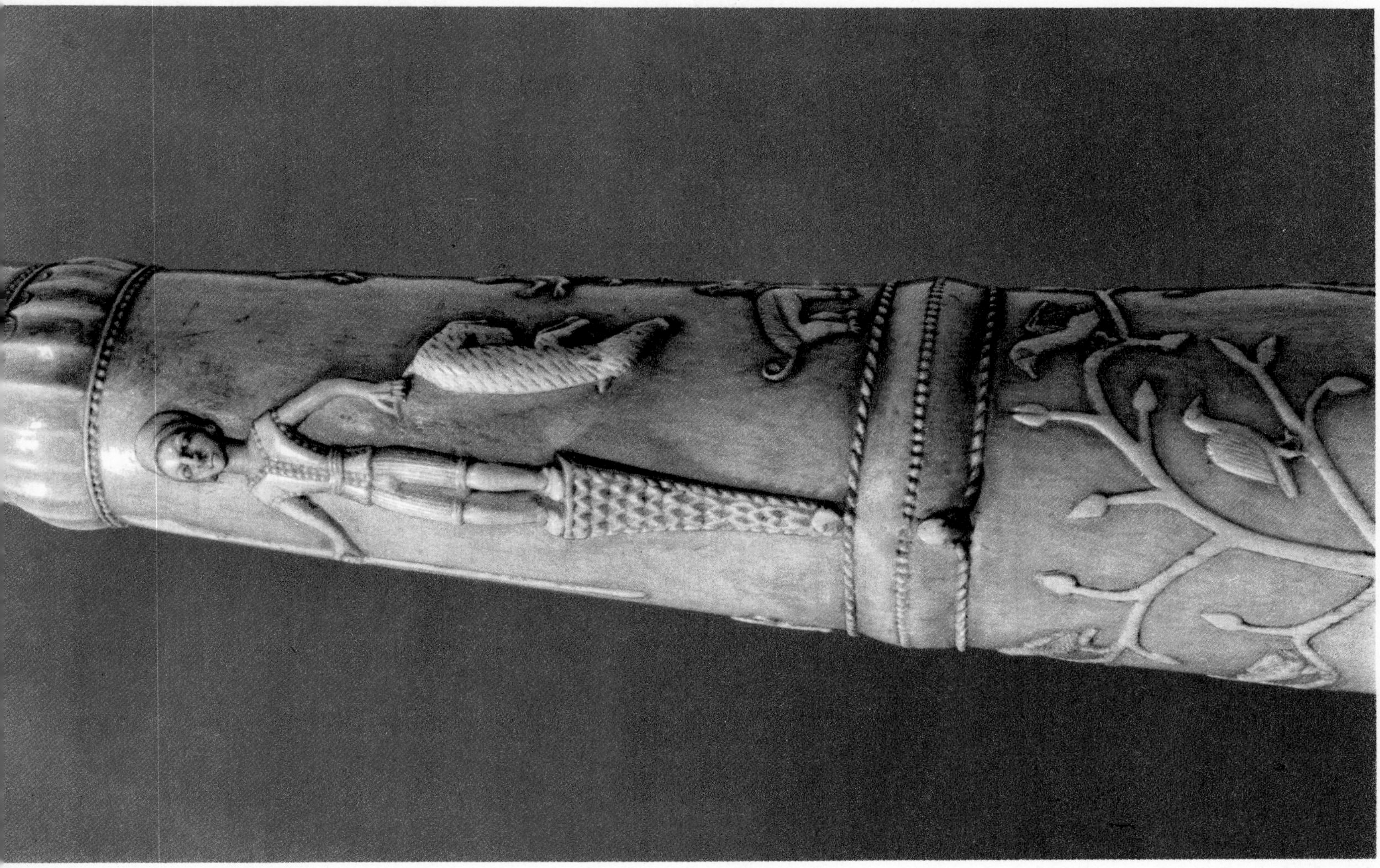

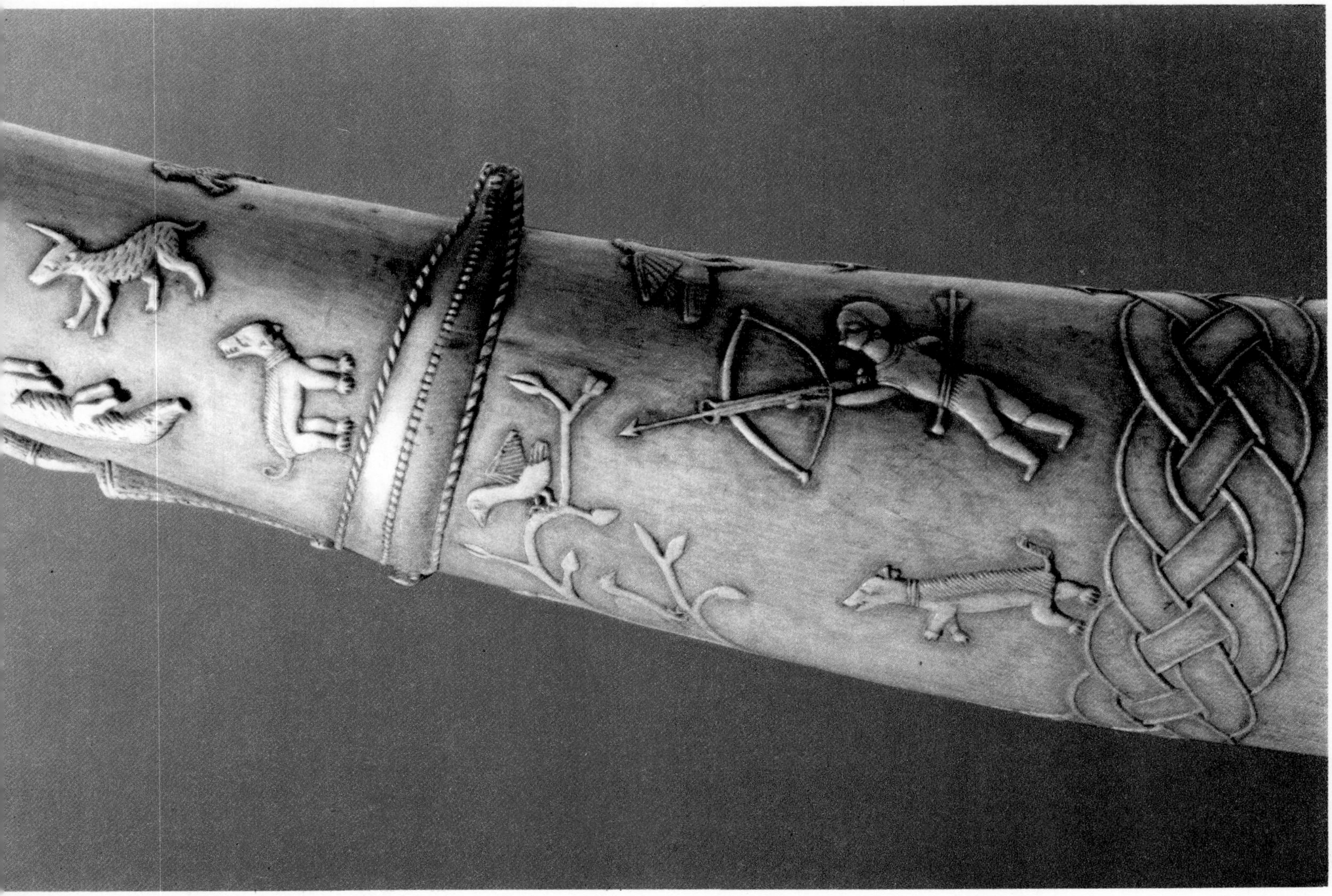

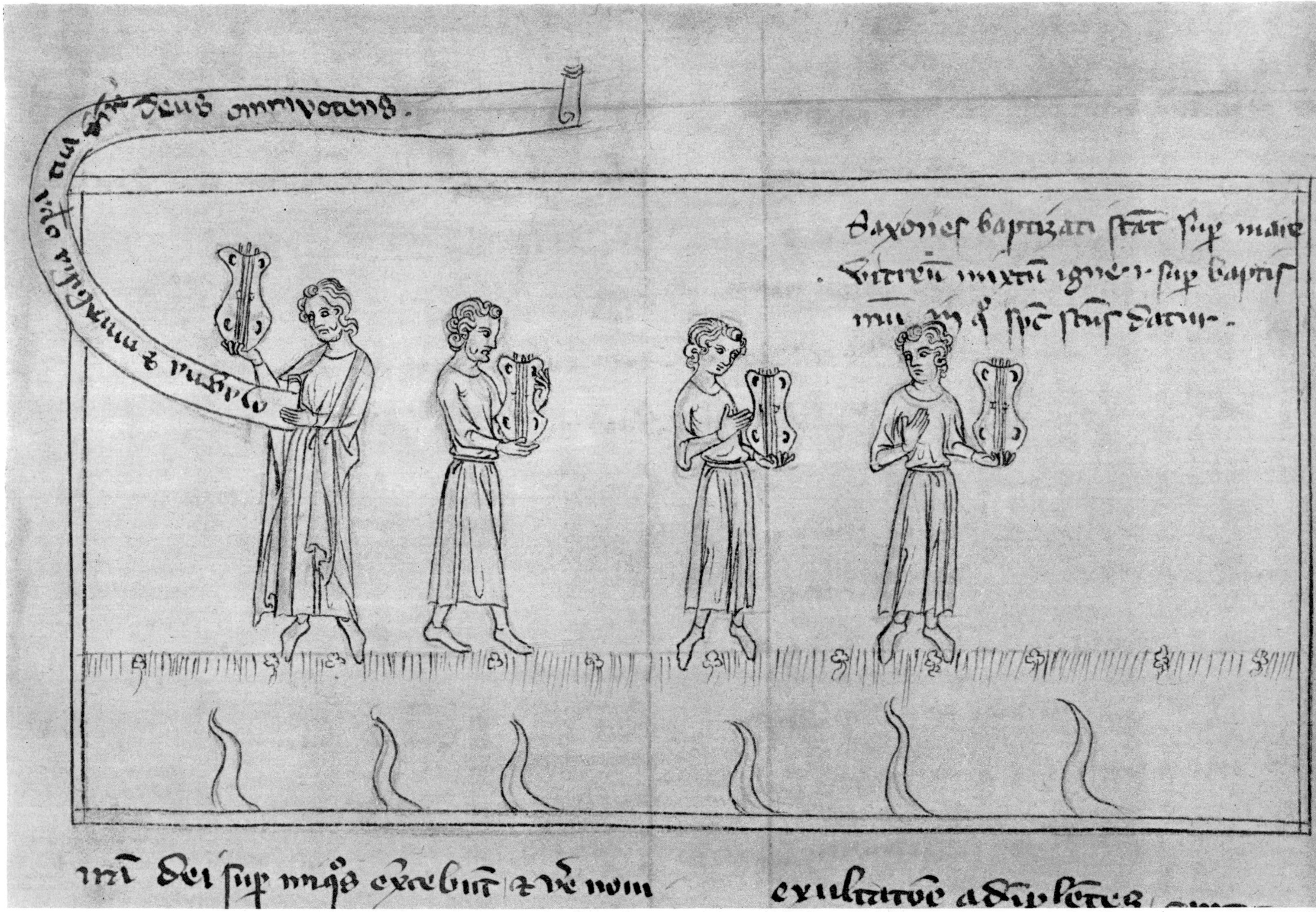

121 *Crots*; Scriptum super apocalypsim, from the end of the fourteenth century. Chapter Library, Prague.

122 Bells, triangle, recorder, jingles, trumpet, harp, shawm, fiddle, lute, organ, helicon, mandora, white zink, harp, trumscheit, psaltery, drums, bell chimes, rattle, clavichord, hurdy-gurdy. Otto von Passau, Codex from 1448. Library of the Gymnasium Casimirianum, Coburg.

123 Jingles, fiddle, lute and psaltery harp.

124 Psaltery harp, one-hand flute with a drum and psaltery; King Wenceslas IV Bible, end of the fourteenth century. State Library, Vienna.

125 Small drum, handbells and drum.

126 Shawm, trumpets, triangle, organ and fiddle; King Wenceslas IV Bible, end of the fourteenth century. State Library, Vienna.

127 Shawm and trumpet.

128 Bohemian wing *(ala bohemica)*; a Krumlov chrestomathy from the beginning of the fifteenth century. National Museum, Prague.

129 Lute: Krumlov chrestomathy of the beginning of the fifteenth century. National Museum, Prague.

130 Psaltery.

131 Mandora, drums and Bohemian wing *(ala bohemica)*; Litoměřice Bible. 1414. Archives, Třeboň.

132 Shepherd's horn, drum, lute and psaltery from the Bible of Queen Christina of Sweden, c. 1420. Vatican Library.

133 Psaltery types of the Bohemian wing. A Latin Bible of the first half of the fifteenth century. Chapter Library, Prague.

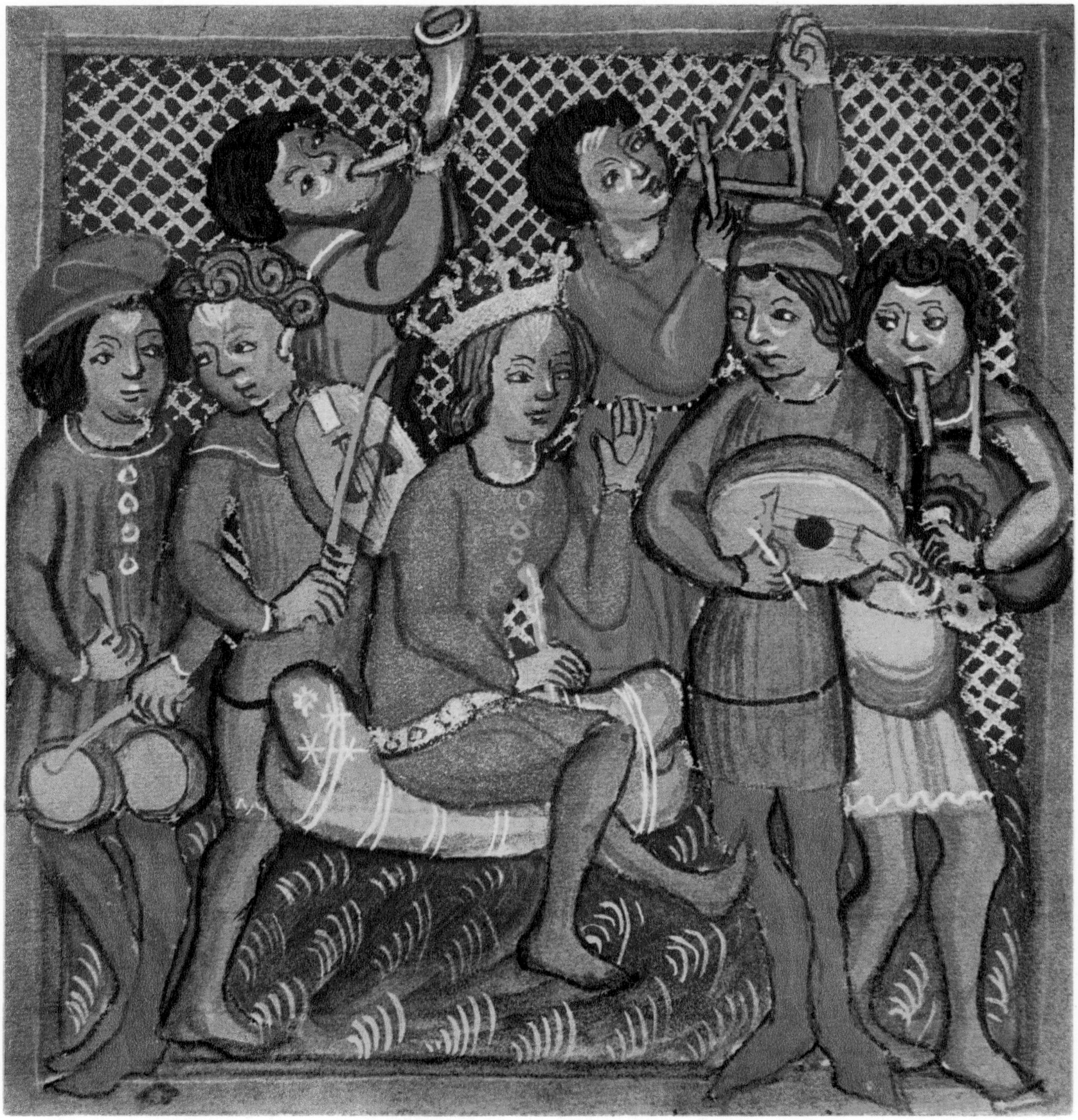

134 Small drums, fiddle, horn, triangle, lute and bagpipes; Olomouc Bible, 1417. University Library, Olomouc.

135 Pommers and trumpets (one trumpet S-shaped); illumination in the Richenthal Chronicle (the Leningrad Manuscript) 1464. University Library, Prague.

136 One-hand flute with small drum, portative organ, dulcimer, tenor pommer, lute, recorder, trumpet, dulcimer; fifteenth century manuscript. City Library, Grenoble.

137 Double flute and lute on a carved ivory comb; fifteenth century French work. National Museum, Prague.

138 Lute on a Venetian enamelled goblet of the end of the fifteenth century.
National Museum, Prague.

139 Small drum, bladder pipe and organ; Lobkovice breviary, 1494. University Library, Prague.

140 Rebec and lute.

141 Clavicytherium or dulcimer with raised stringboard; detail from a wooden altar dating from the end of the fifteenth century. Parish church of Kefermarkt, Upper Austria.

142—143 Trumpets and wind-cap shawms (Rauschpfeife); Litoměřice breviary, 1520.

144 Harp and lute; Litoměřice breviary, 1520.

145—146 Black (curved) zink, bass pommer. Harp and *viola da braccio*. Mladá Boleslav gradual, 1570—1572. District Museum, Mladá Boleslav.

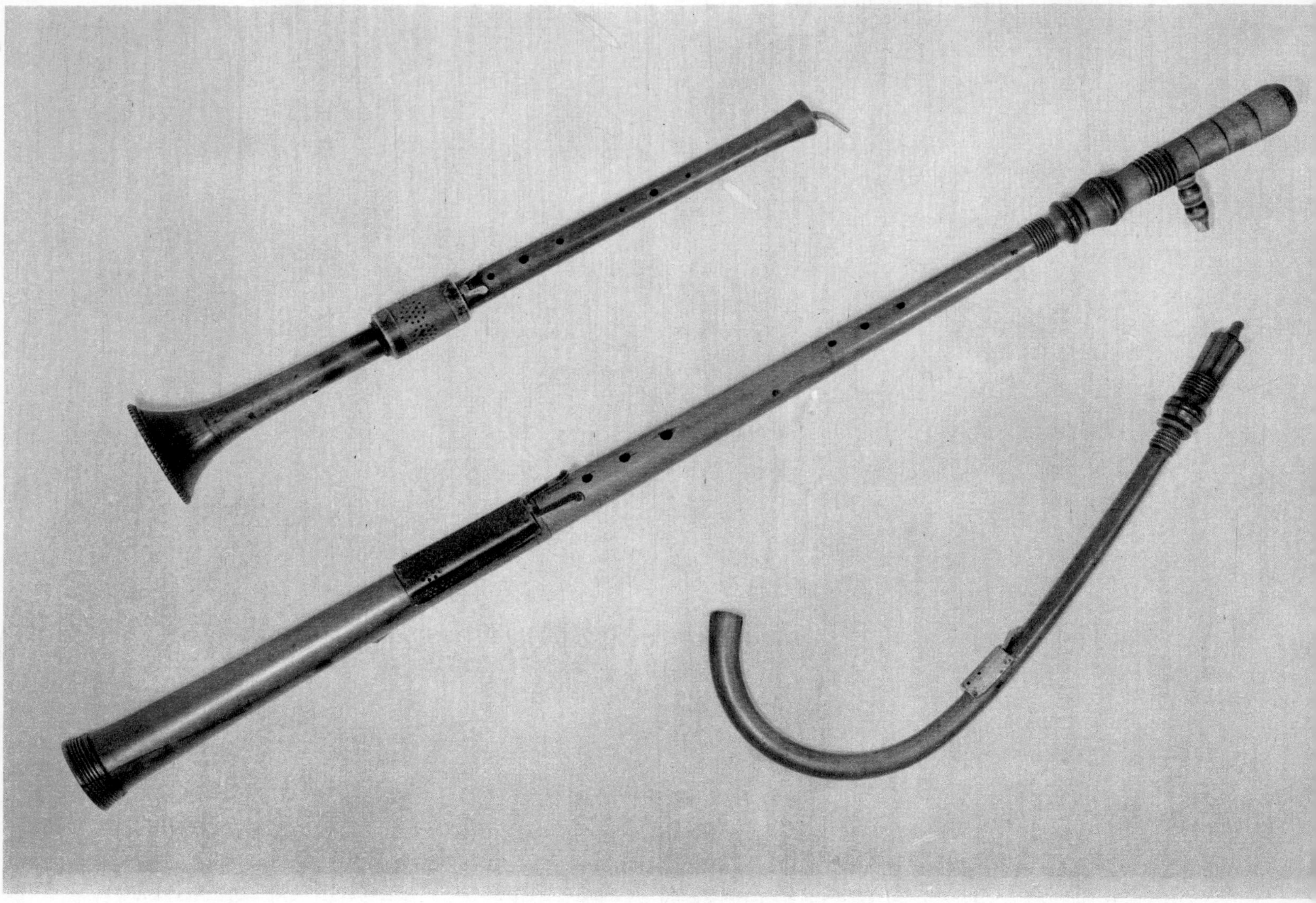

147—149 Alto pommer, grand bass wind-cap shawm and alto cromorne, sixteenth century. National Museum, Prague.

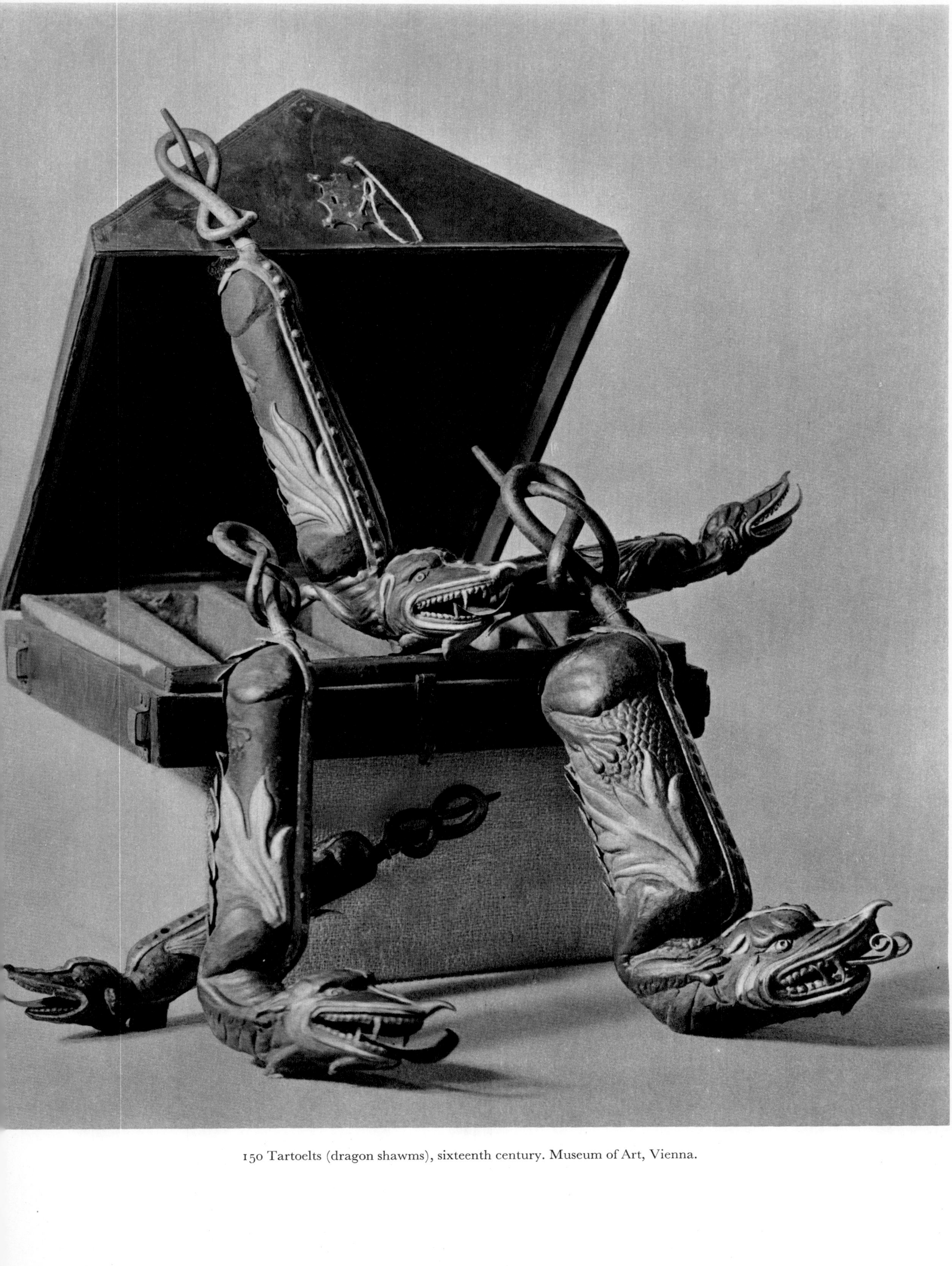

150 Tartoelts (dragon shawms), sixteenth century. Museum of Art, Vienna.

151 Recorder; Jan Kupecký (1667—1740). National Museum, Budapest.

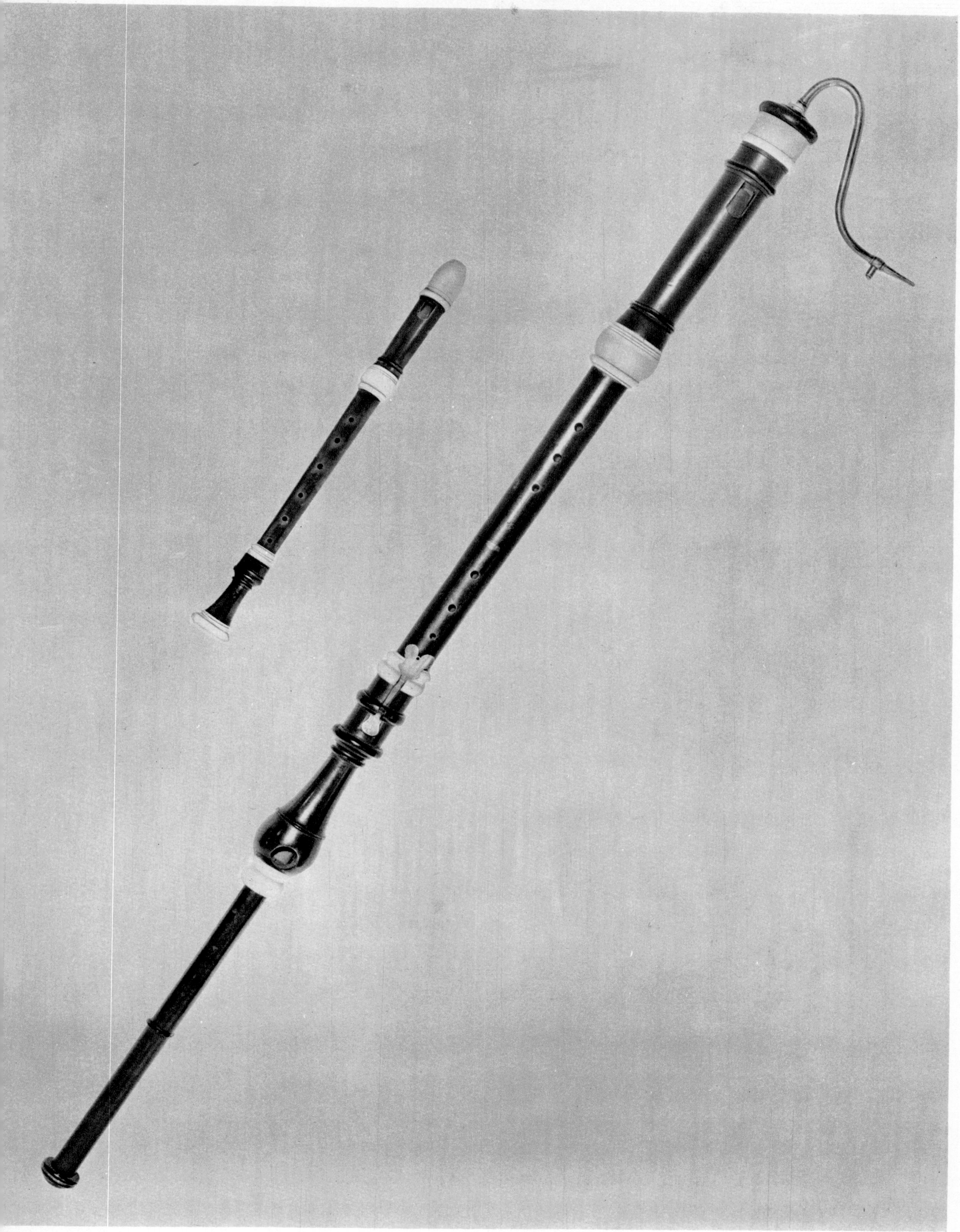

152—153 Alto and bass recorder made by P. I. Bressan, seventeenth century. National Museum, Prague.

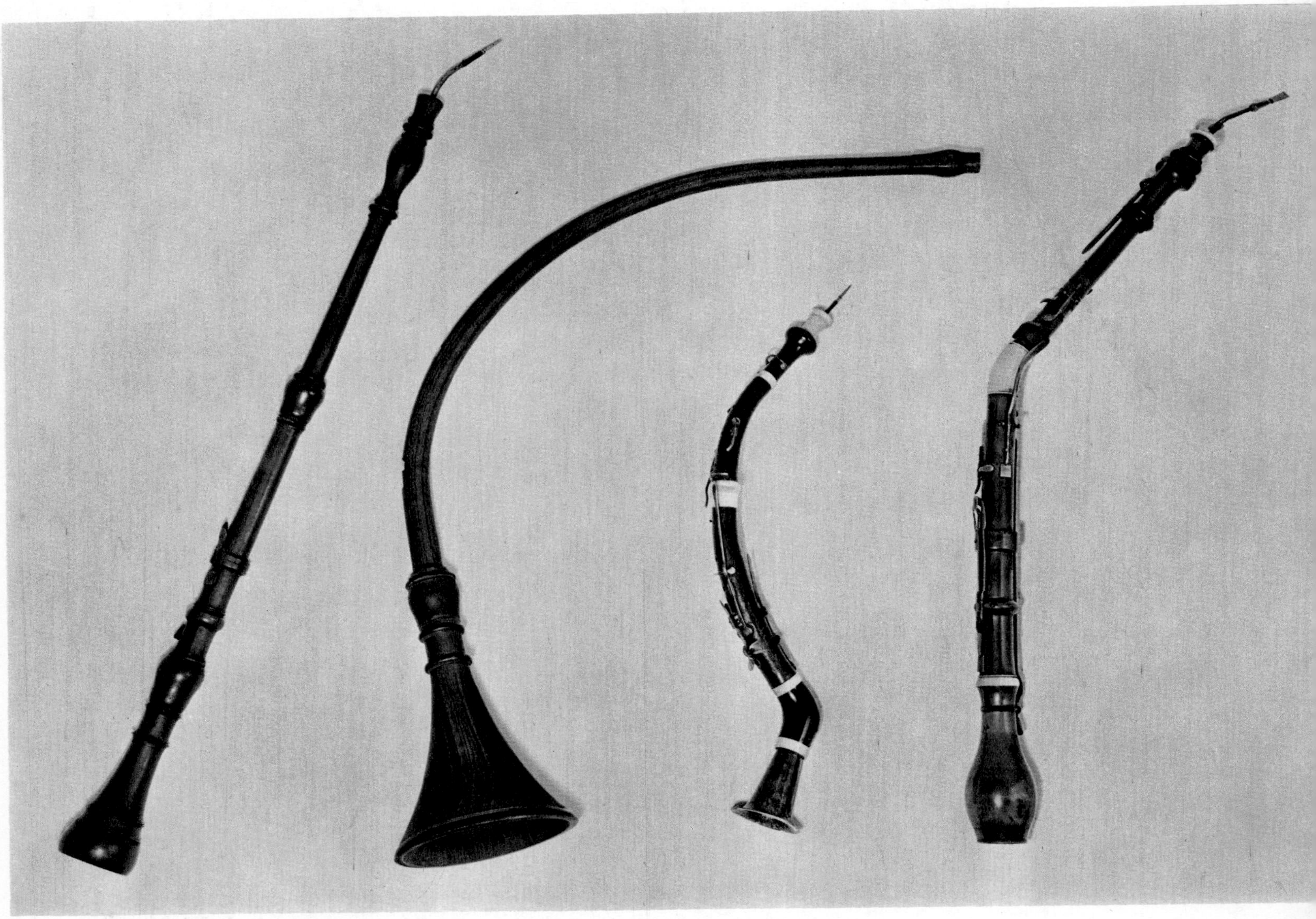

154—157 Hunting oboe by Fridrich, seventeenth century; and English horns (cors anglais) made in Bohemia, seventeenth to nineteenth century. National Museum, Prague.

158 Transverse flute; Jan Kupecký (1667—1740).

159—161 Oliphant belonging to the Polish King Jan Sobieski, 1683, and details. National Museum, Prague.

IOANNES SOBIESK
REXPOLON.ETM.D.L
MDCLXXXIII

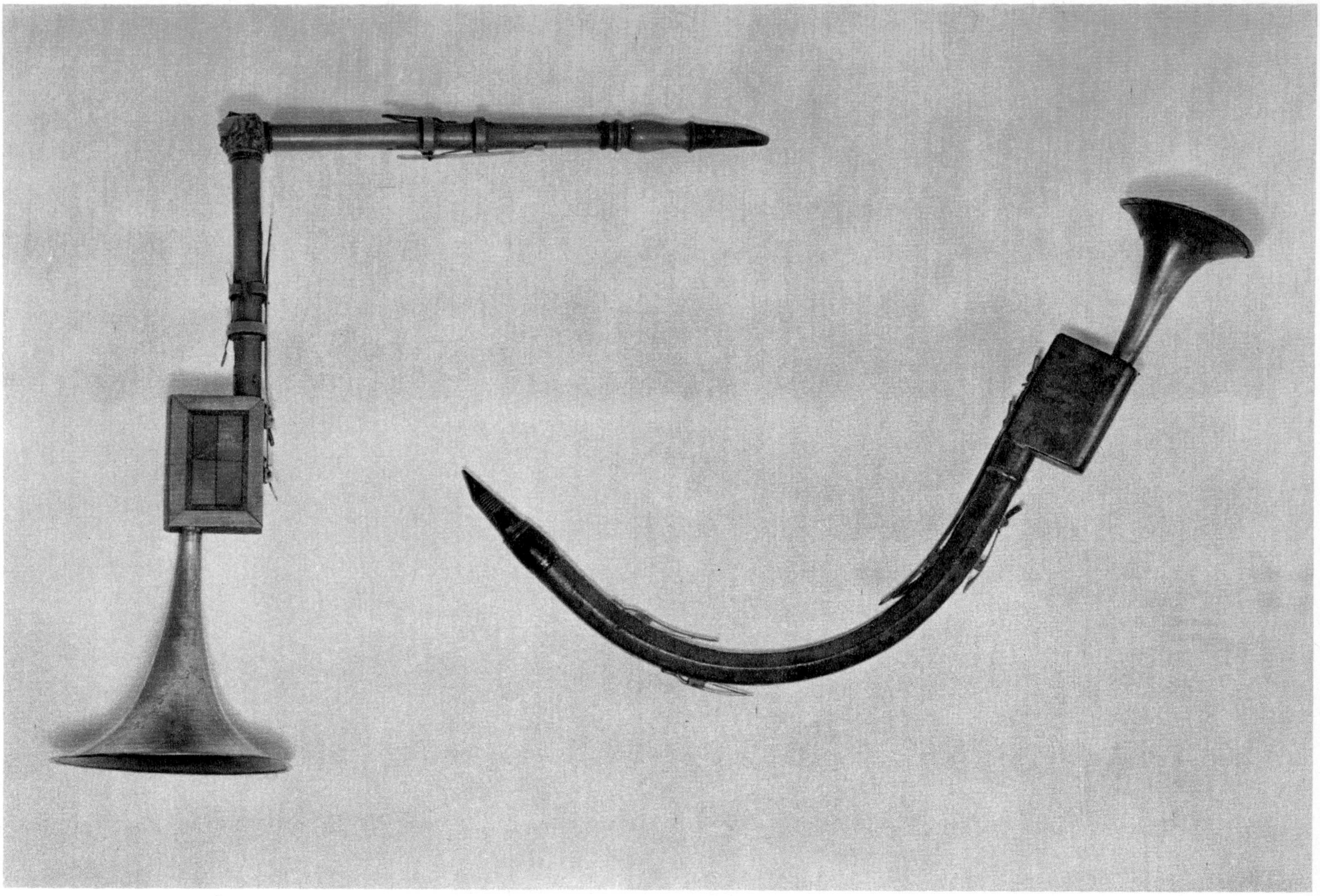

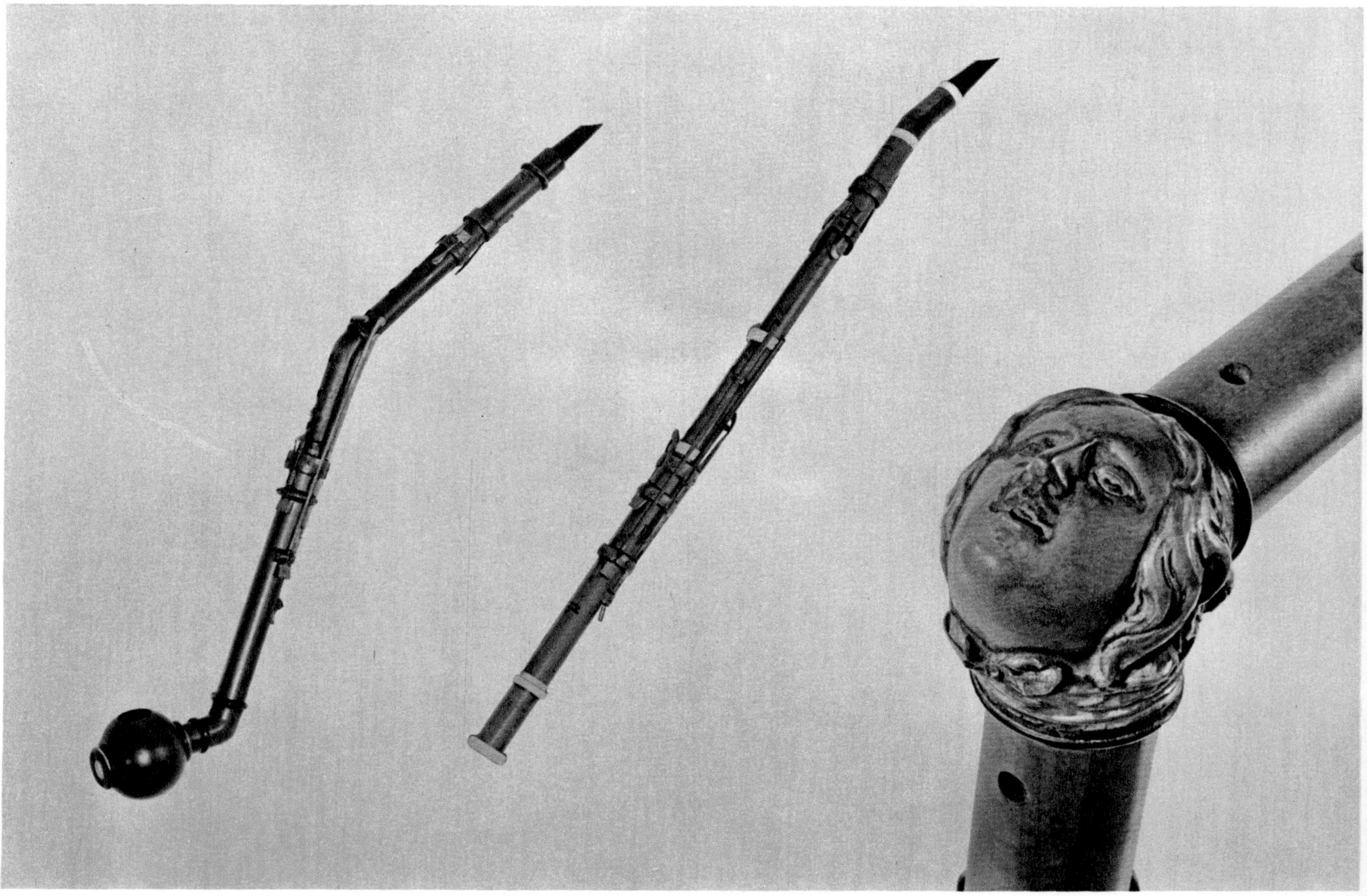

162—165 Czech basset-horns of the eighteenth and nineteenth centuries and detail of the first basset horn.
National Museum, Prague.

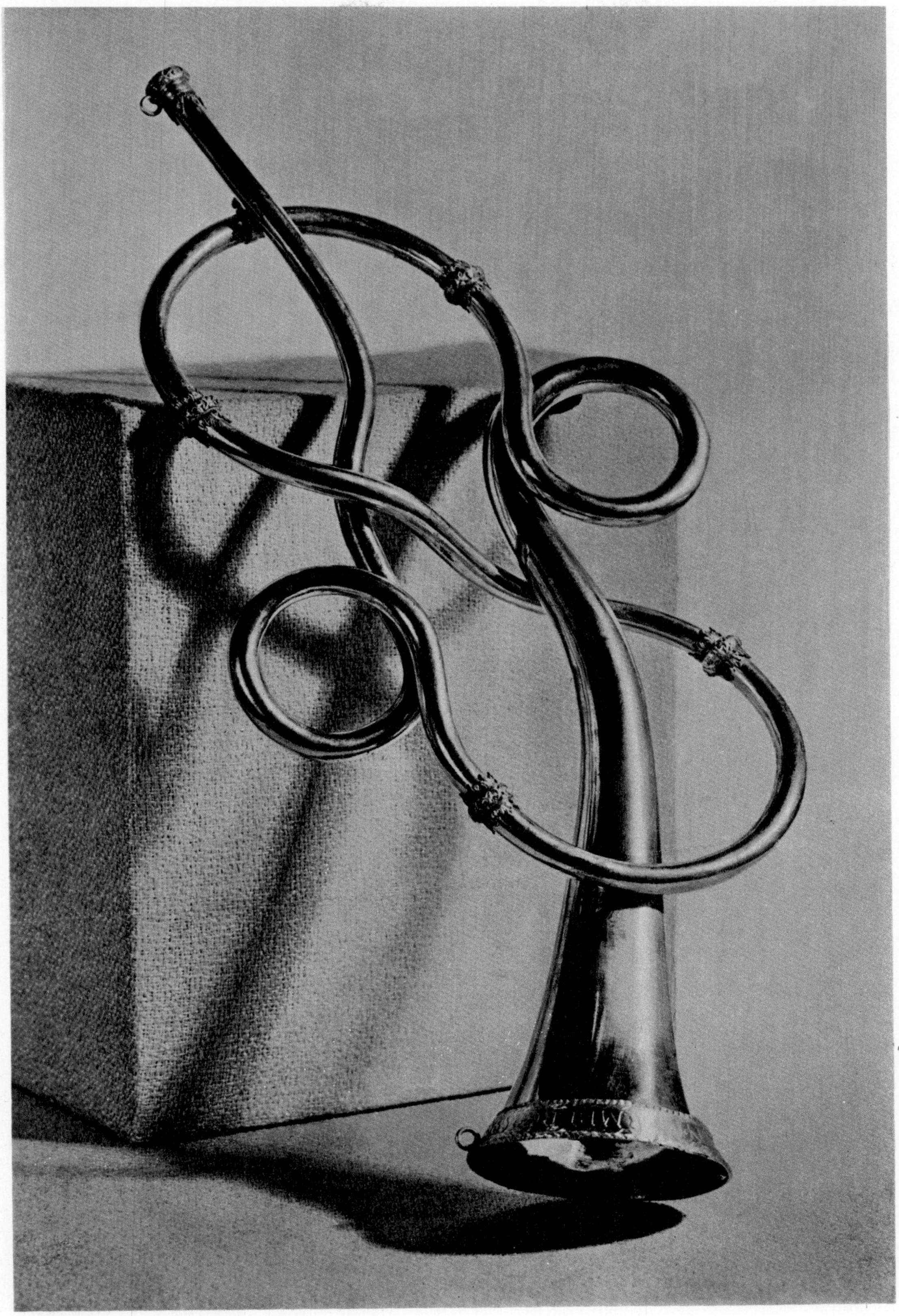

166 Trumpet made by the Nüremberg instrument maker Antonius Schnitzer, 1598. Museum of Art, Vienna, from the collection of the Friends of Music in Vienna.

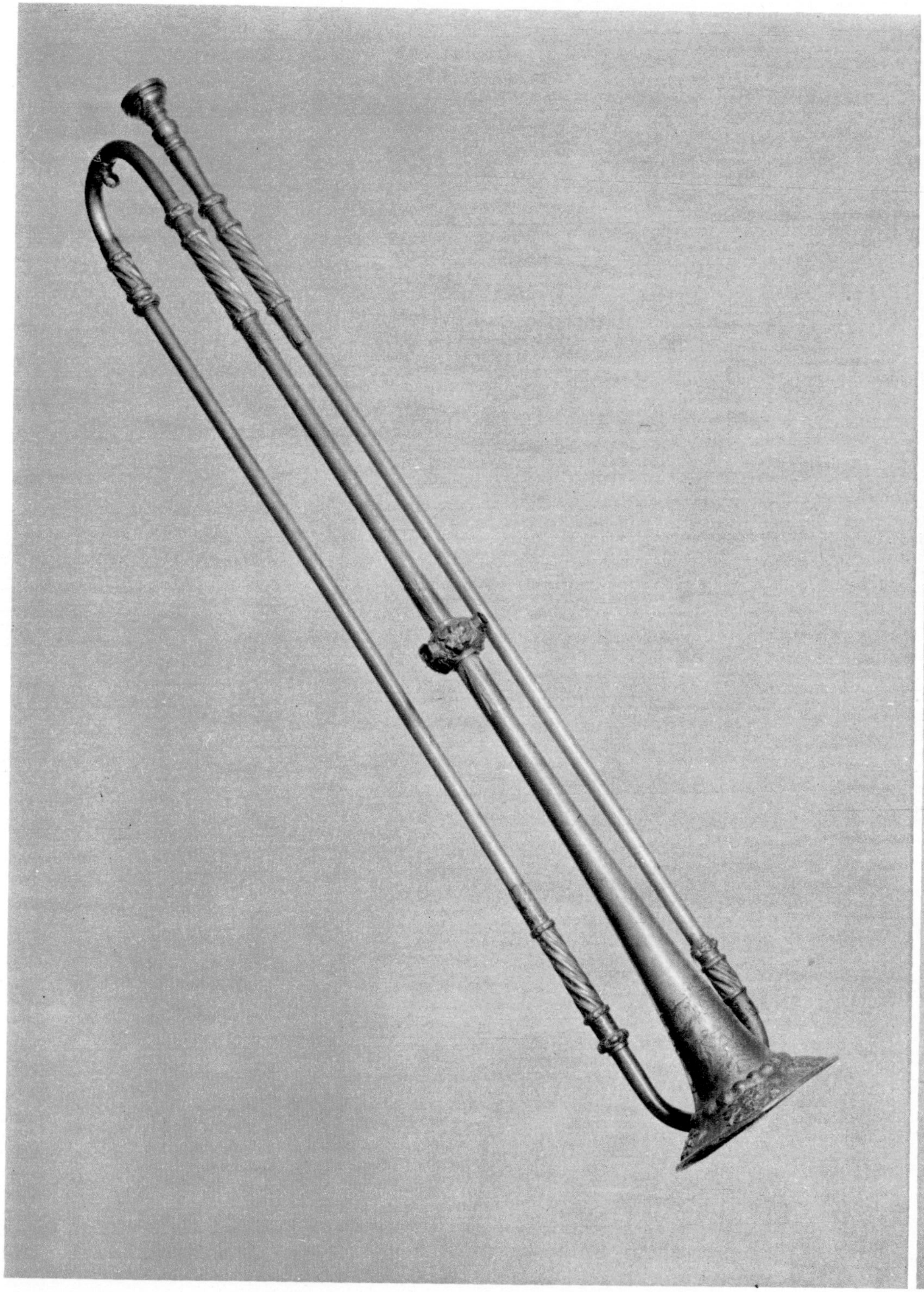

167 *Trompeta clarina* from the Lobkovice collection, made by Michael Leichamschneider, Vienna 1716; silver, gilded, and inlaid with semi-precious stones.

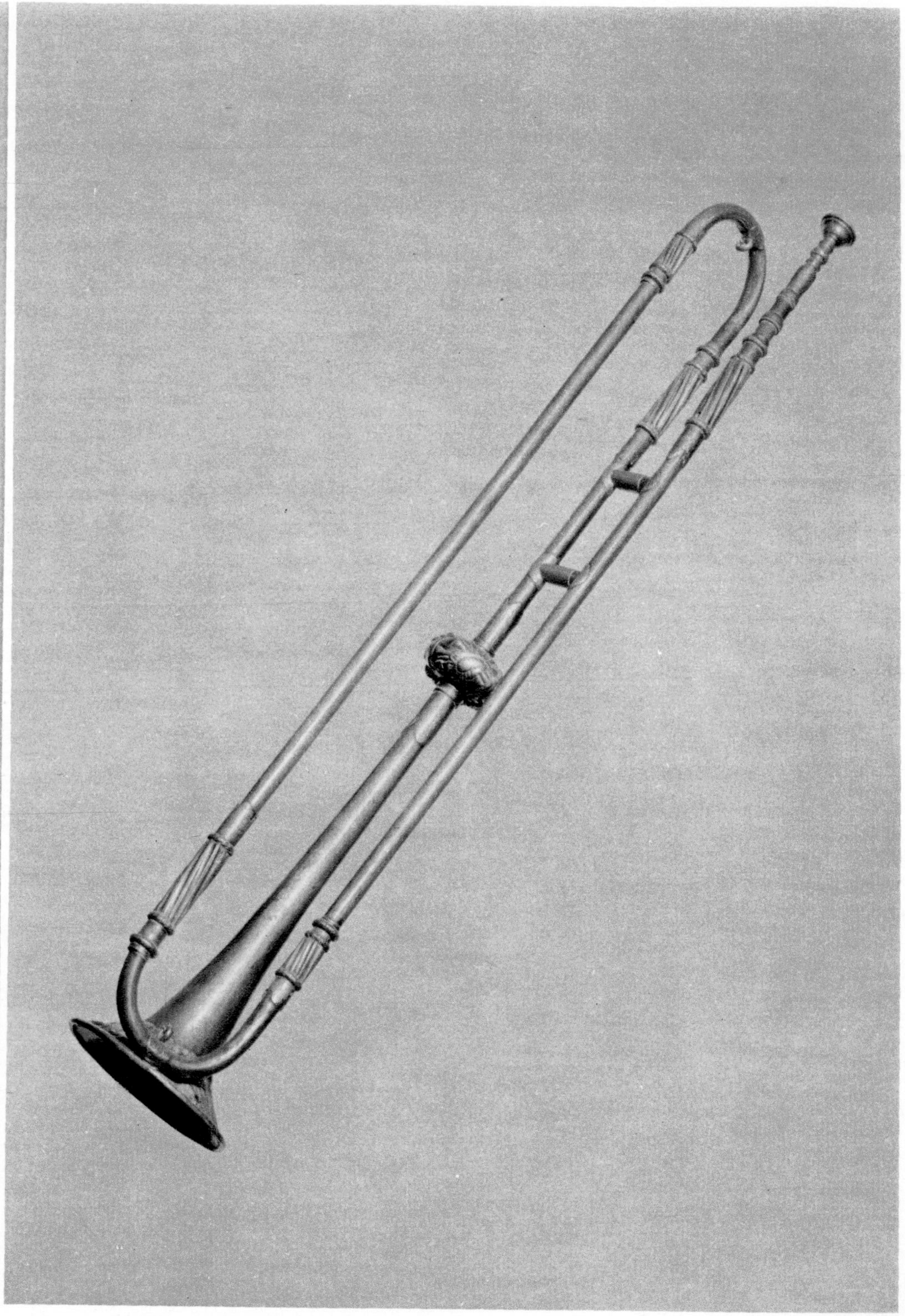

168 Gilded silver *trompeta clarina* belonging to the King of Saxony Augustus III; eighteenth century. National Museum, Prague

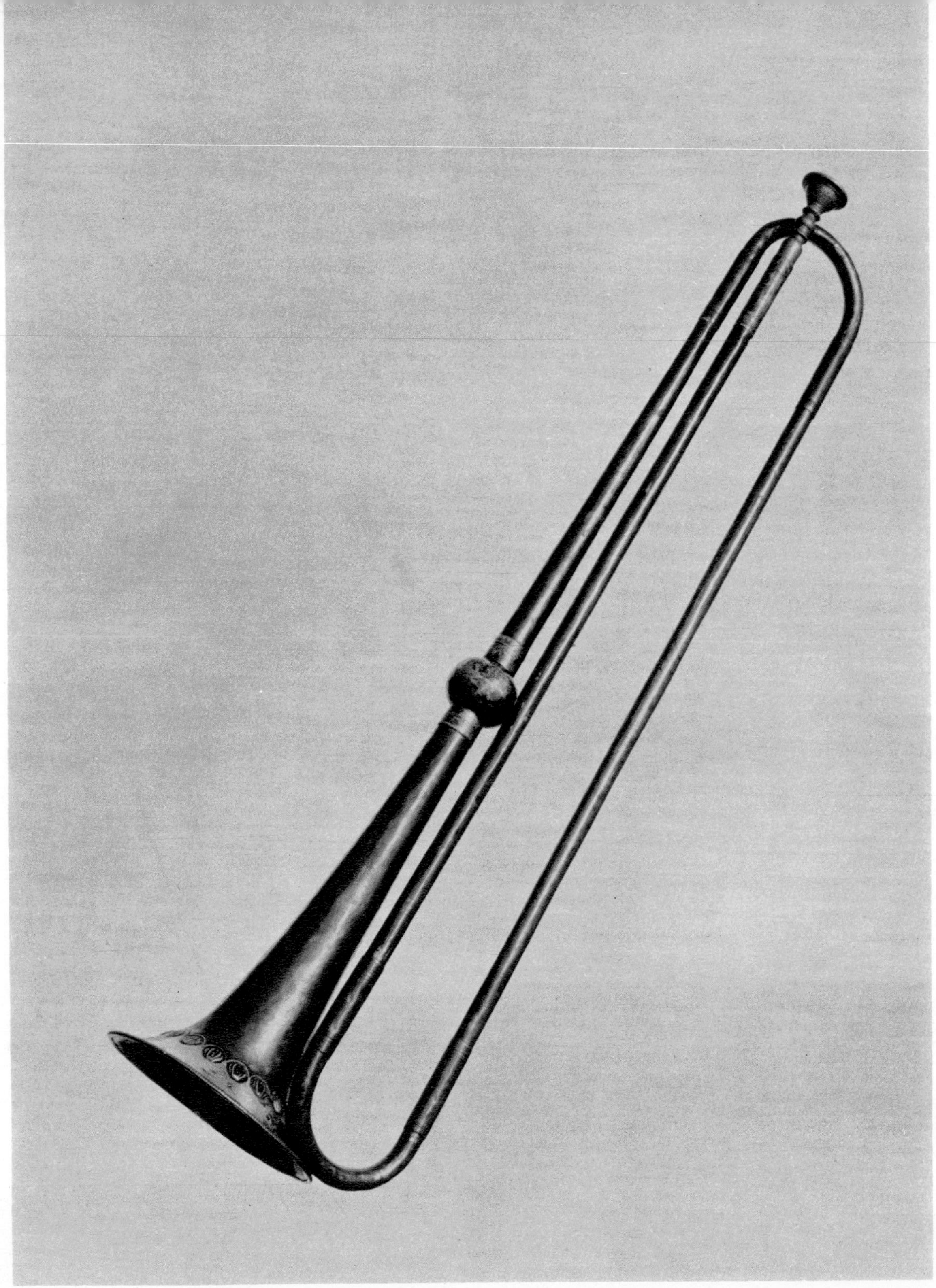

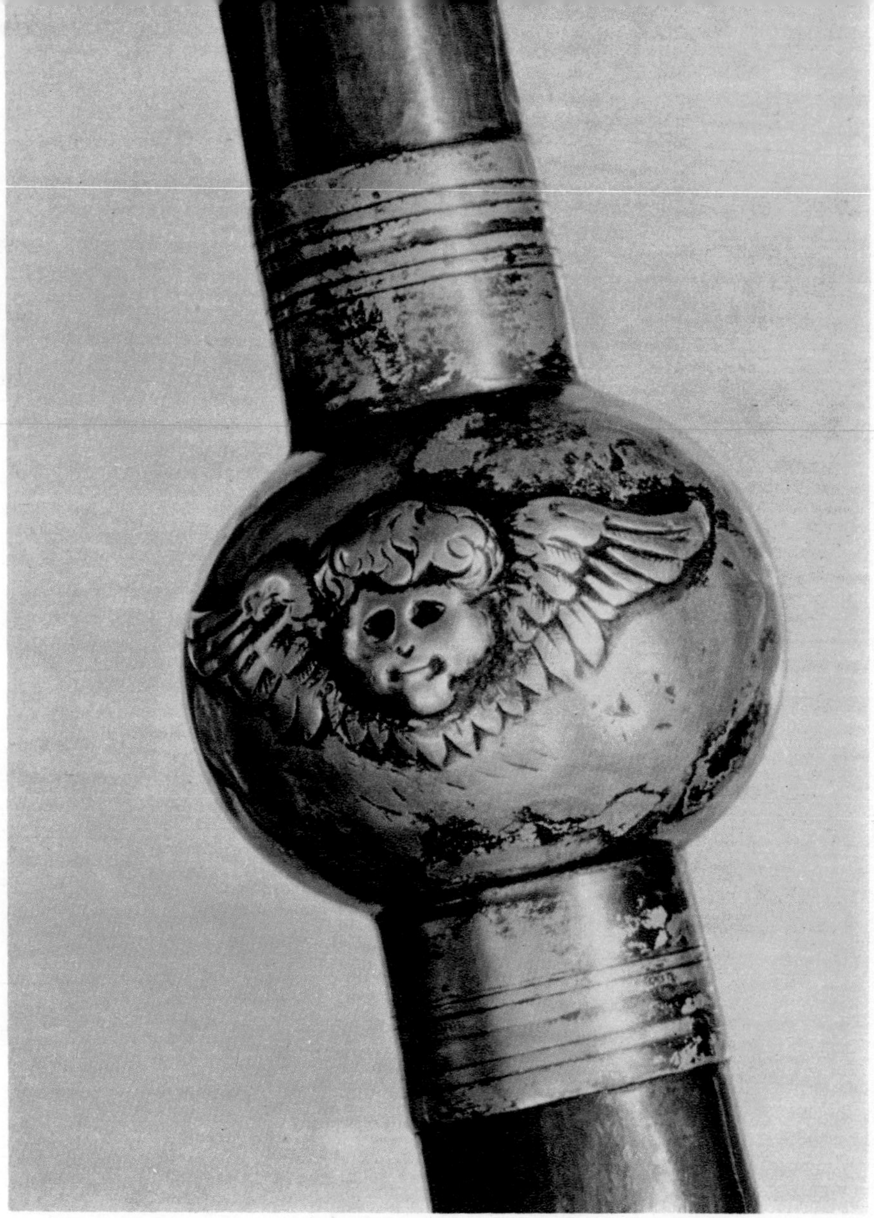

169—170 *Trompeta clarina* made by the Prague instrument maker Bauer, eighteenth century, and the pommel of this trumpet showing wrought metal ornamentation. National Museum, Prague.

171 Organ, flute, violin and 'cello; painting on a Czech goblet from the middle of the eighteenth century.
Museum of Industrial Arts, Prague.

172 Harp and French horns; painting on a Czech goblet from the middle of the eighteenth century.
Museum of Industrial Arts, Prague.

173—174 Bassoon and French horn; eighteenth century Viennese porcelain. Museum of Industrial Arts, Prague.

175 Recorder, black (curved) zink, lute, viola, *viola da gamba* and trumpet; wood carving from the royal throne of the Castle of Prague, second half of the seventeenth century. City Museum, Prague.

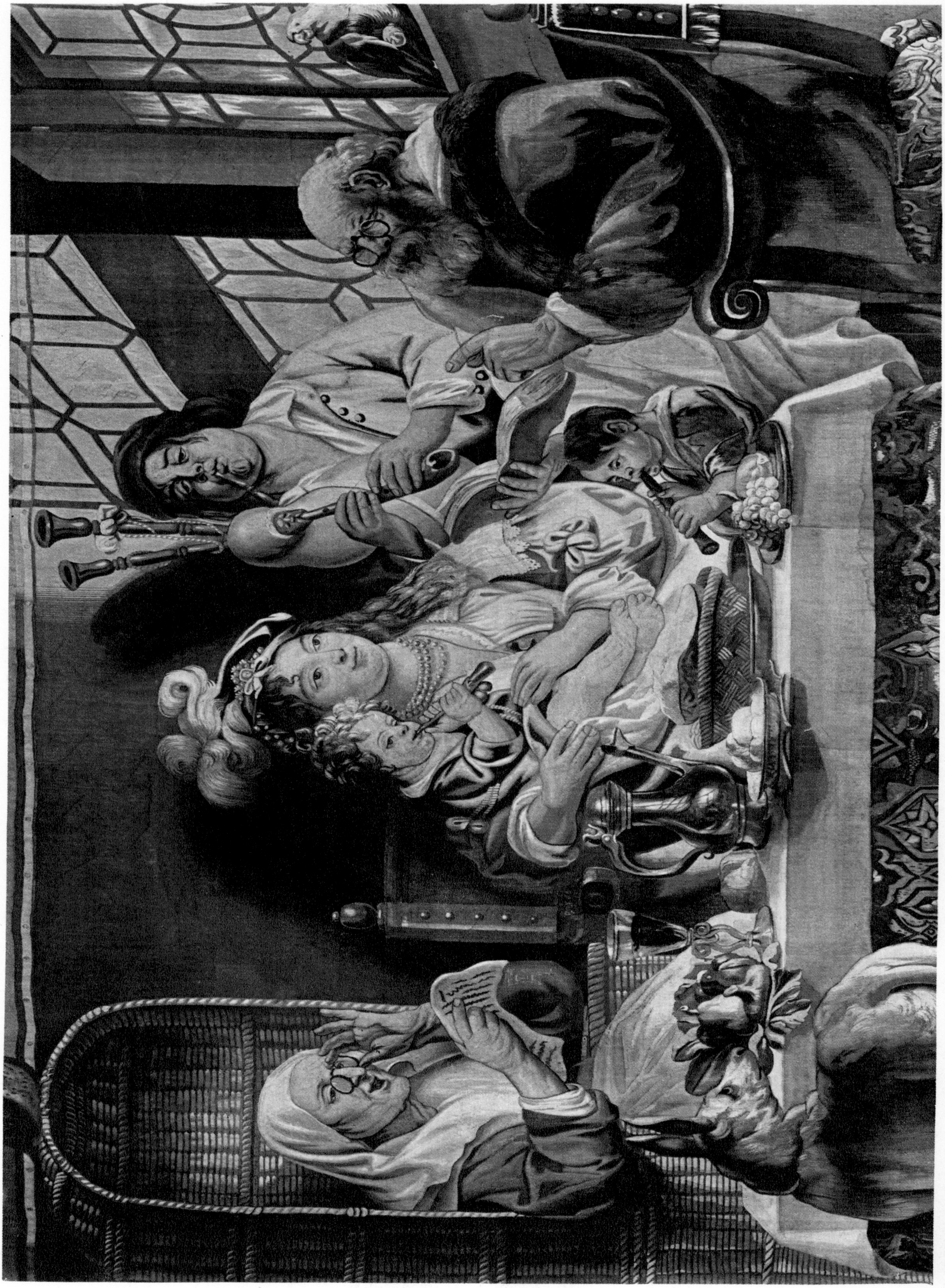

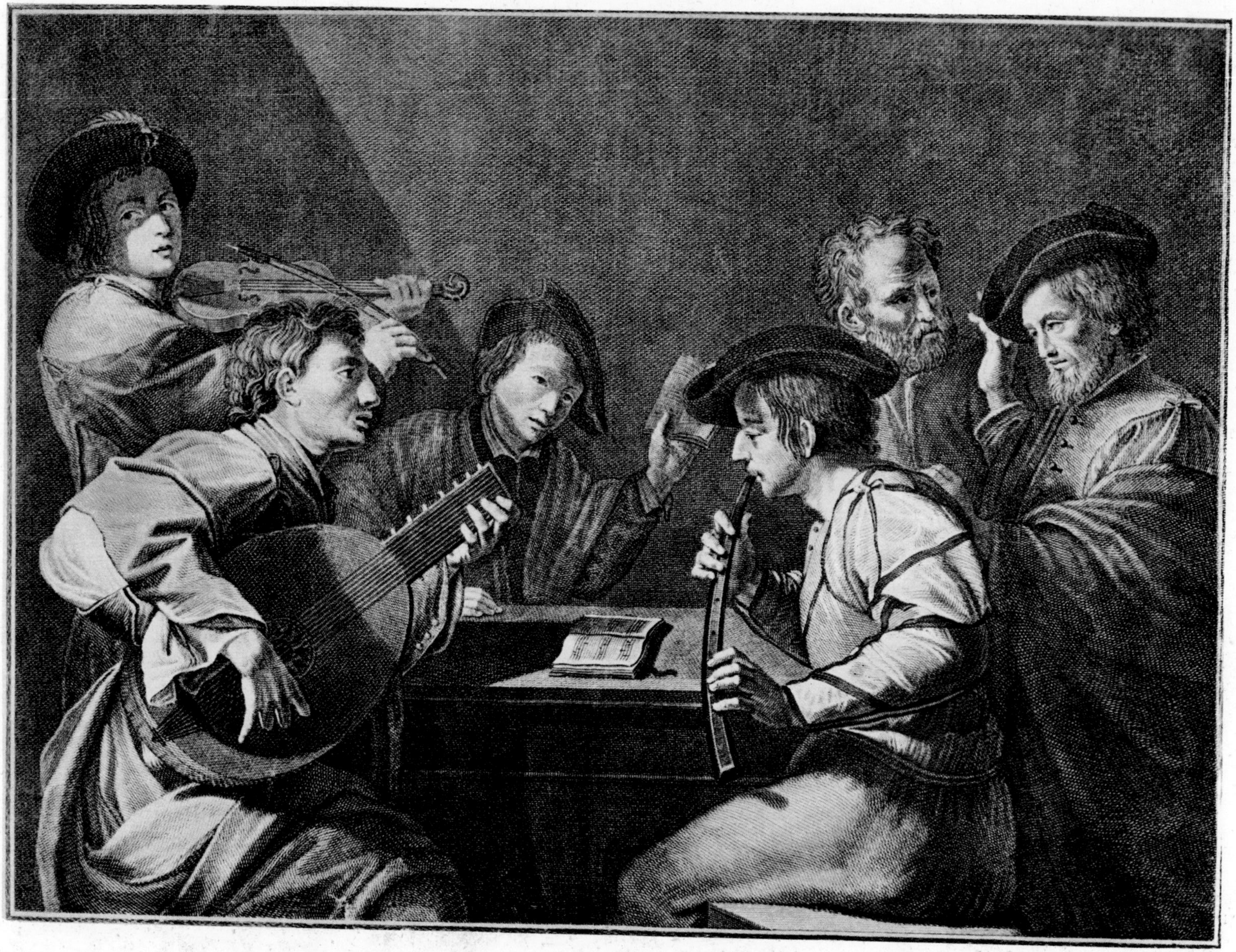

177 Lute, violin and black (curved) zink; Italian engraving of the year 1784. National Museum, Prague.

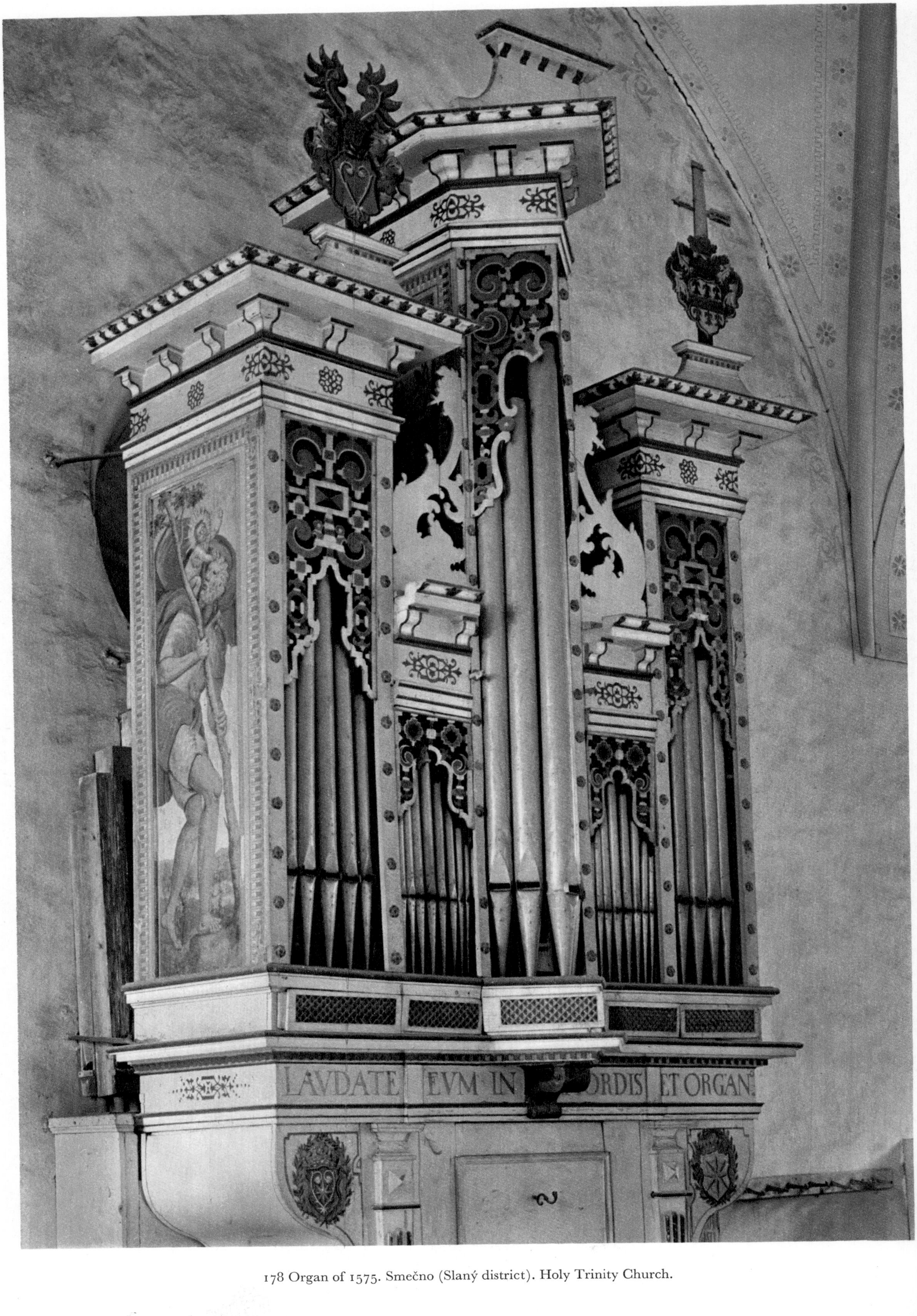


178 Organ of 1575. Smečno (Slaný district). Holy Trinity Church.

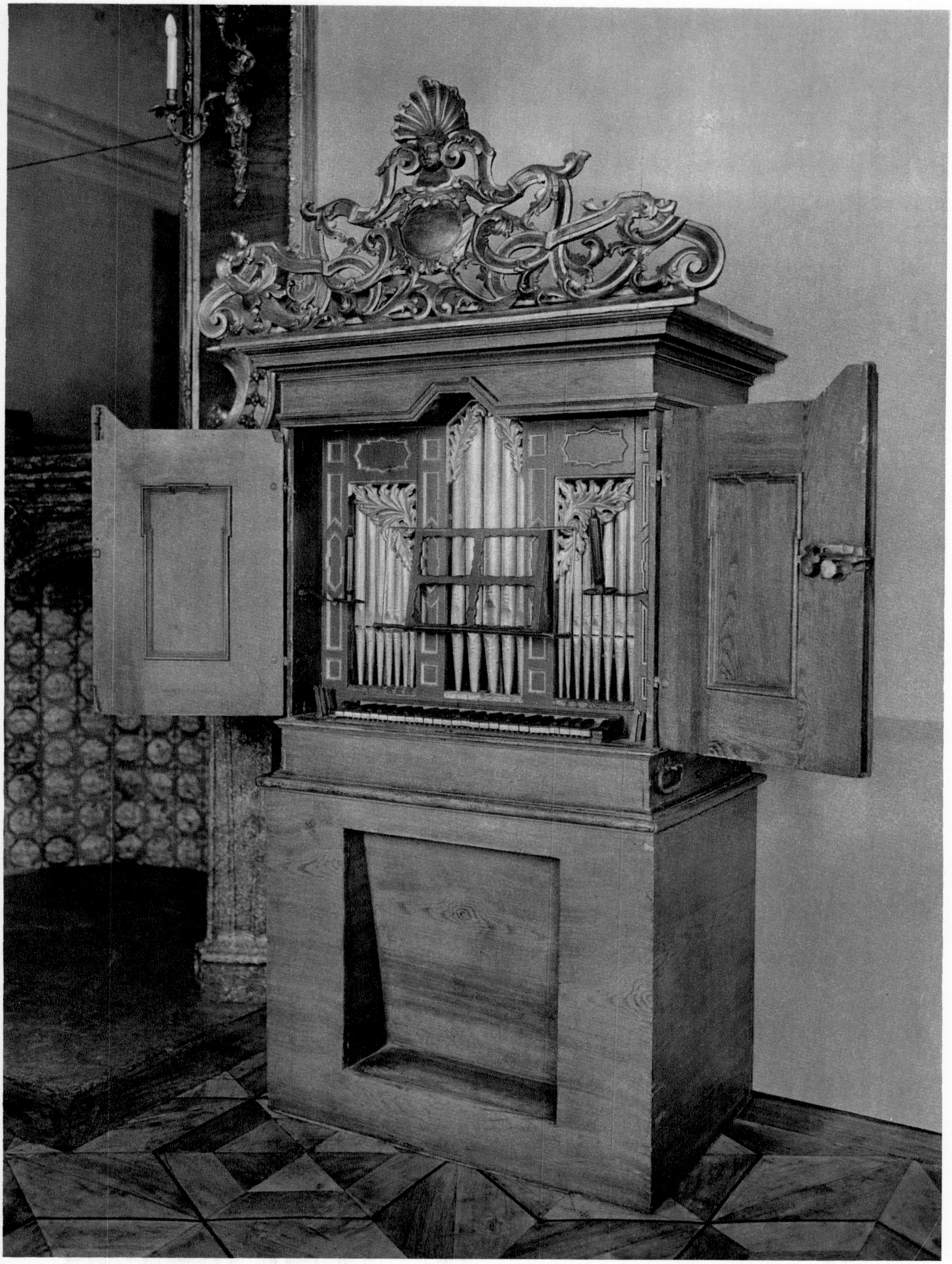

179 Portable Czech organ (positive), eighteenth century. National Museum, Prague.

180 Michael Engler organ, 1745, St Maurice Church, Olomouc.

181 Baroque organ, made by the Brno organ-makers Adam Sieber and Antonín Richter. Holy Hill, near Olomouc.

182 Small portable Czech organ (portative), eighteenth century. National Museum, Prague.

183 Lute; Jan Kupecký (1667—1740).

184 Double-pedal harp made by Erard Frères, Paris, mid-nineteenth century. National Museum, Prague.

ST. CECILIA.
divine Cecilia came,
Inventress of the vocal frame;
The sweet enthusiast, from her sacred store,
Enlarg'd the former narrow bounds,
And added length to solemn sounds,
Engraved by W. Bond.

185 Pedal harp with hook action; coloured engraving from the end of the eighteenth century. National Museum, Prague.

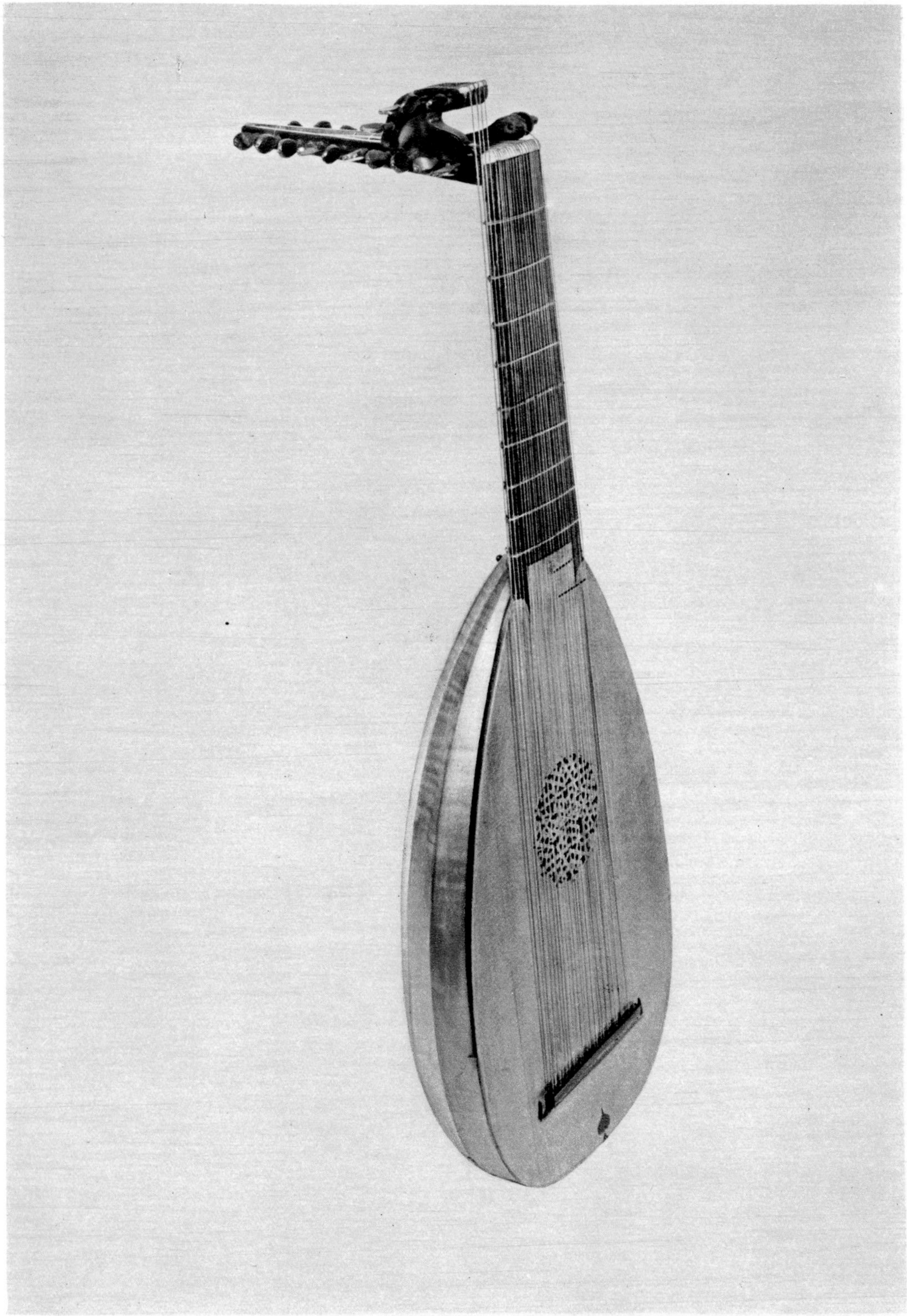

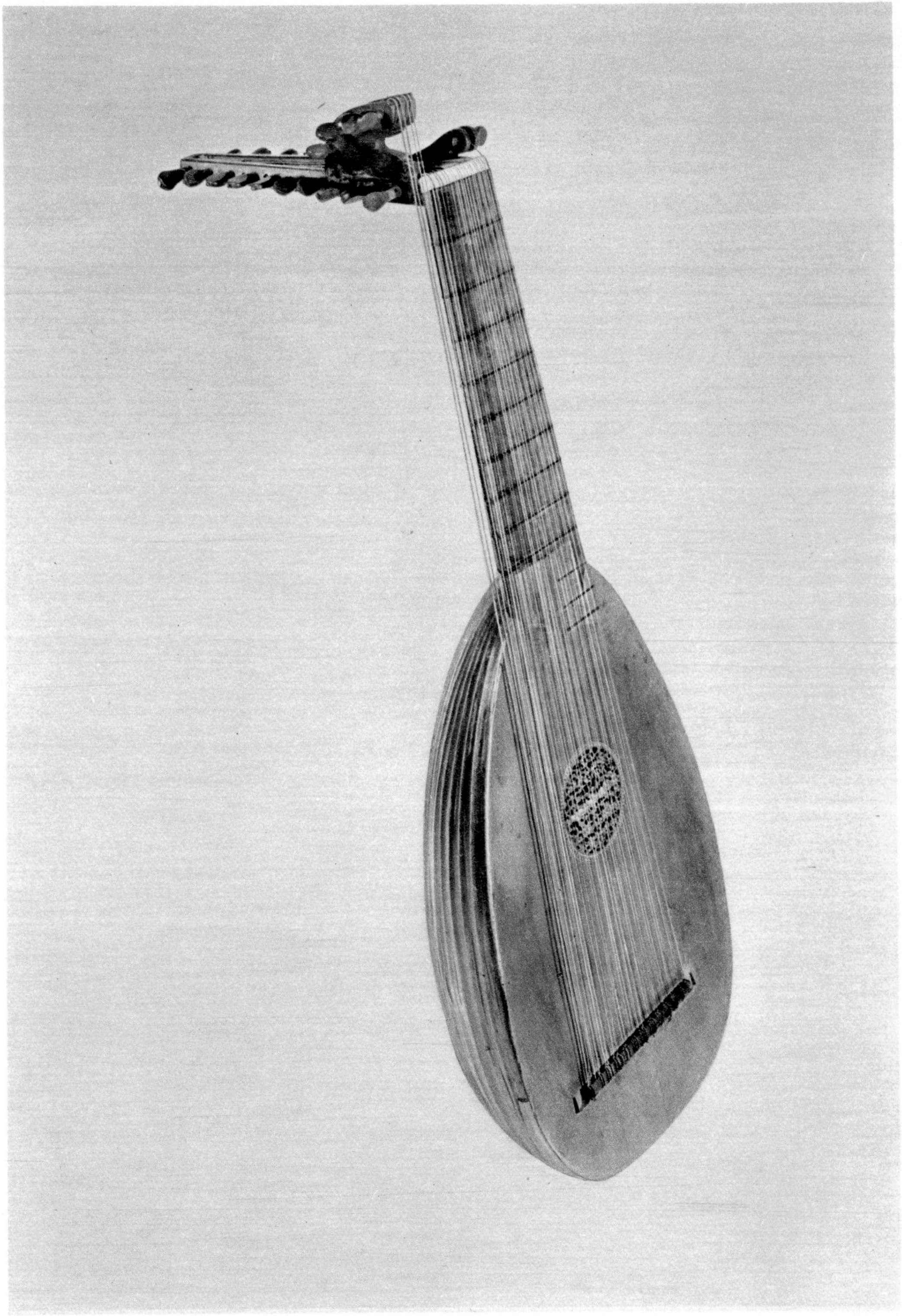

186—187 Lute made by Max Unverdorben of Venice in the sixteenth century, and one by Thomas Edlinger of Prague at the end of the seventeenth century.

188—189 The rosettes of both lutes. National Museum, Prague.

190 Lute; unknown painter of the seventeenth century. National Museum, Prague.

191 Flute, violin and chitarrone (George Frederick Handel as a young musician in Hamburg); eighteenth century French engraving. National Museum, Prague.

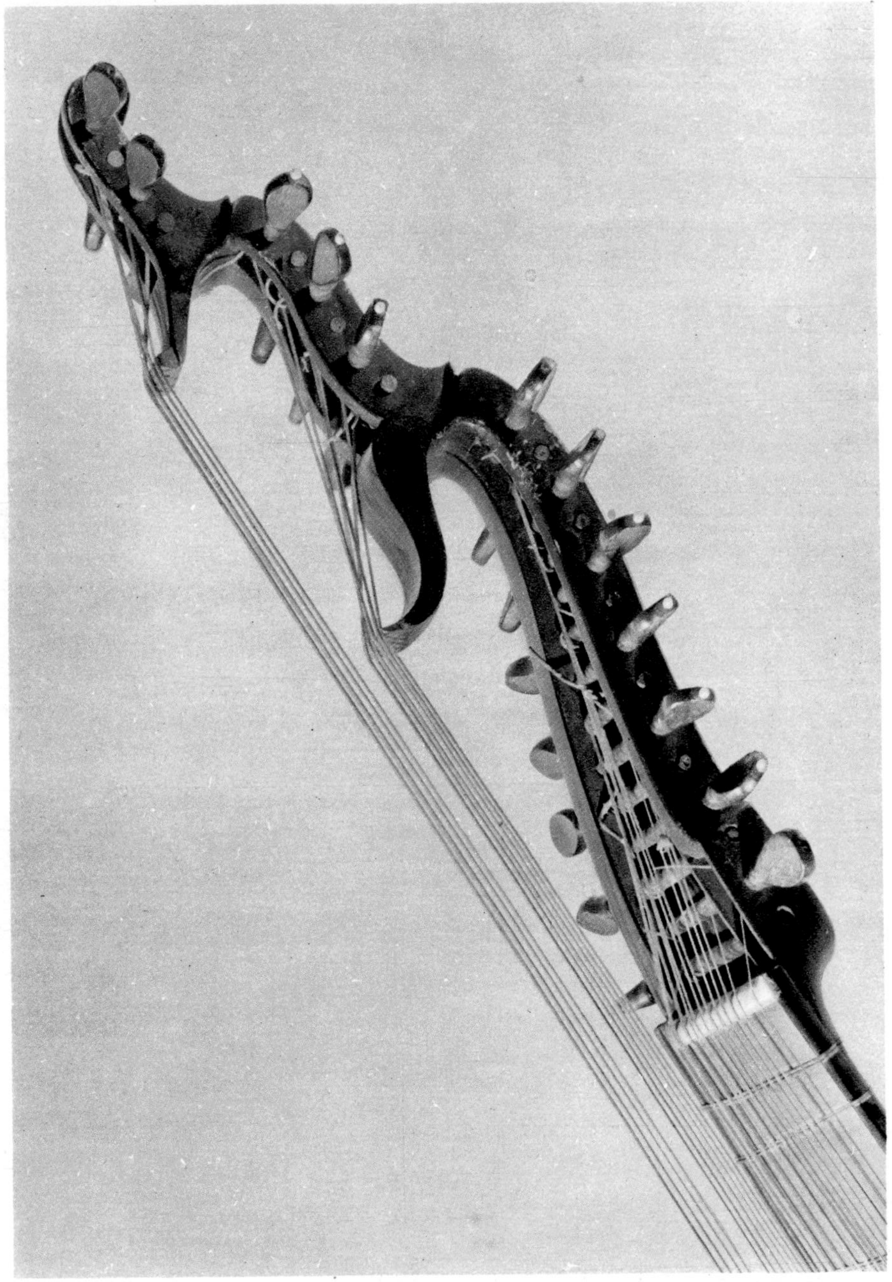

192—193 Theorbo and detail of the triple pegbox made by the Olomouc maker of lutes and violins Martin Bruner in 1764. National Museum, Prague.

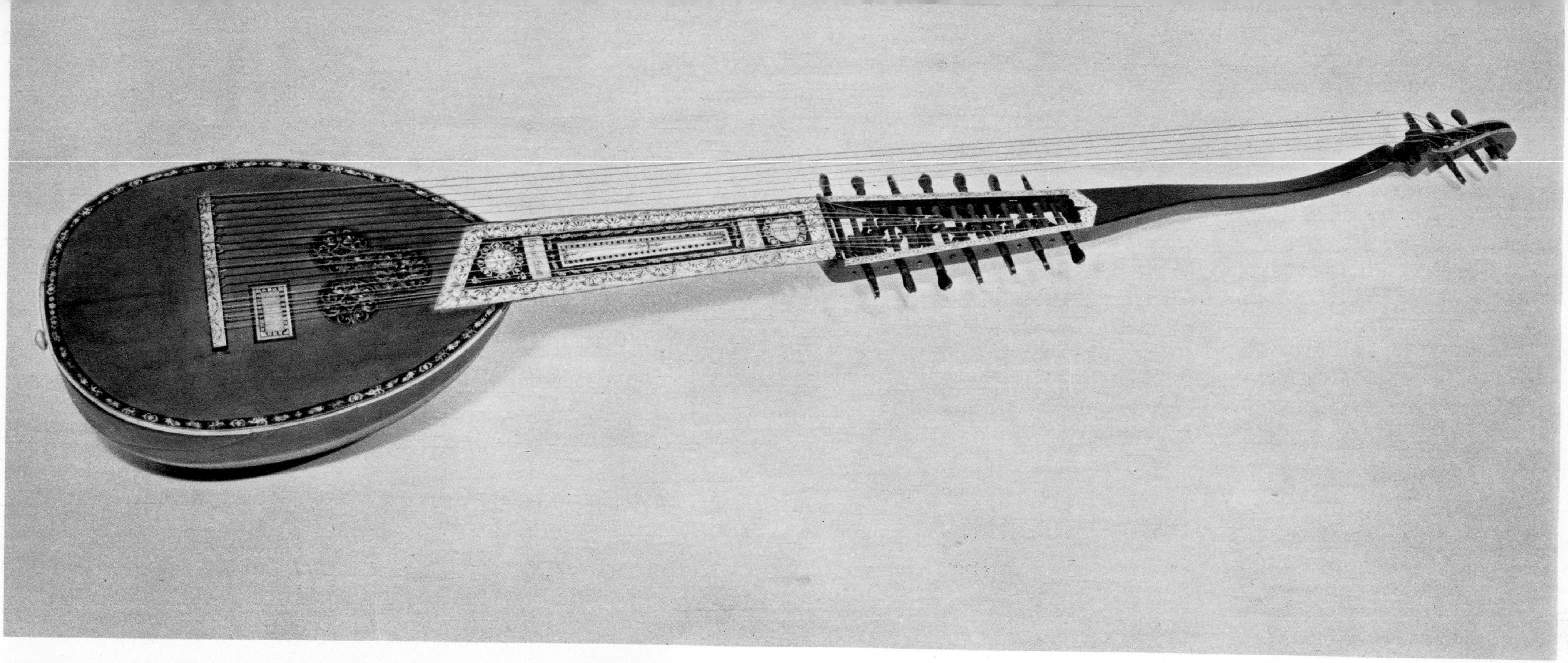

194—195 Chitarrone and detail of the rosettes; made by the Prague lute maker Martin Schott, 1680. National Museum, Prague.

196—197 Czech *guitar battente* and one made by the Prague lute maker Andreas Ott at the end of the seventeenth century. National Museum, Prague.

198—199 Guitar and detail of the rosette; made by the Viennese lute maker Matthias Fux in 1692. National Museum, Prague.

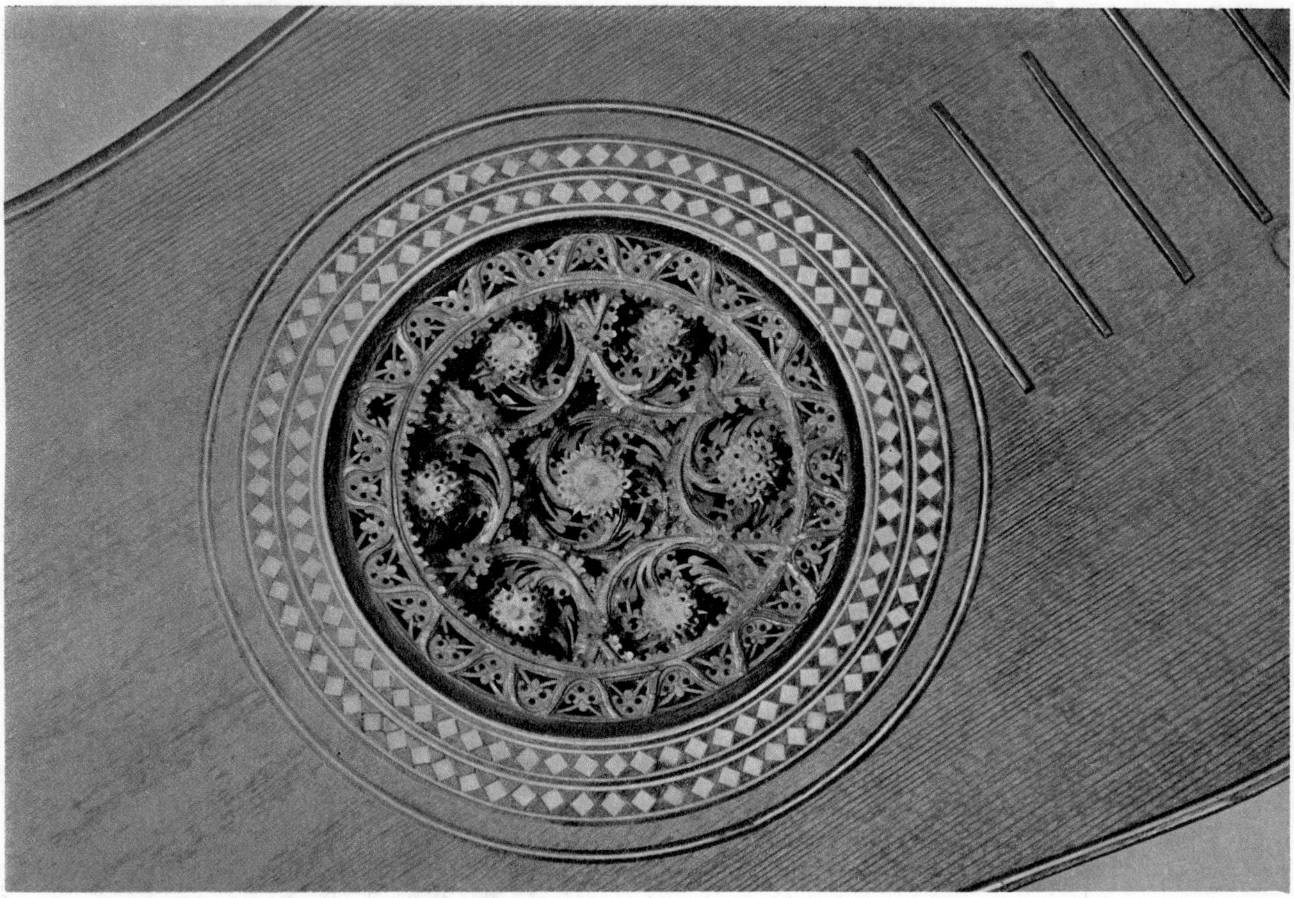

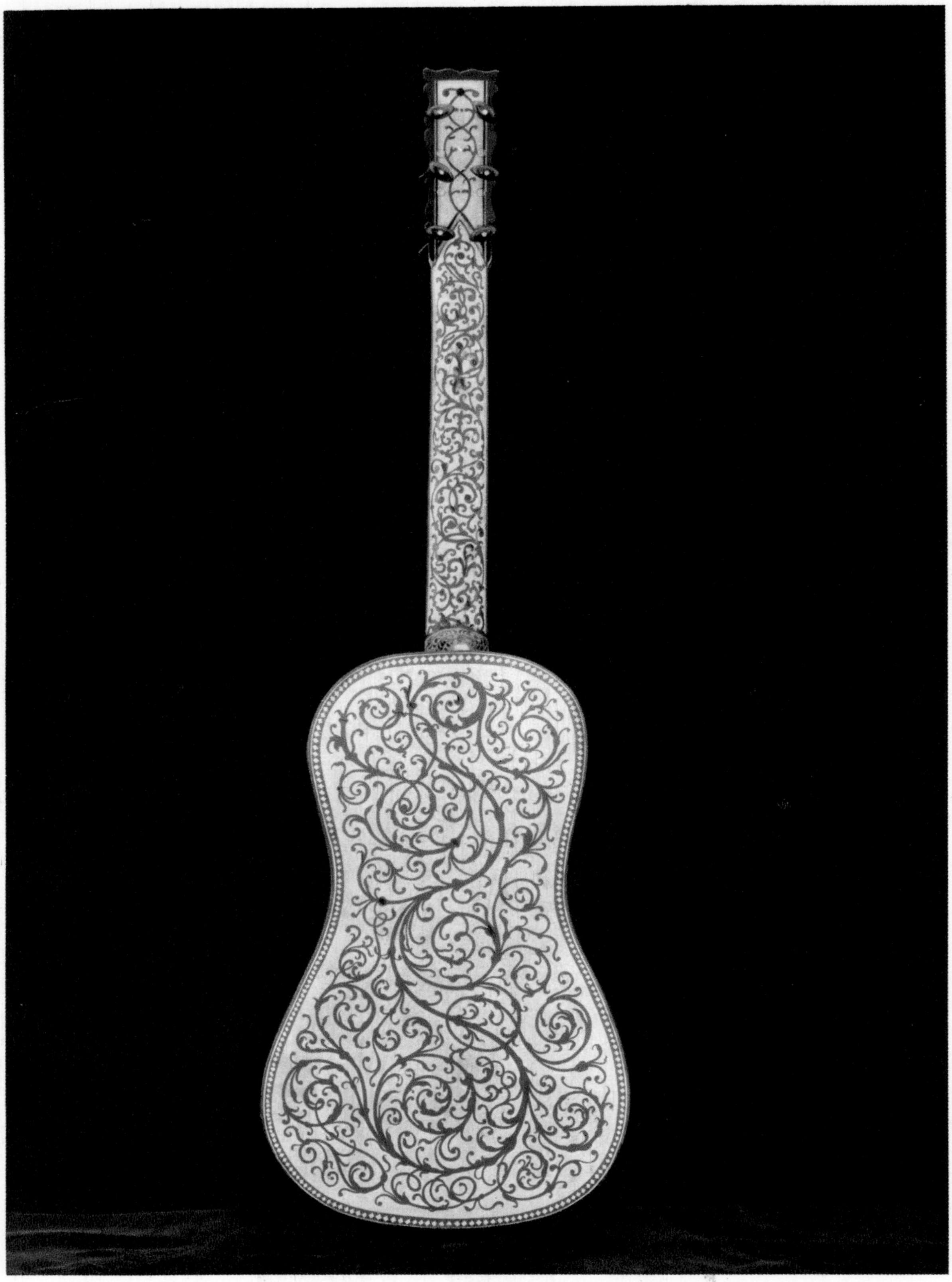

200 Back of the guitar made by G. Sellas.

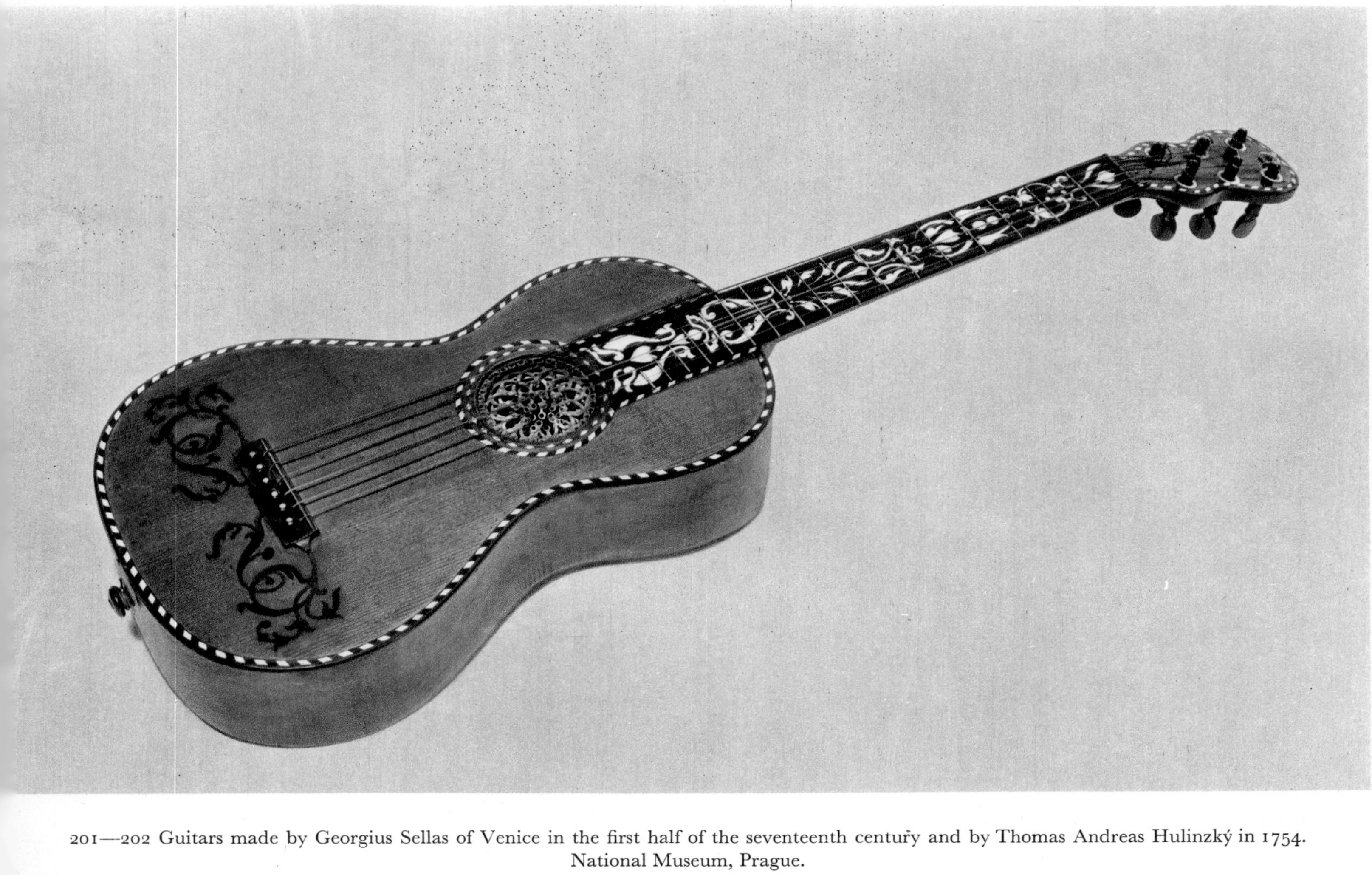

201—202 Guitars made by Georgius Sellas of Venice in the first half of the seventeenth century and by Thomas Andreas Hulinzký in 1754. National Museum, Prague.

203 Cistra made by Girolamo de Virchi in Brescia, 1754, for Archduke Ferdinand of Tyrol.
Museum of Art, Vienna.

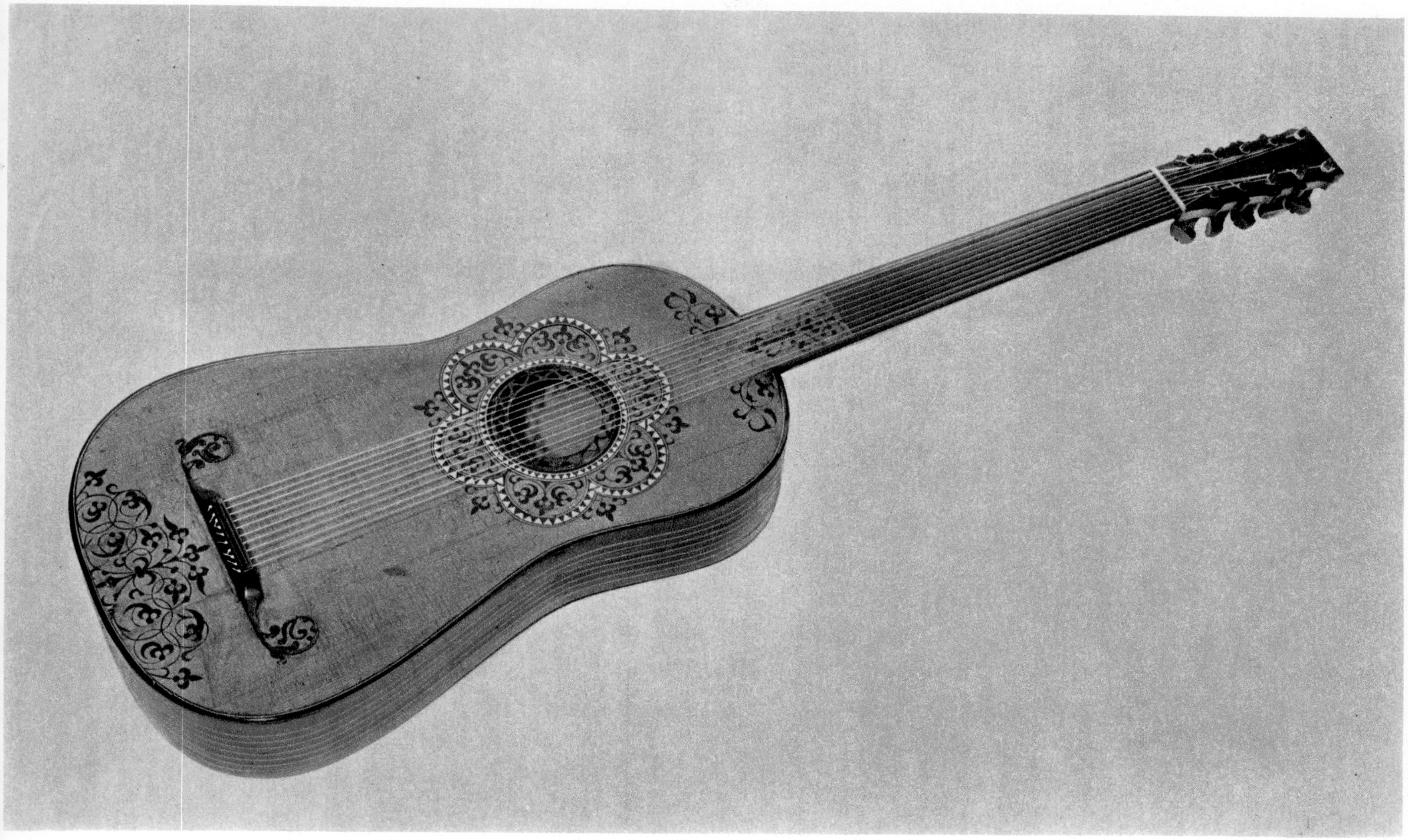

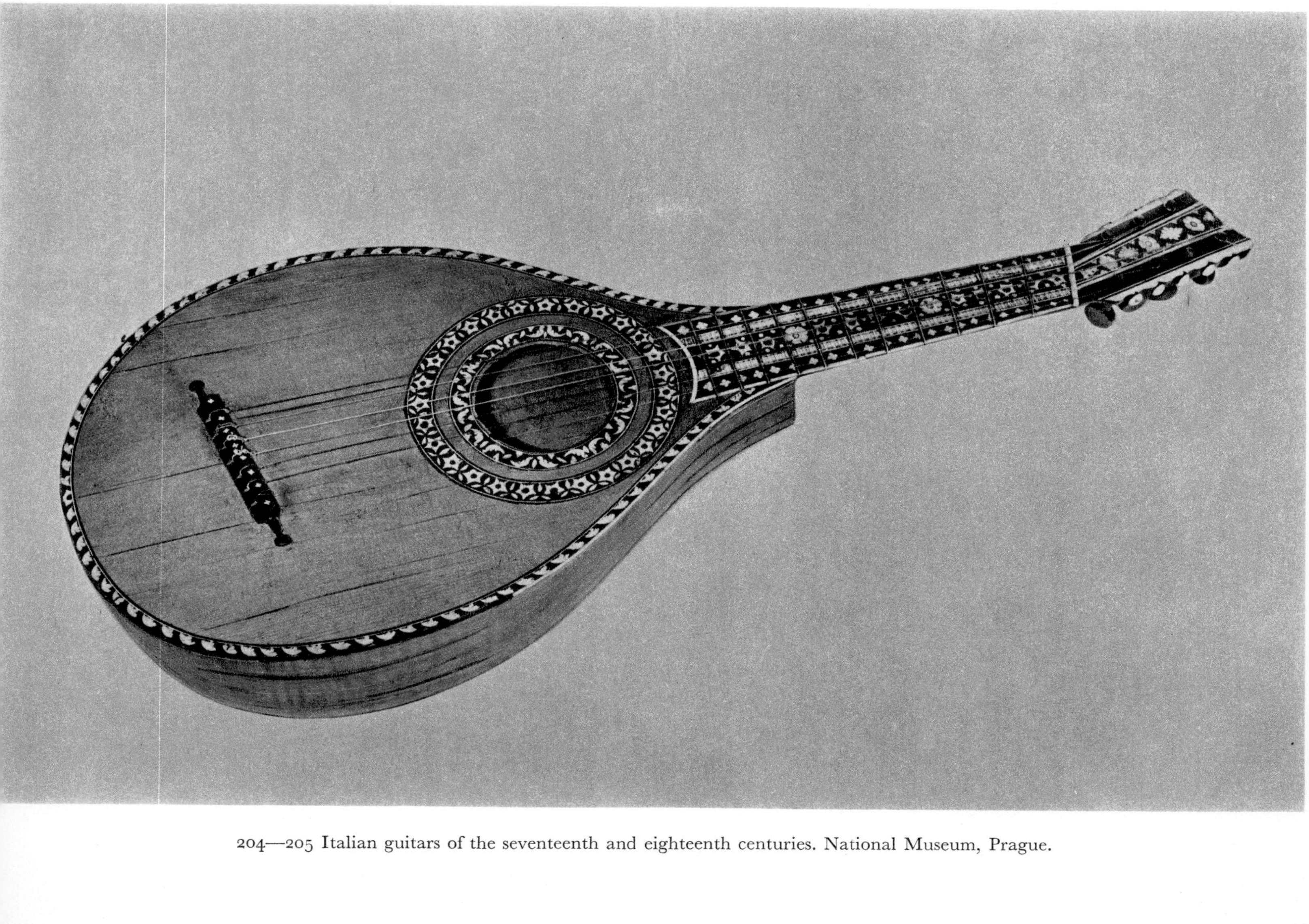

204—205 Italian guitars of the seventeenth and eighteenth centuries. National Museum, Prague.

206—207 Cistra made by Maximilian Zacher, Breslau, 1751, and one by Johannes Michael Willer, Prague, 1799.
National Museum, Prague.

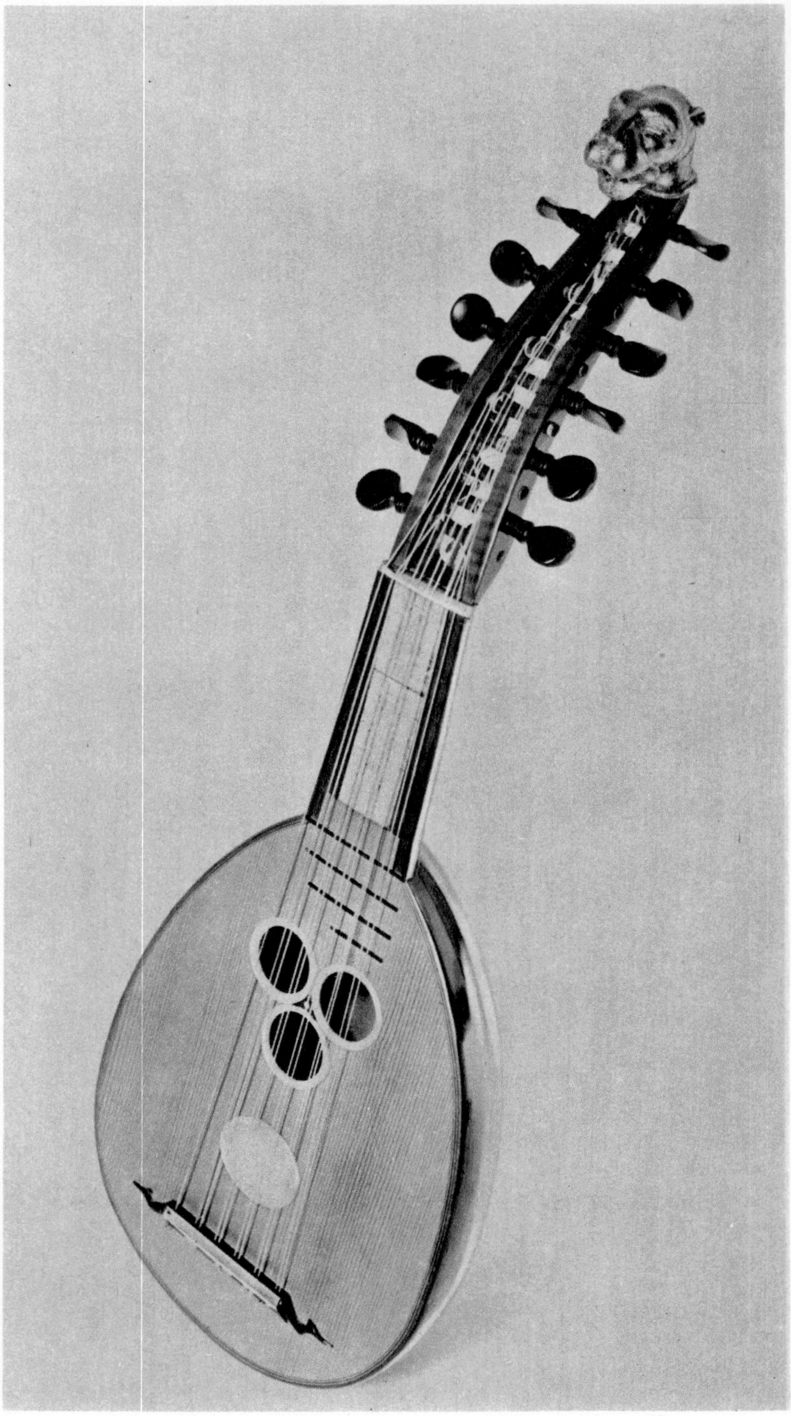

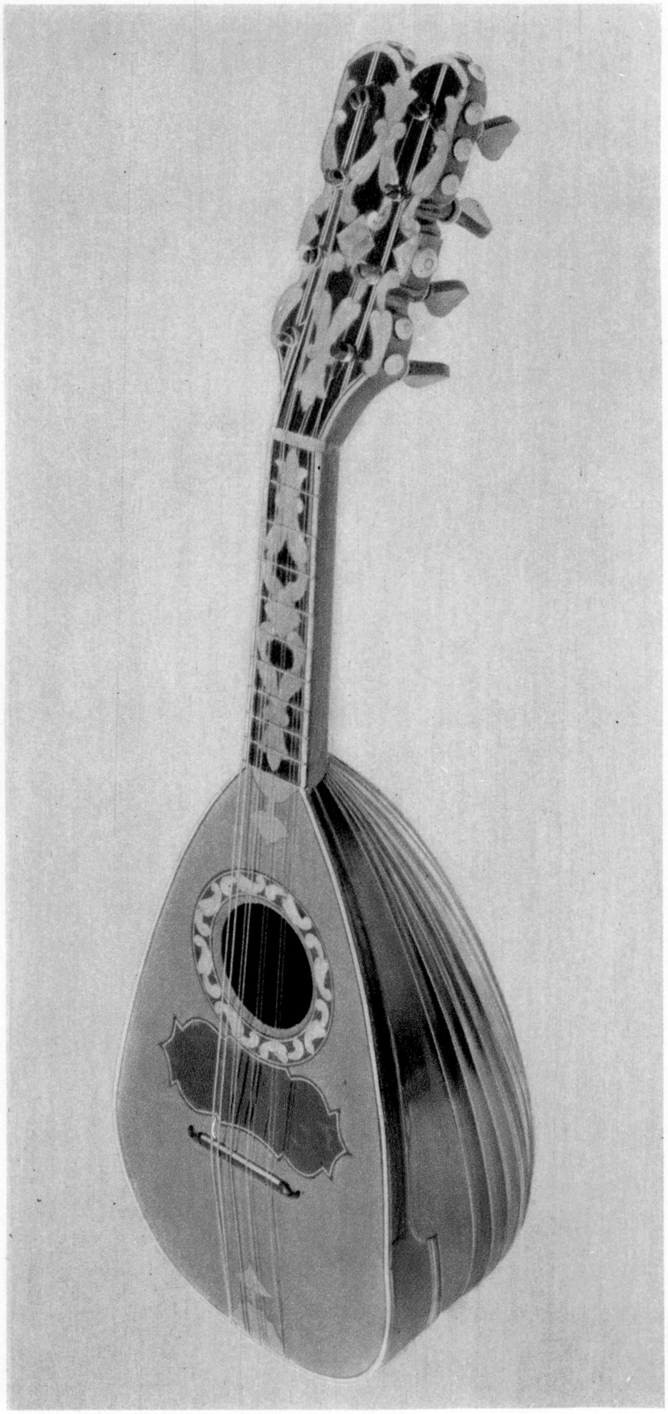

208—209 Milanese mandoline by Francesco Plesbler, Milan, 1773, and Neapolitan mandoline made by Johann Jobst Franck, Dresden, 1789. National Museum, Prague.

210 The oldest double virginals, the work of Hans Ruckers of Antwerp, 1581. Metropolitan Museum of Art, New York.

211 Lutes, shawms and flutes. Detail of the painting of the lid of Hans Ruckers' double virginals, 1581. Metropolitan Museum of Art, New York.

212 Seventeenth century dulcimer from H. Boddington's collection.

213 Dulcimer (tympanum), French engraving of the seventeenth century.

214 Grand clavichord made by Francesco Neri of Rimini (Italy) in the seventeenth century. City Museum, Prague.

215 Clavicytherium made by Marinus Kaiser for the Emperor Leopold I in the second half of the seventeenth century. Museum of Art, Vienna.

216 Harpsichord with keyboard of mother-of-pearl and tortoise-shell. Seventeenth century.

217 The eighteenth century Czech piano on which Wolfgang Amadeus Mozart played in January 1787 in the Ladies'College in Prague.
National Museum, Prague.

218 Joseph Haydn's two-manual harpsichord, made by Burkat Shudi and John Broadwood, London, 1775. Museum of Art, Vienna (from the collection of the Friends of Music).

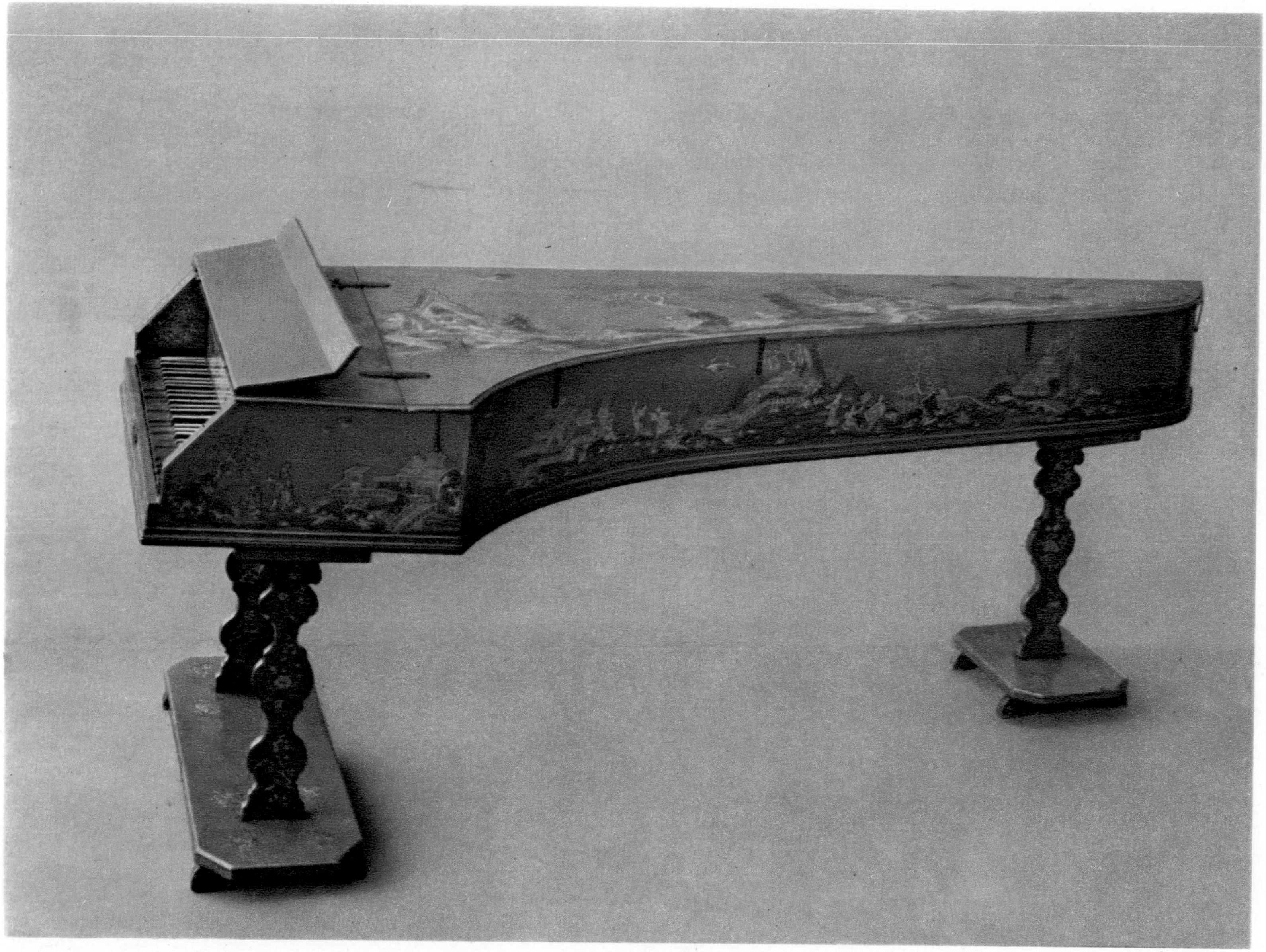

219 Eighteenth century harpsichord. National Museum, Prague.

220 Czech giraffe piano from the first half of the nineteenth century. National Museum, Prague.

221 Pyramid piano with a clock, made by Leopold Sauer, Prague, at the beginning of the nineteenth century. City Museum, Prague.

222 Table piano made by Leopold Sauer, Prague, at the beginning of the nineteenth century. City Museum, Prague.

223 Flute, lute and drone; Johannes Steen (1626—1679). National Gallery, Prague.

224 Trumscheit *(tromba marina)*; engraving from F. Bonanni's book *Cabinetto armonico*, Rome, 1722. National Museum, Prague.

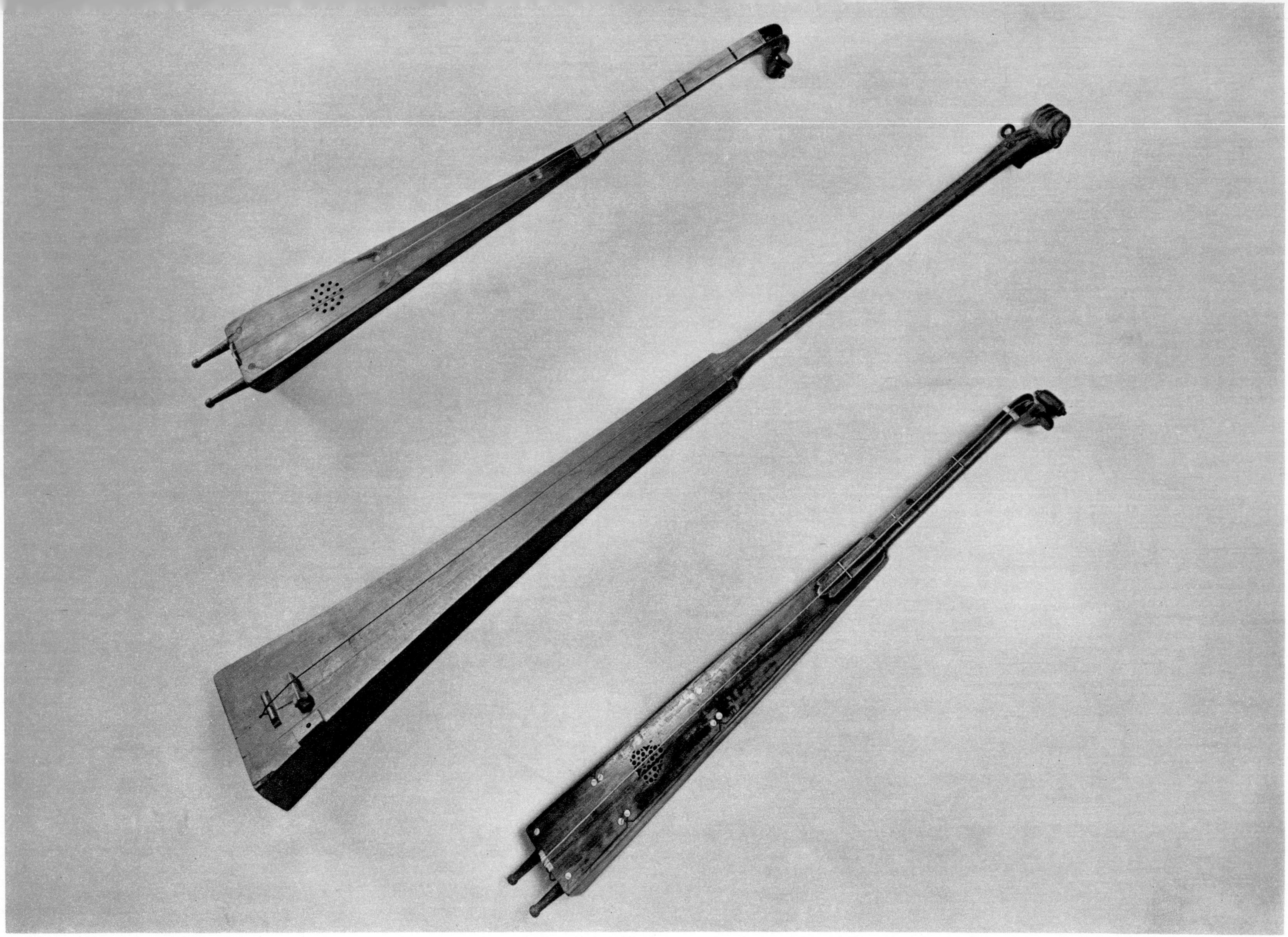

225—227 Trumscheits of the seventeenth and eighteenth centuries. National Museum, Prague.

228 *Lira da braccio*; Johannes Andrea, Verona 1511. Museum of Art, Vienna.

229 Tenor, alto and descant *viola da gamba* and lute; painting dated 1614 on part of a wooden ceiling in the former Pauline Monastery in Prague. City Museum, Prague.

230 Tenor *viola da gamba;* Johannes Verkolje (1650—1693).

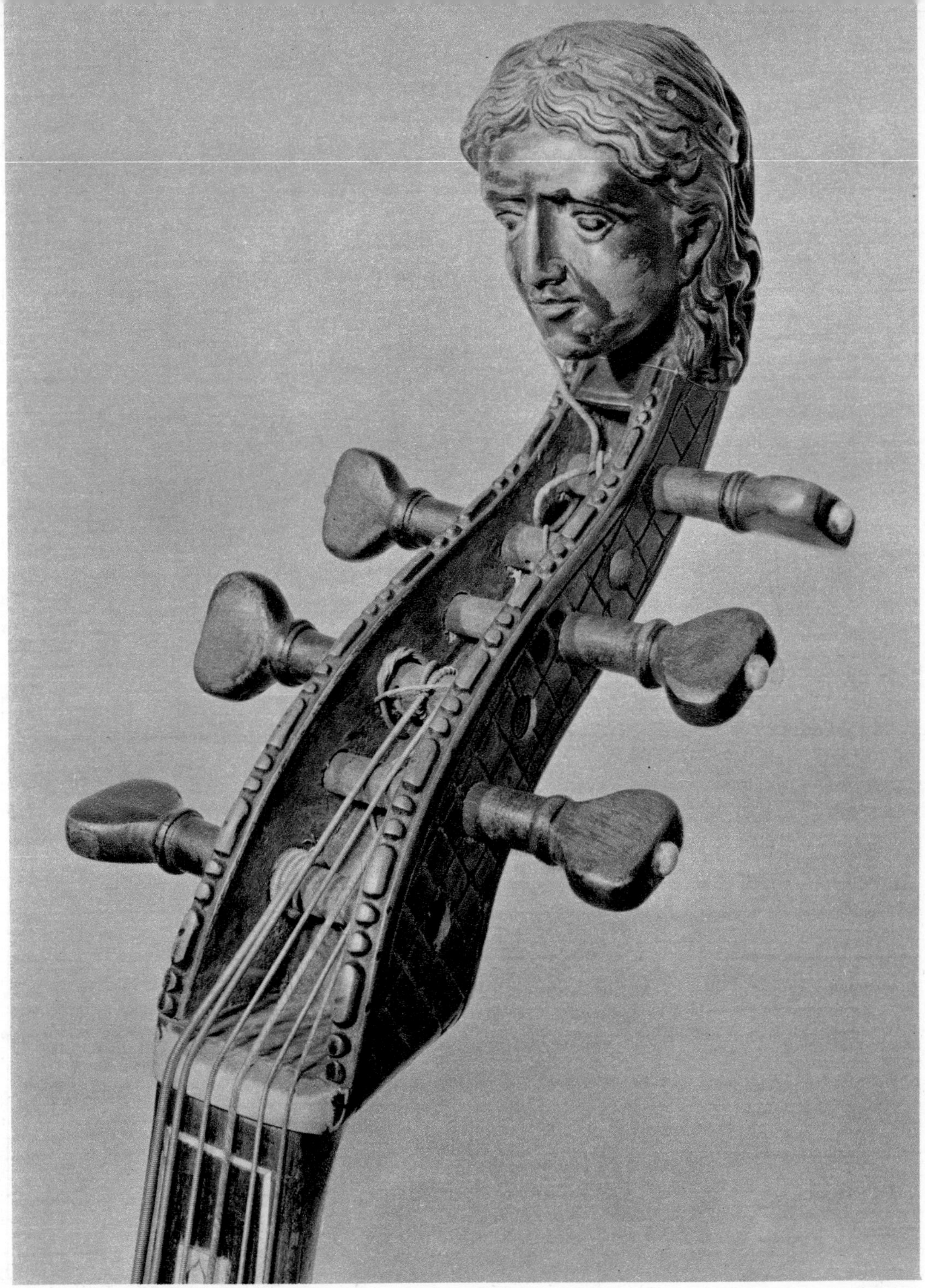

231—232 **Tenor** *viola da gamba* and detail of the neck and pegbox; Johannes Udalricus Eberle, Prague, 1740. National Museum, Prague.

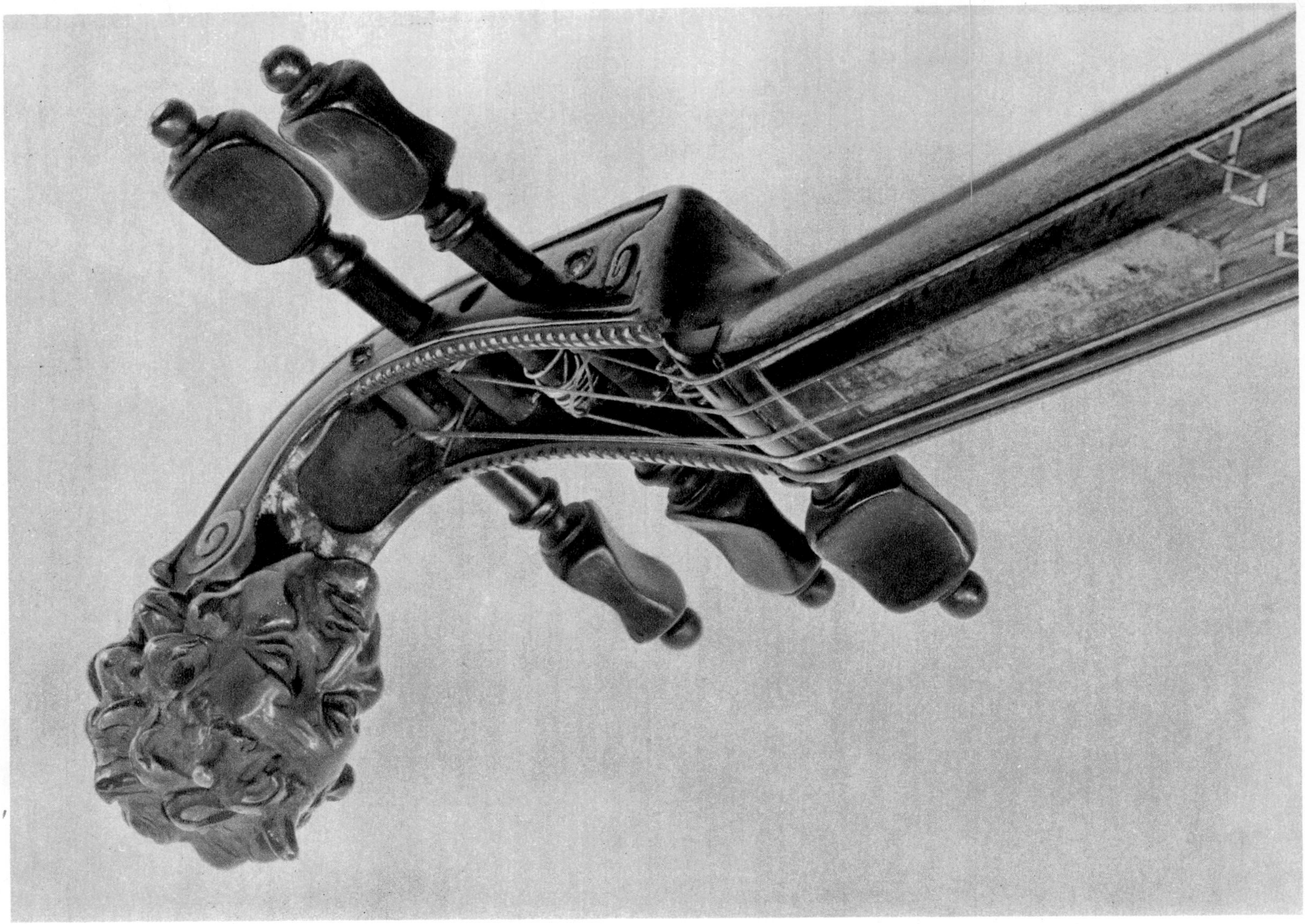

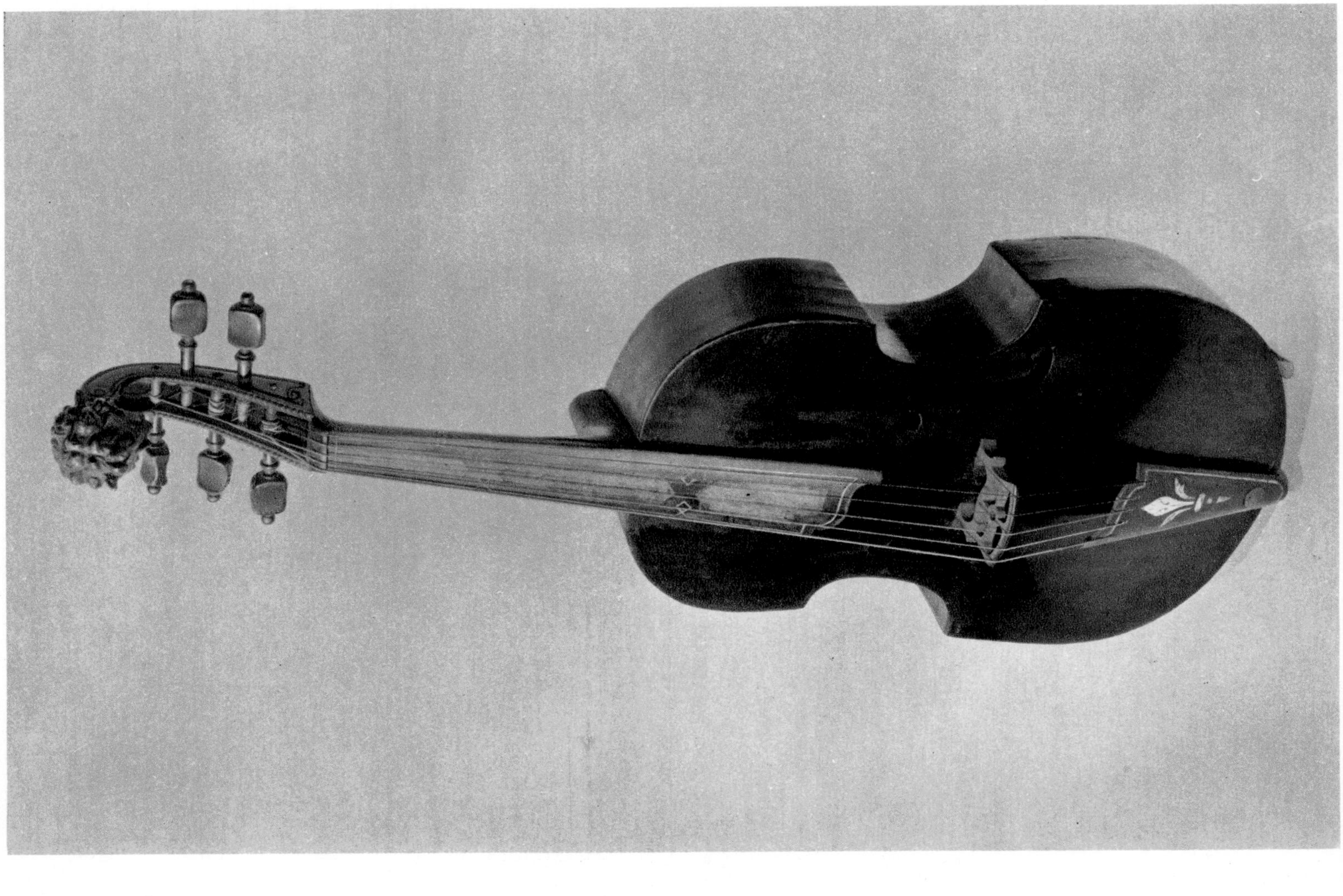

235—236 *Viola di bordone* (barytone) and detail of the neck and pegbox; eighteenth century. National Museum, Prague.

237 Lutes and violin; unknown Italian painter of the seventeenth century. National Museum, Prague.

238 Trumpets, kettle-drum, violin, shawm, lute and *viola da gamba*; unknown Flemish painter of the middle of the seventeenth century. National Museum, Prague.

239—240 *Viola d'amore* and English violetta (really an alto *viola d'amore* with double the number of sympathetic strings) made by Johannes Udalricus Eberle, Prague 1758 and 1727. National Museum, Prague.

241 Necks of Czech *violas d'amore*, eighteenth century. National Museum, Prague.

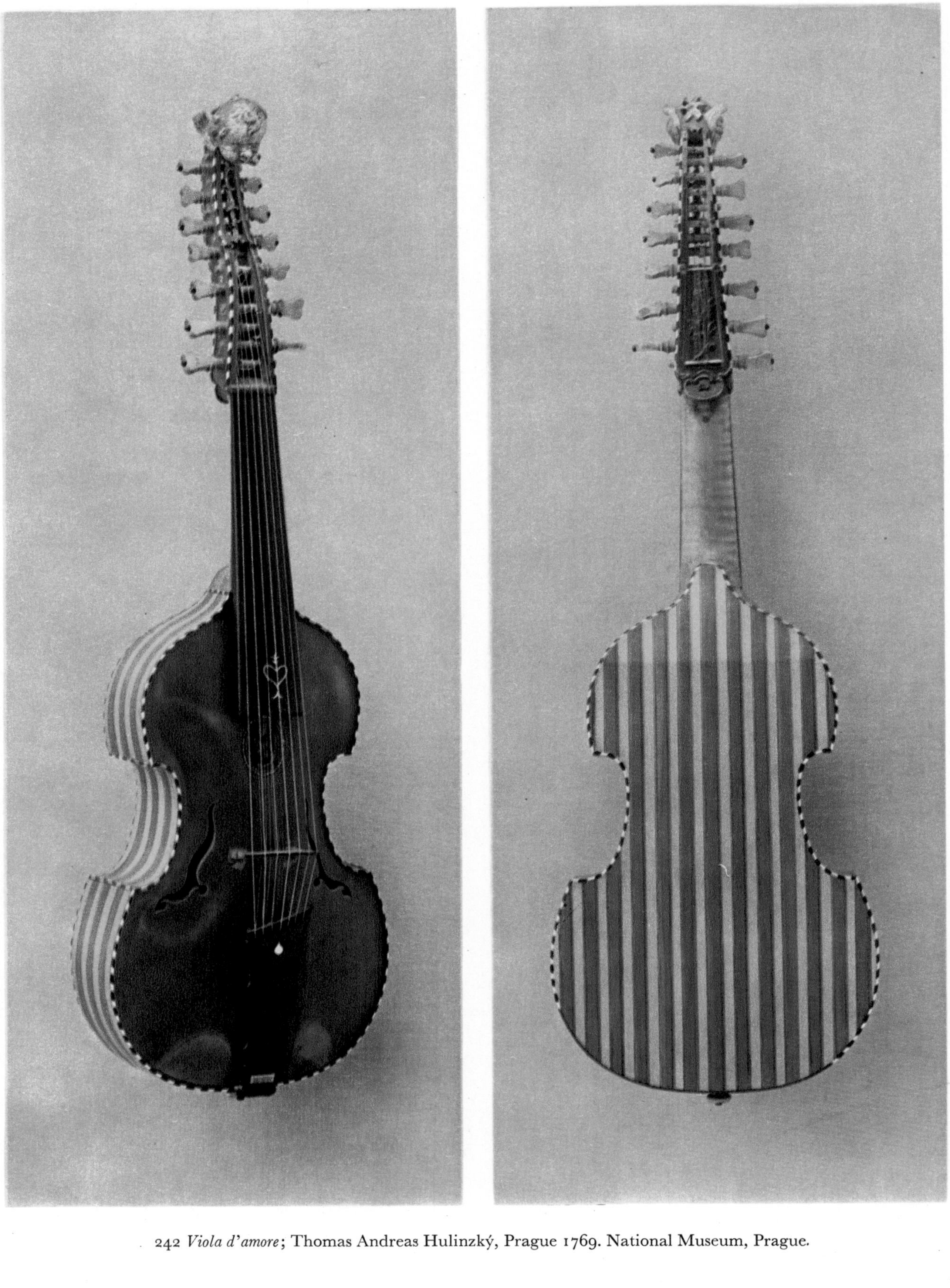

242 *Viola d'amore*; Thomas Andreas Hulinzký, Prague 1769. National Museum, Prague.

243 Jan Kubelík's violin, called the Emperor, made by Antonio Stradivari in 1715.

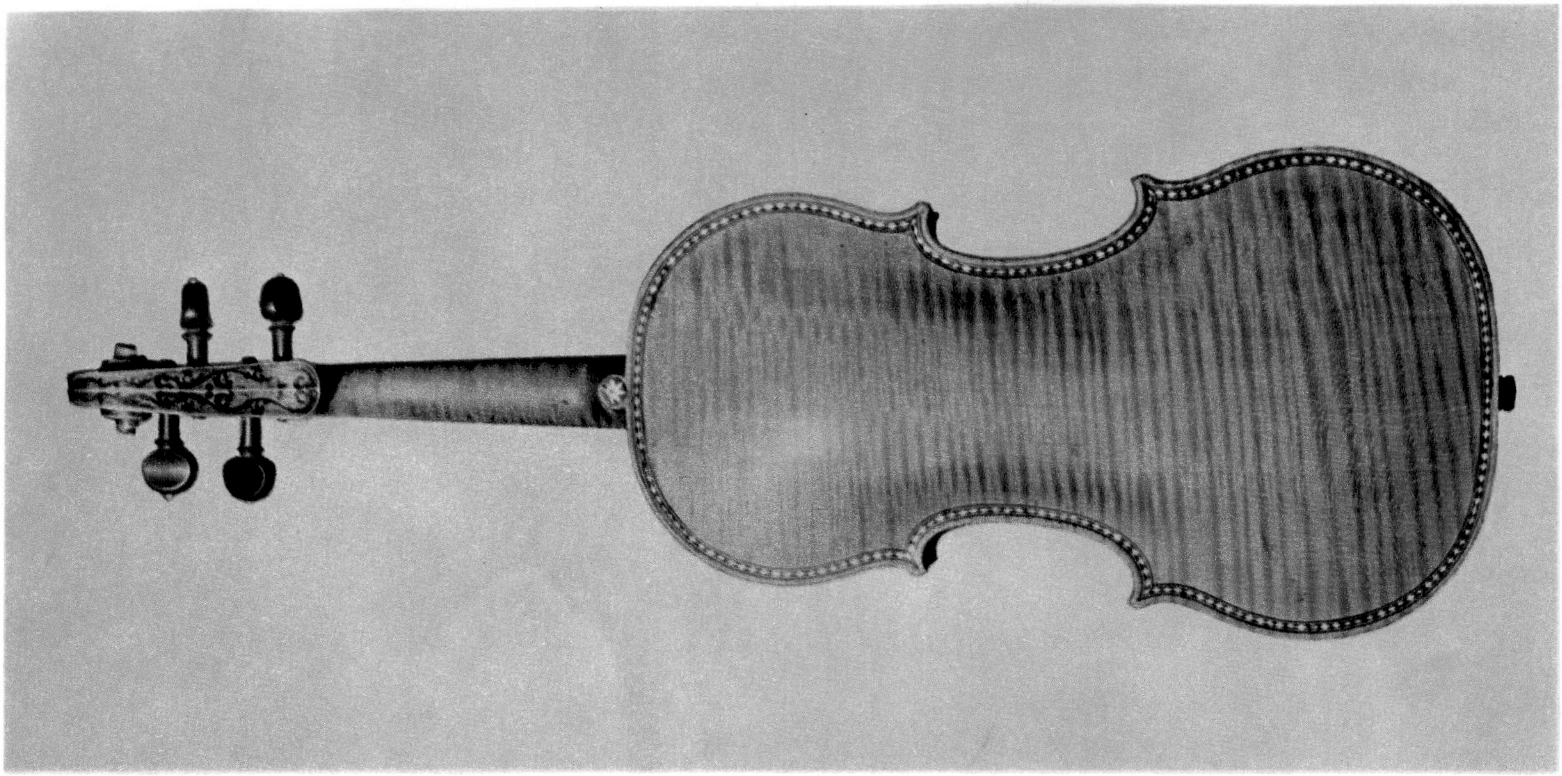
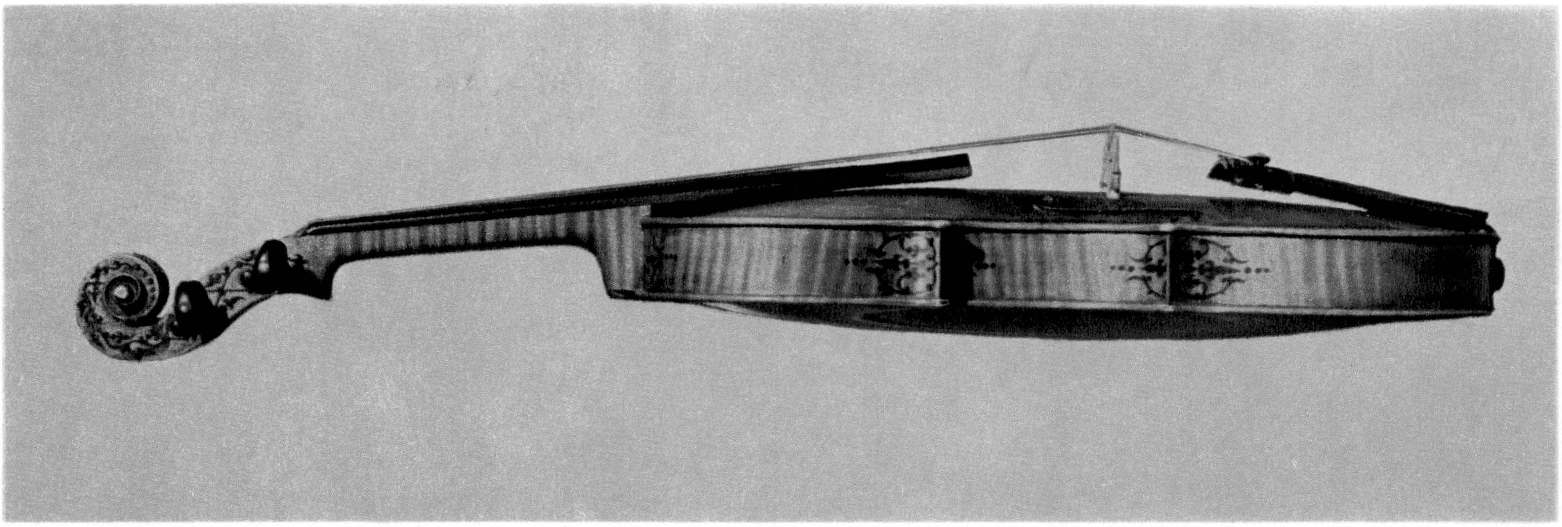
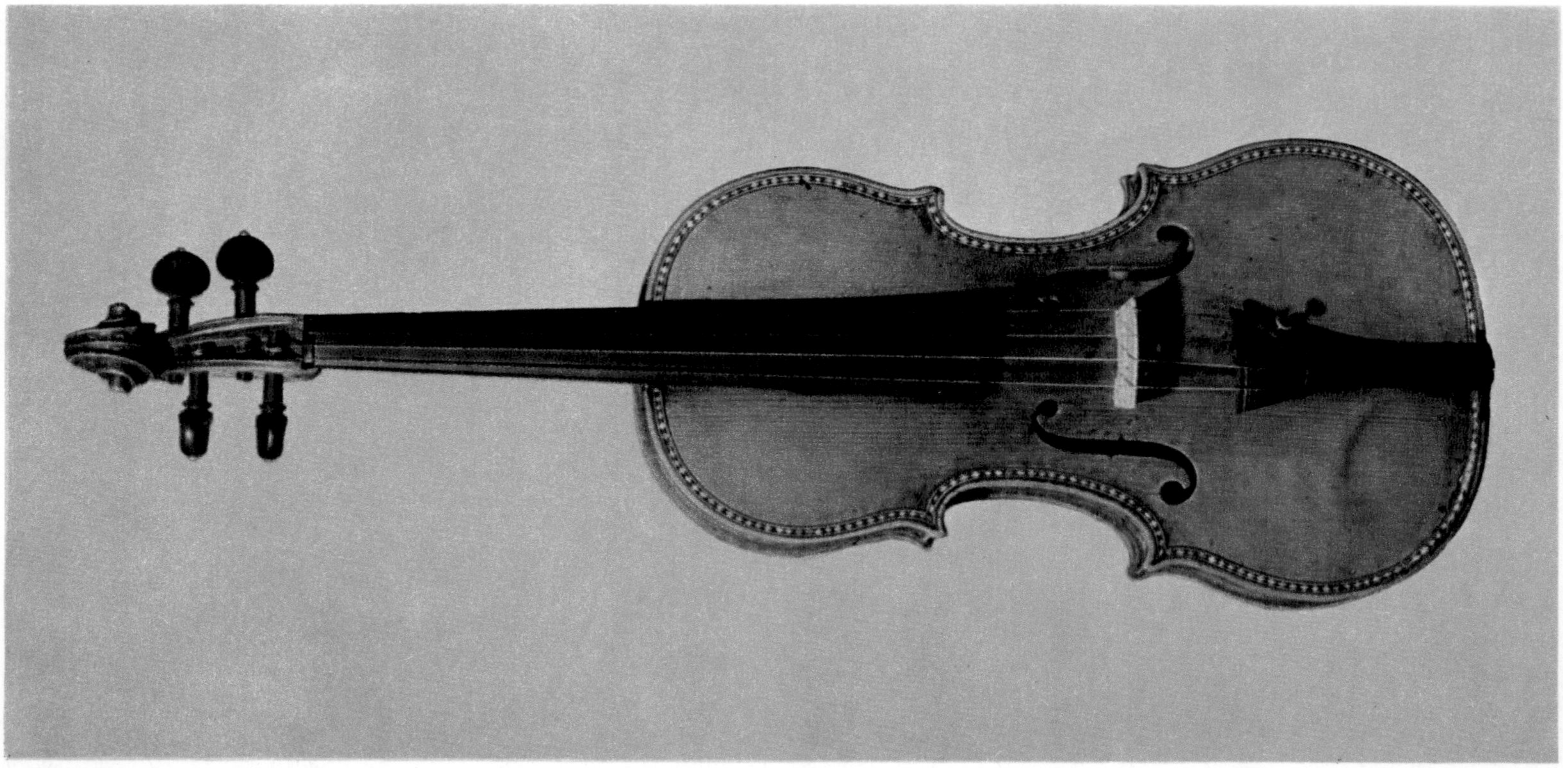

245 Flute, lute, 'cello and violin; Johann Georg Platzer (1704—1761). National Museum, Prague (deposited by the National Gallery).

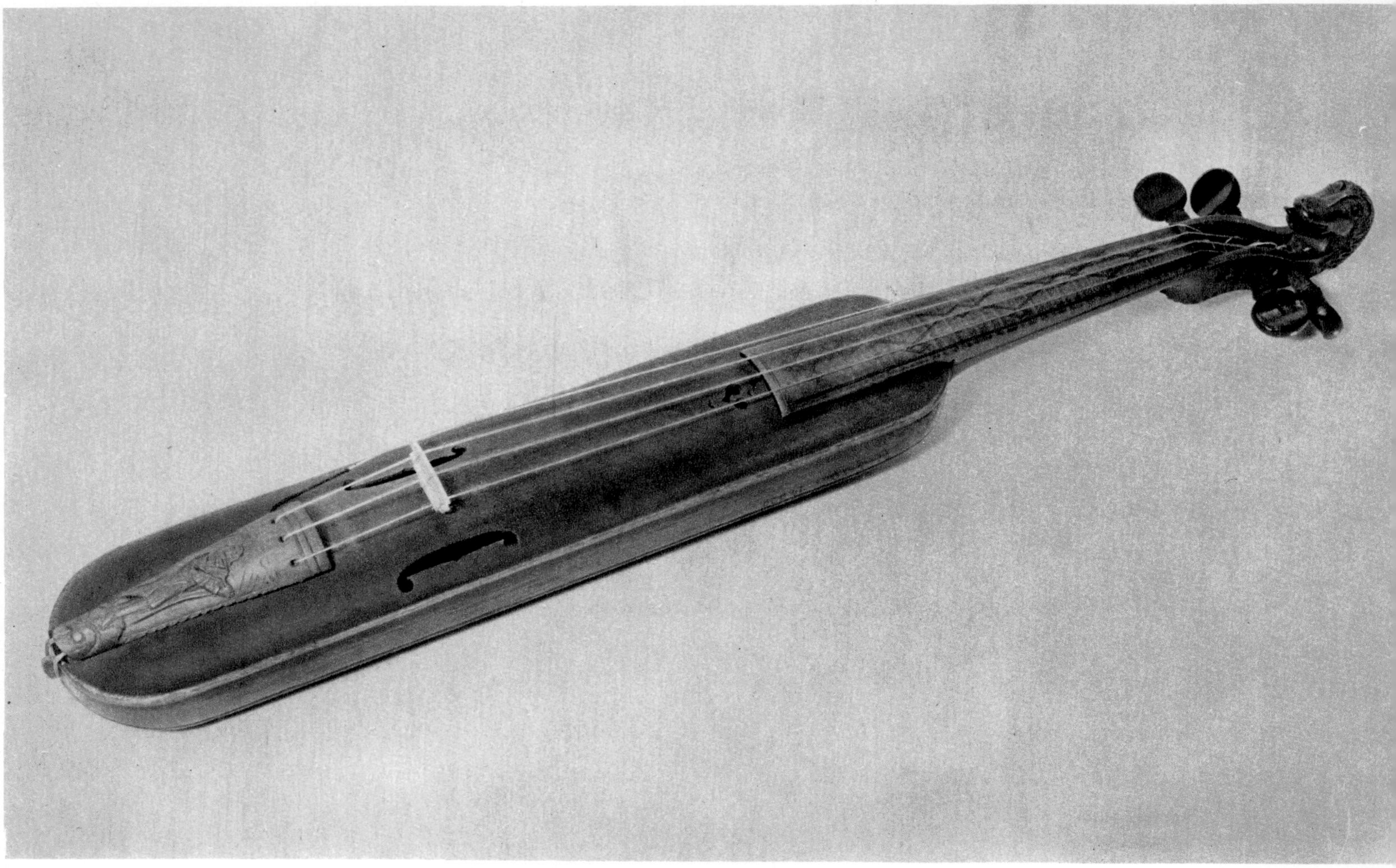

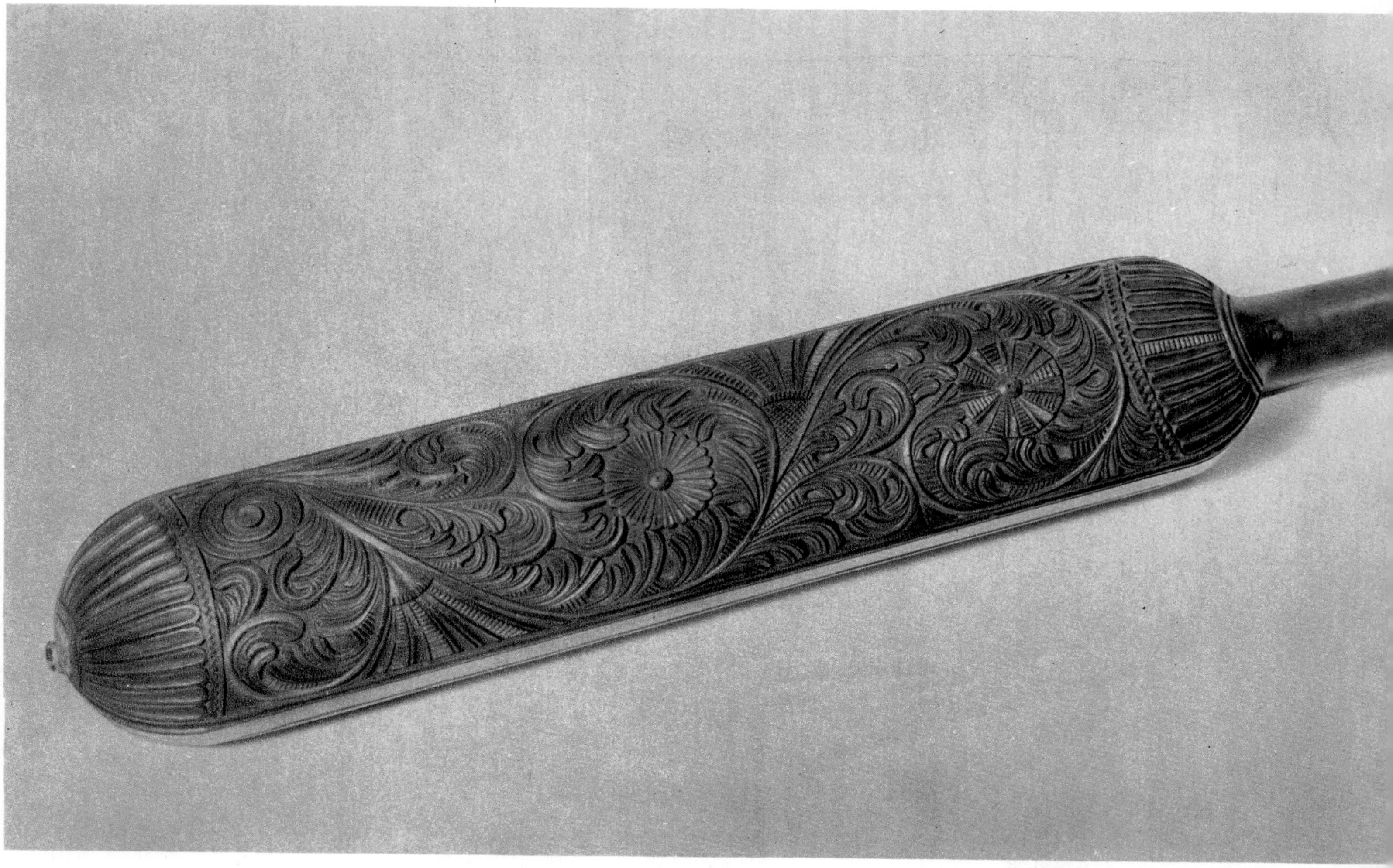

246—247 Italian sordine and detail of its base; seventeenth century. National Museum, Prague.

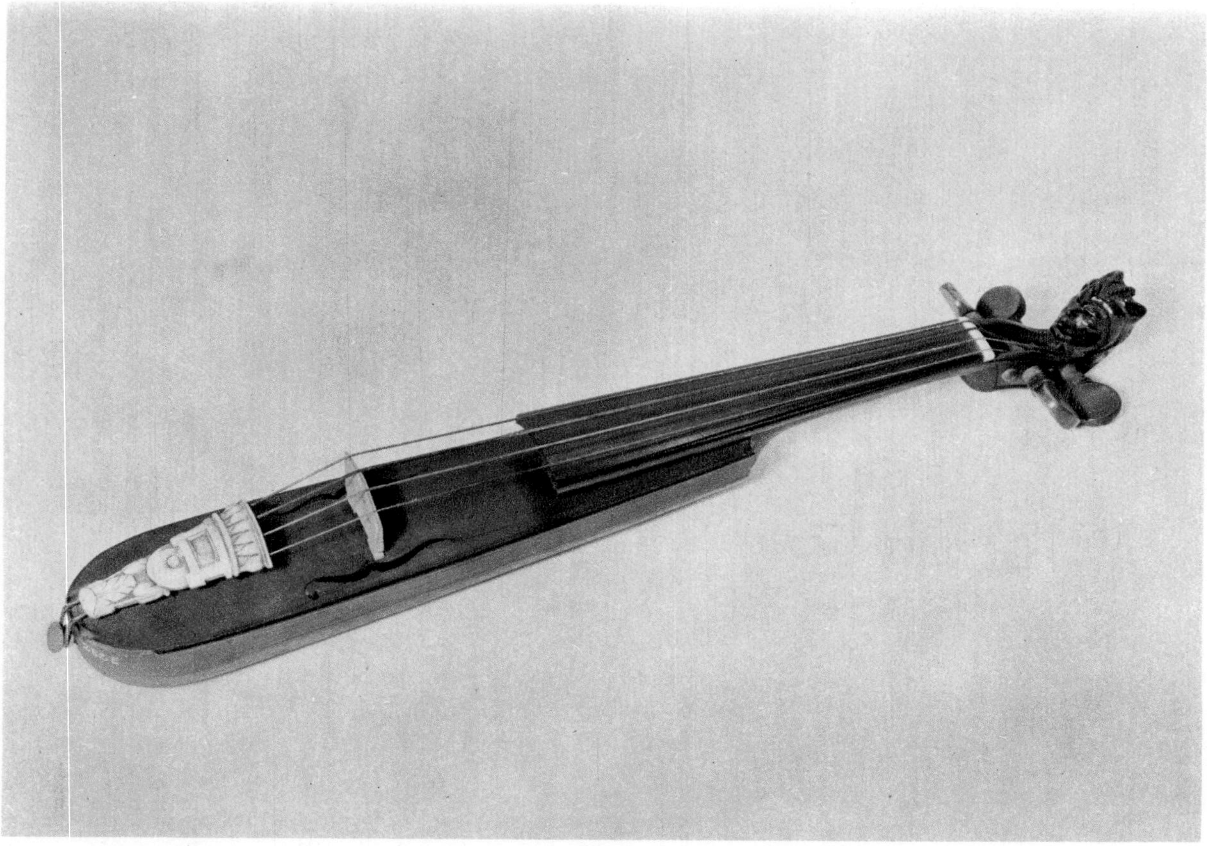

248—249 Pochette (small violin played by dancing masters) made by the Chomutov violin maker Johannes Rauch in the eighteenth century, and eighteenth century sordine. National Museum, Prague.

250 Hurdy-gurdy and violin; unknown eighteenth century painter. National Museum, Prague (deposited by the National Gallery).

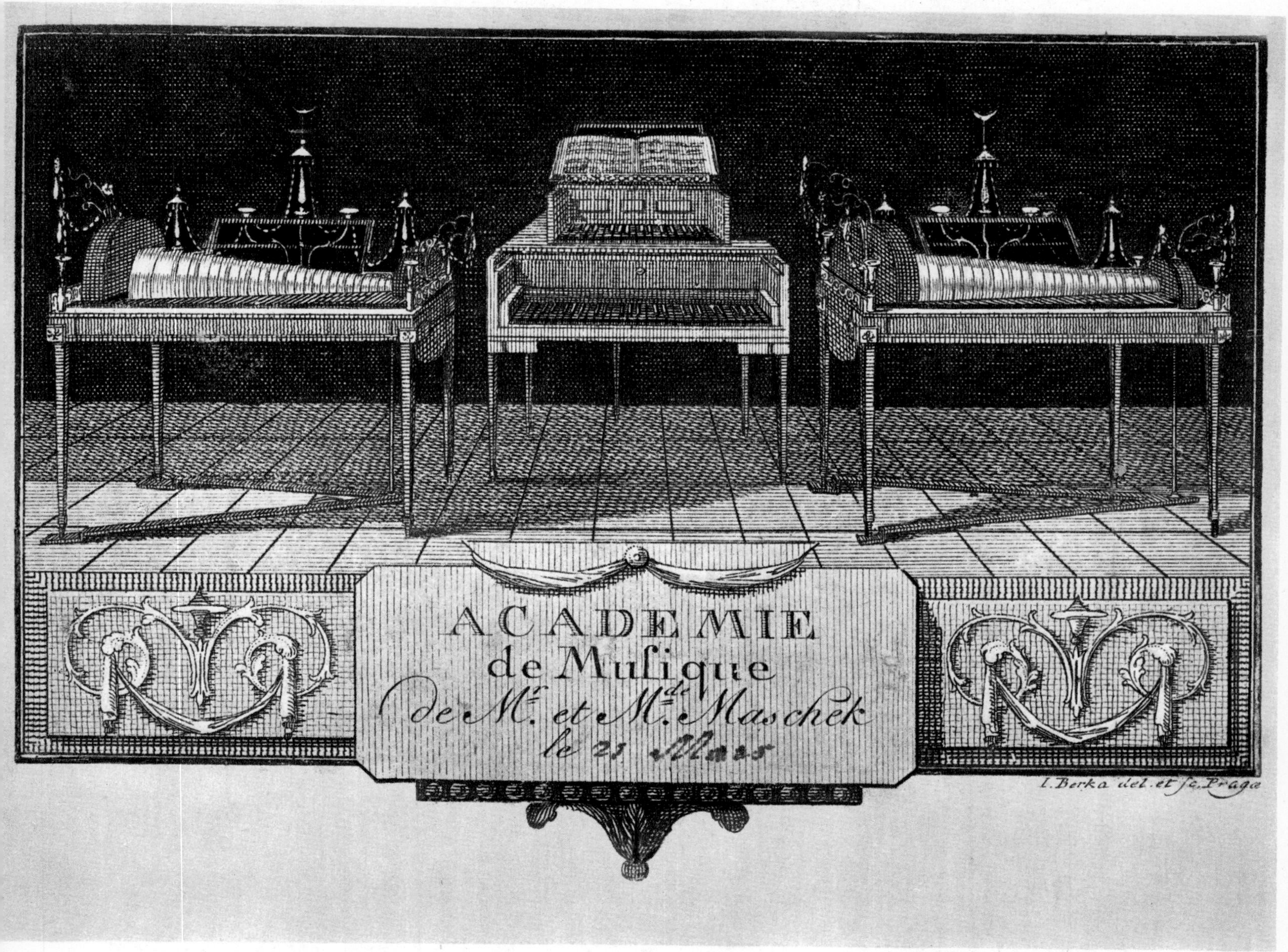


251 Glass harmonicas and keyboard chimes; engraving from the first half of the nineteenth century, on a poster advertising the Czech performers, Mr and Mrs Mašek. National Museum, Prague.

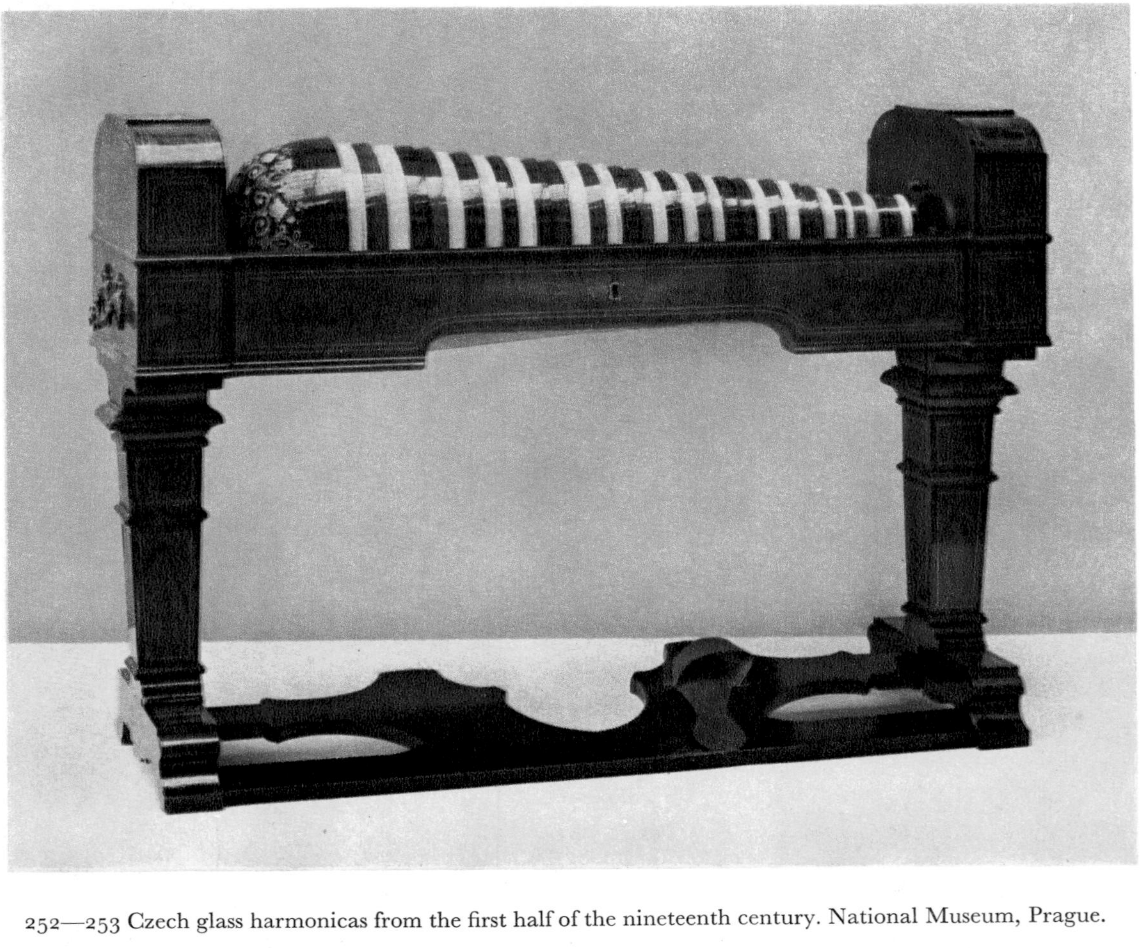

252—253 Czech glass harmonicas from the first half of the nineteenth century. National Museum, Prague.

254 The drum of the Prague maltsters' guild, 1639. City Museum, Prague.

255 Transverse flute, xylophone, viola and violin; unknown Czech painter of the second half of the seventeenth century. National Museum, Prague.

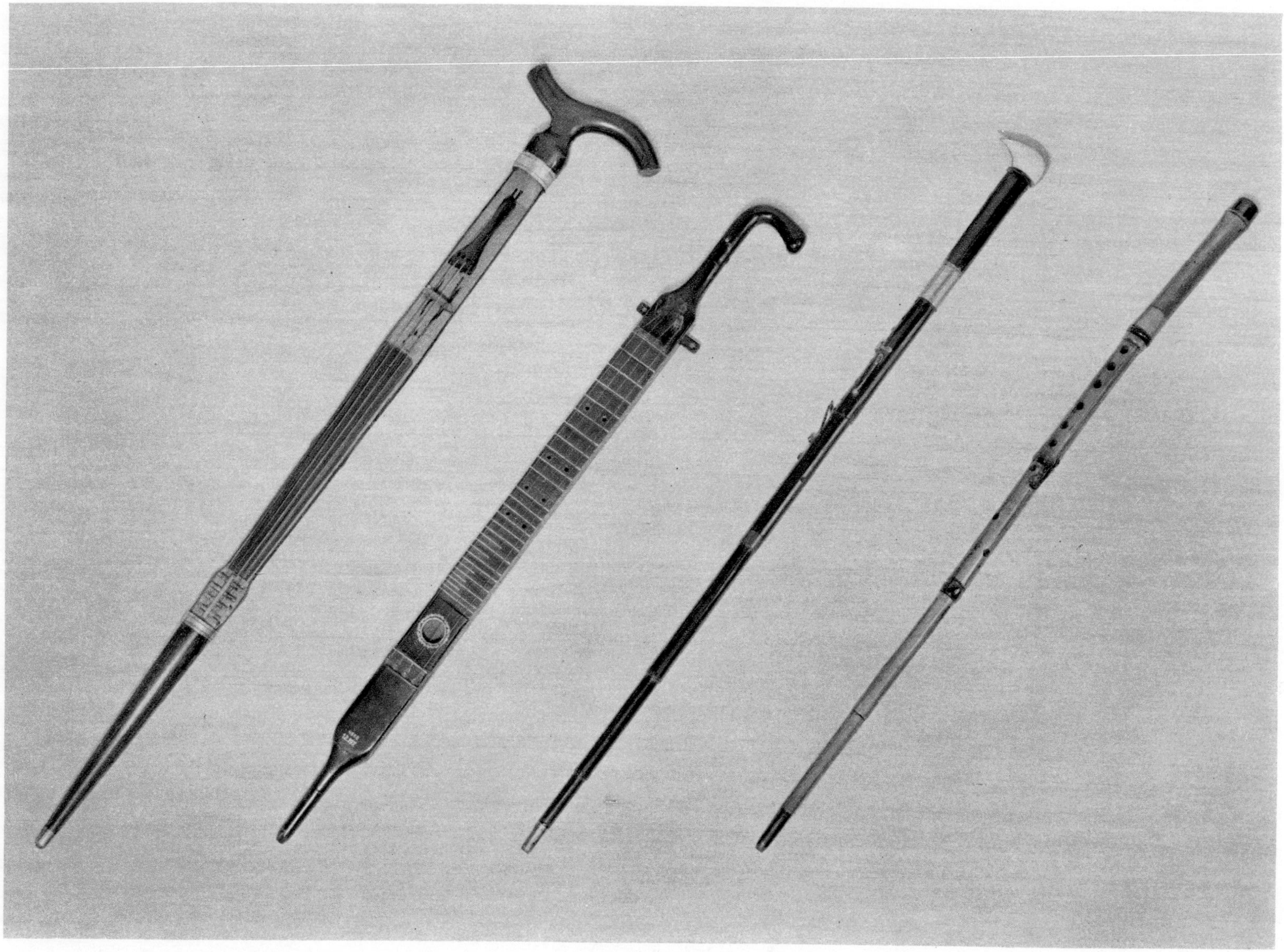

256—259 Instruments in walking sticks, early nineteenth century: violin, guitar, *chakan* and flute. National Museum, Prague.

260 Czech physharmonica from the beginning of the nineteenth century. National Museum, Prague.

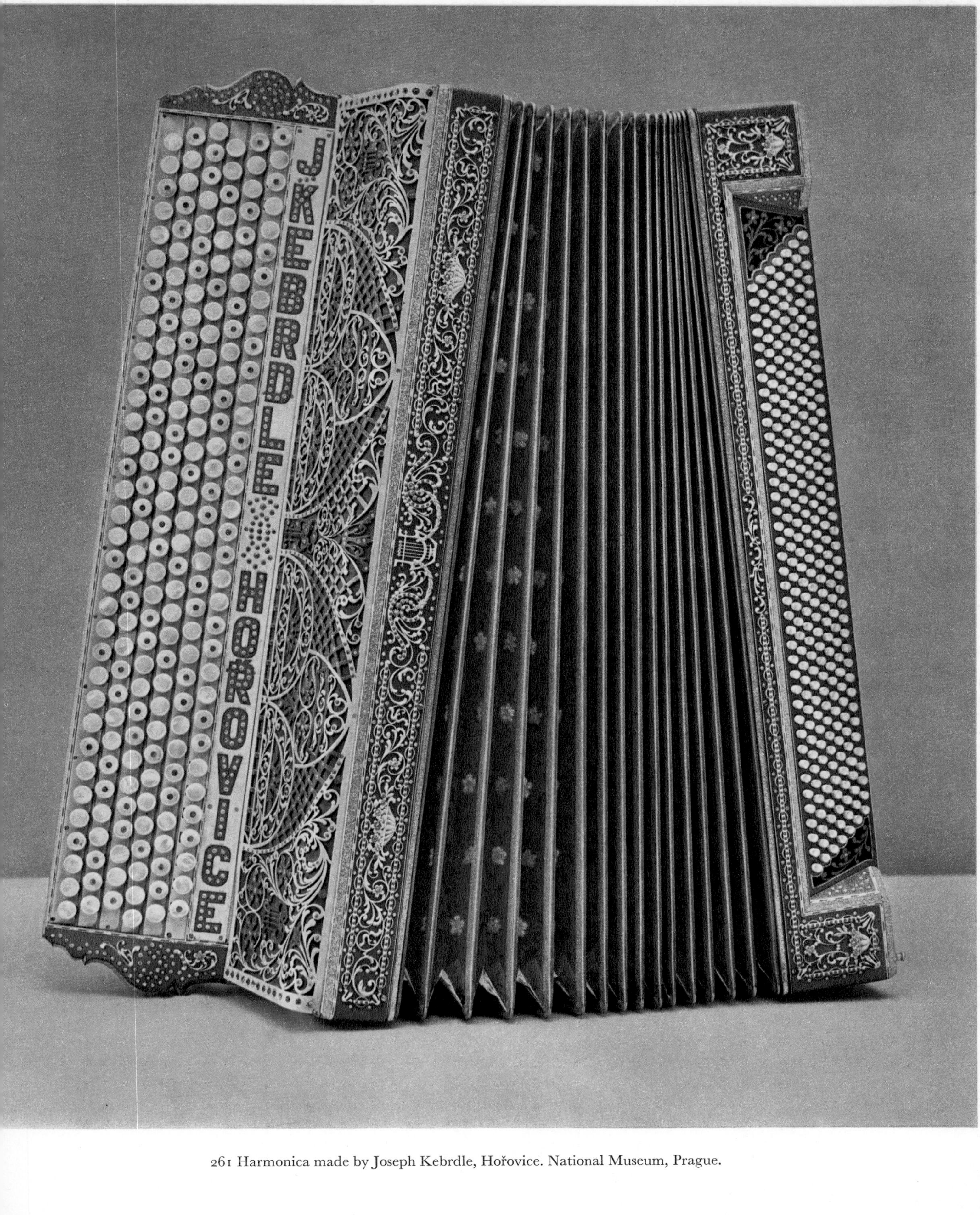


261 Harmonica made by Joseph Kebrdle, Hořovice. National Museum, Prague.

262 A Chinese Pavilion of the eighteenth century. National Museum, Prague.

263—264 Terpodion and a view of the mechanism with a wooden roller; first half of the nineteenth century.
Moravian Museum, Brno.

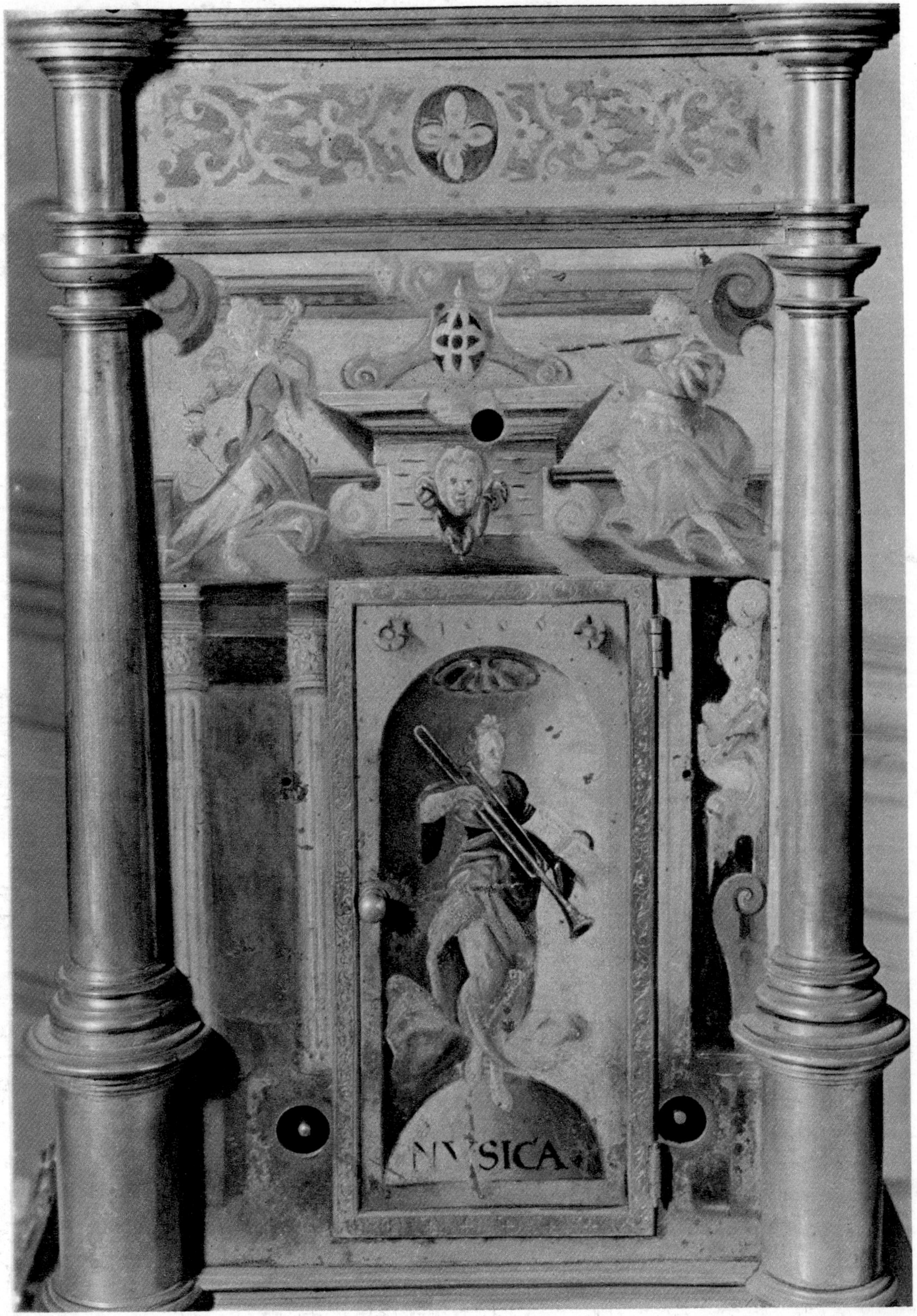


265—266 Musical clock, 1596, and detail of the left side with musical instruments: tenor *viola da gamba*, transverse flute and trombone. Mathematical Room, Klementinum, Prague.

269—270 Hooked harp and barrel-organ. Types of Prague musicians. Coloured engraving by F. K. Wolf from the beginning of the nineteenth century. National Museum, Prague.

271—272 Mechanical pointed harp (harfonetta) from the end of the eighteenth century, and detail of the back part of the body, National Museum, Prague.

273—274 Modern electric organ on the Unit system and the keyboard. Pantheon of the National Museum, Prague.

Vyp. jazyků
B
D
Crescendo
Žaluzie I.
Žaluzie II.
Žaluzie II 2
P
F
TT
A
C
Vyp.crescenda
Vyp.komb.
MF
PL

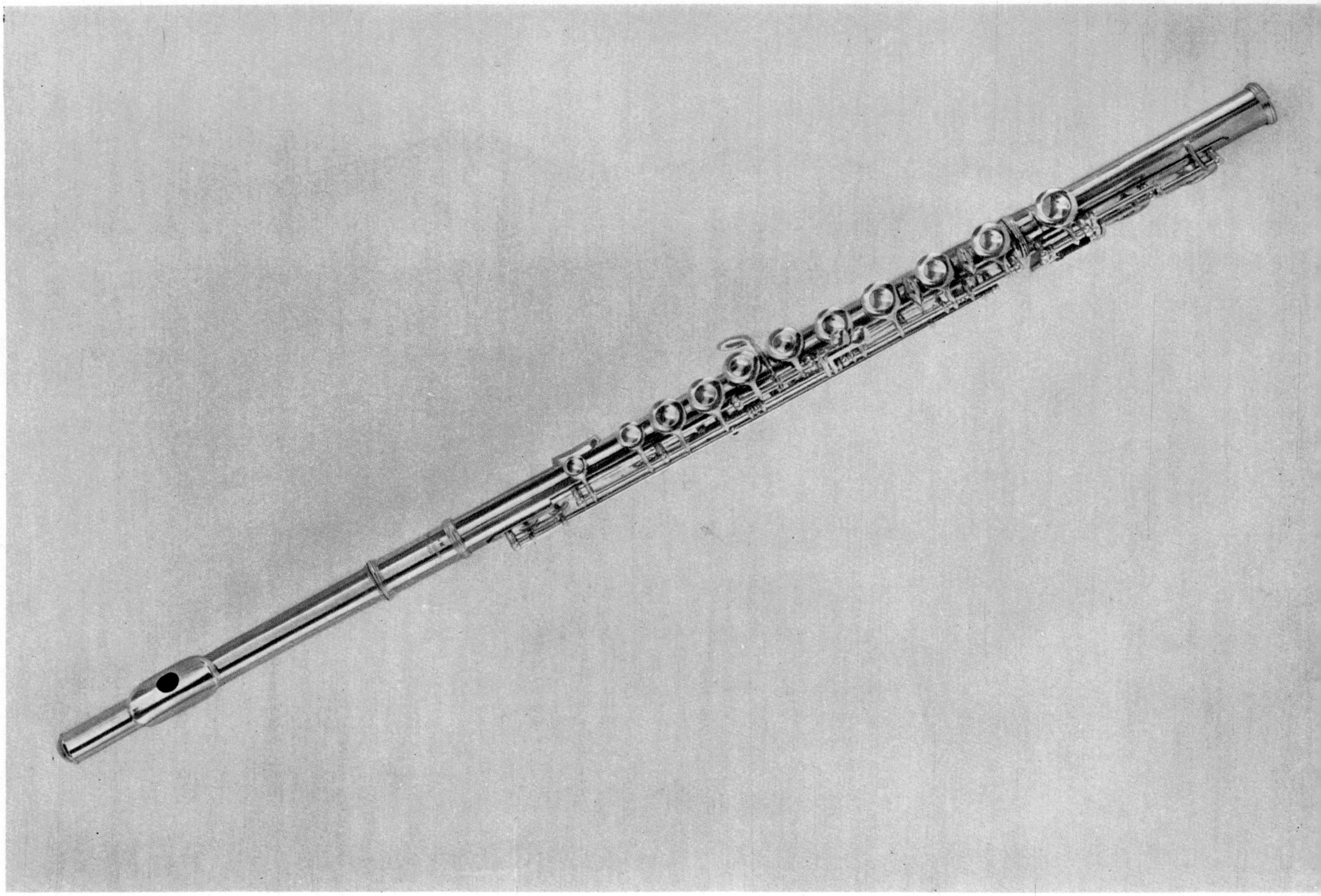

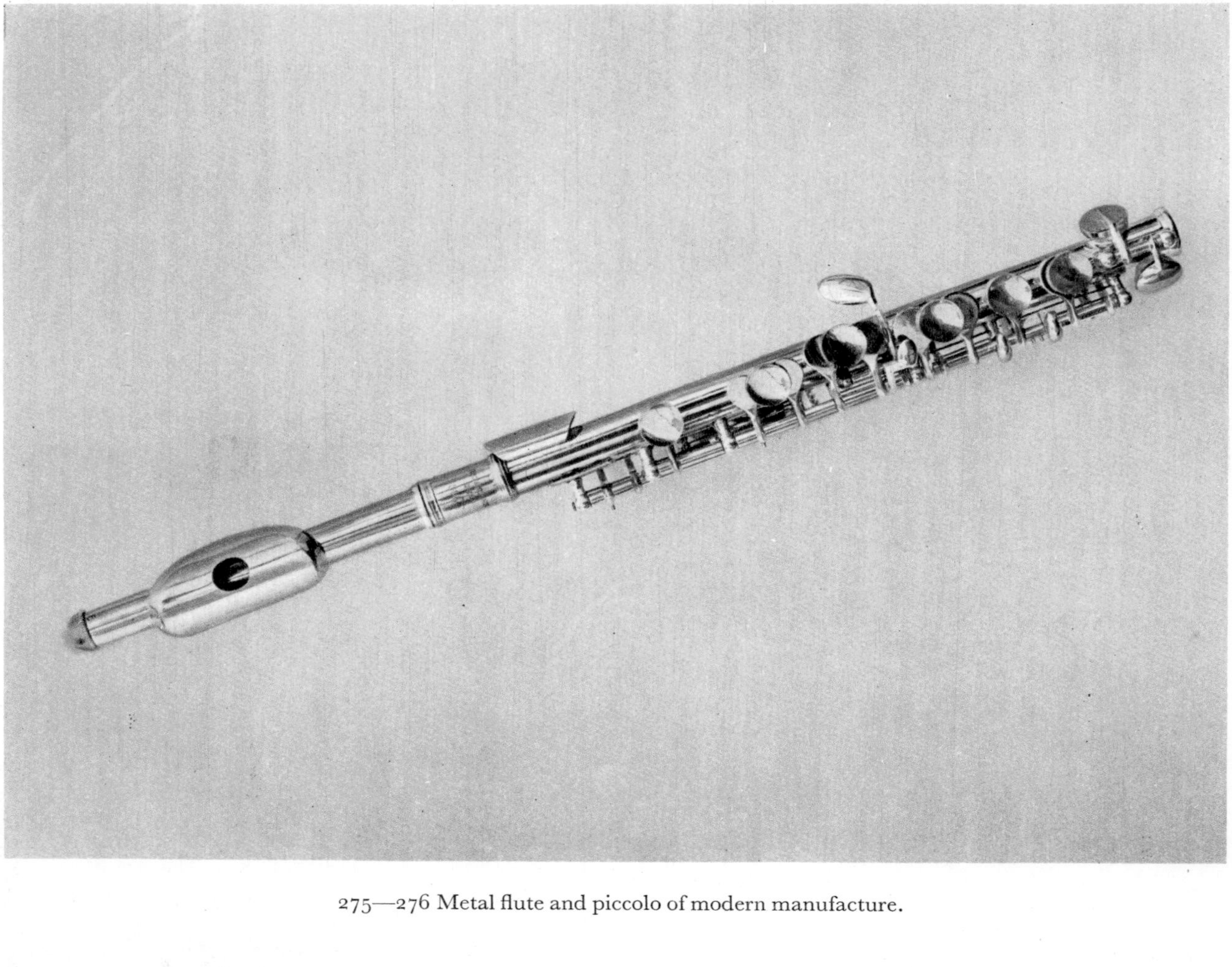

275—276 Metal flute and piccolo of modern manufacture.

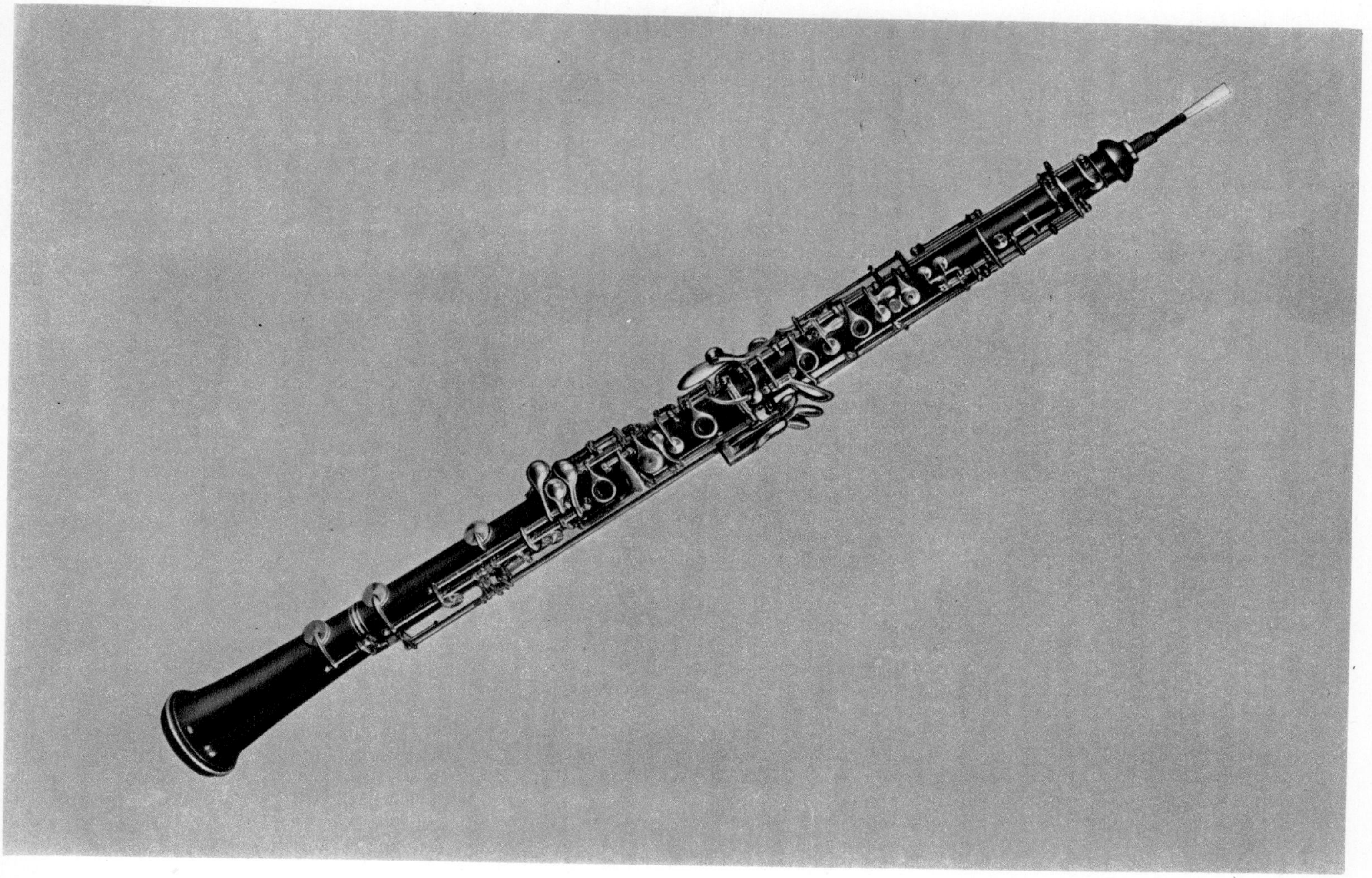

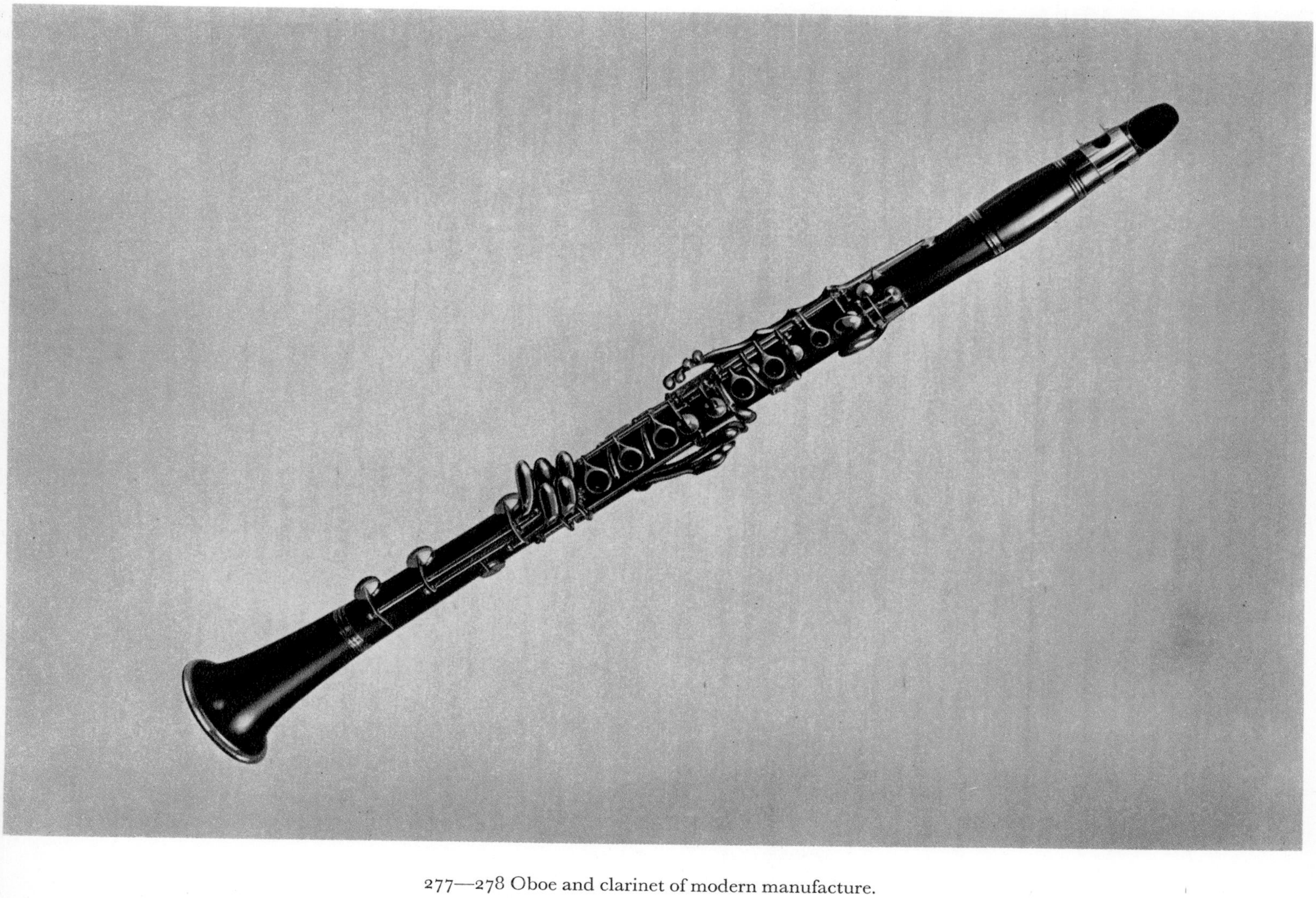

277—278 Oboe and clarinet of modern manufacture.

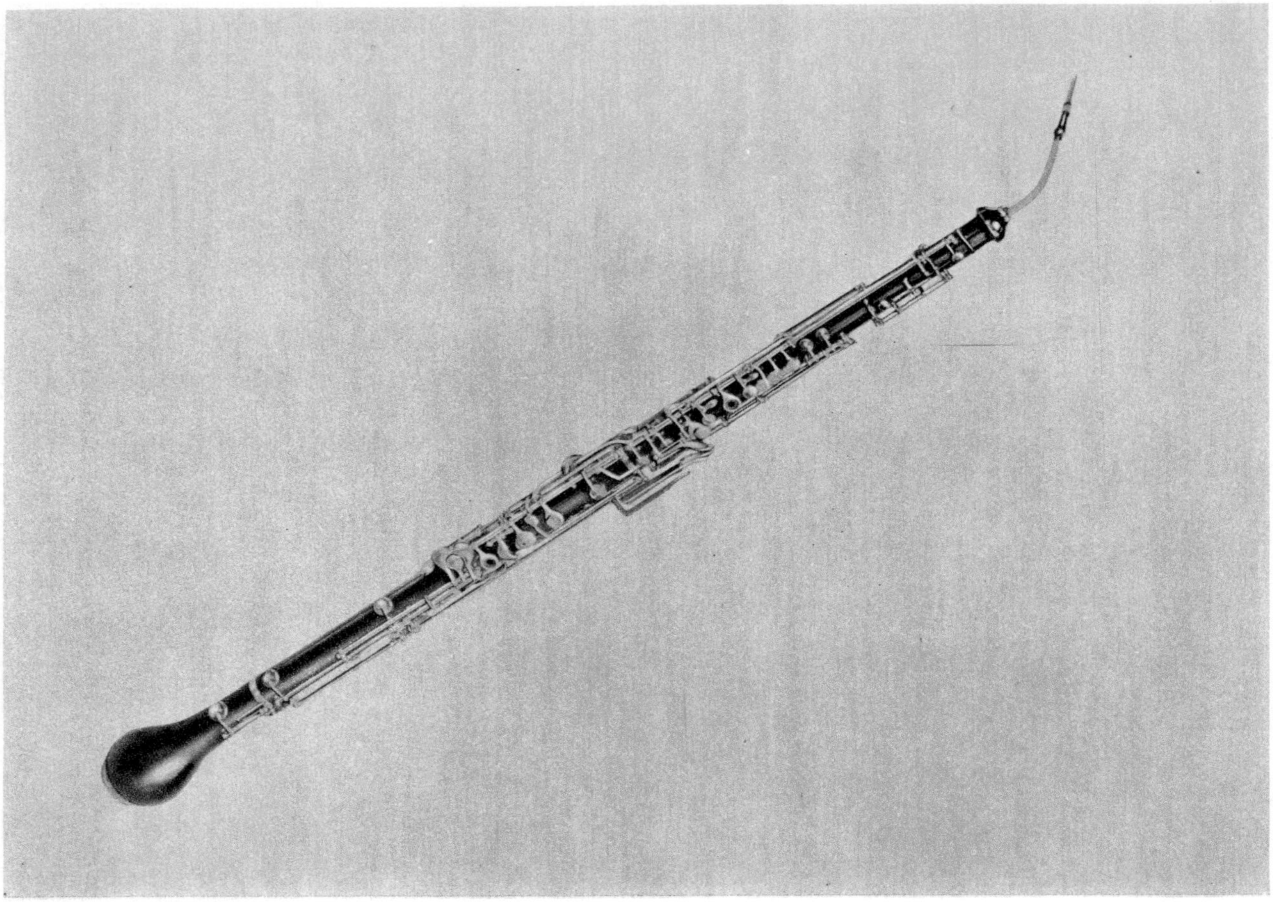

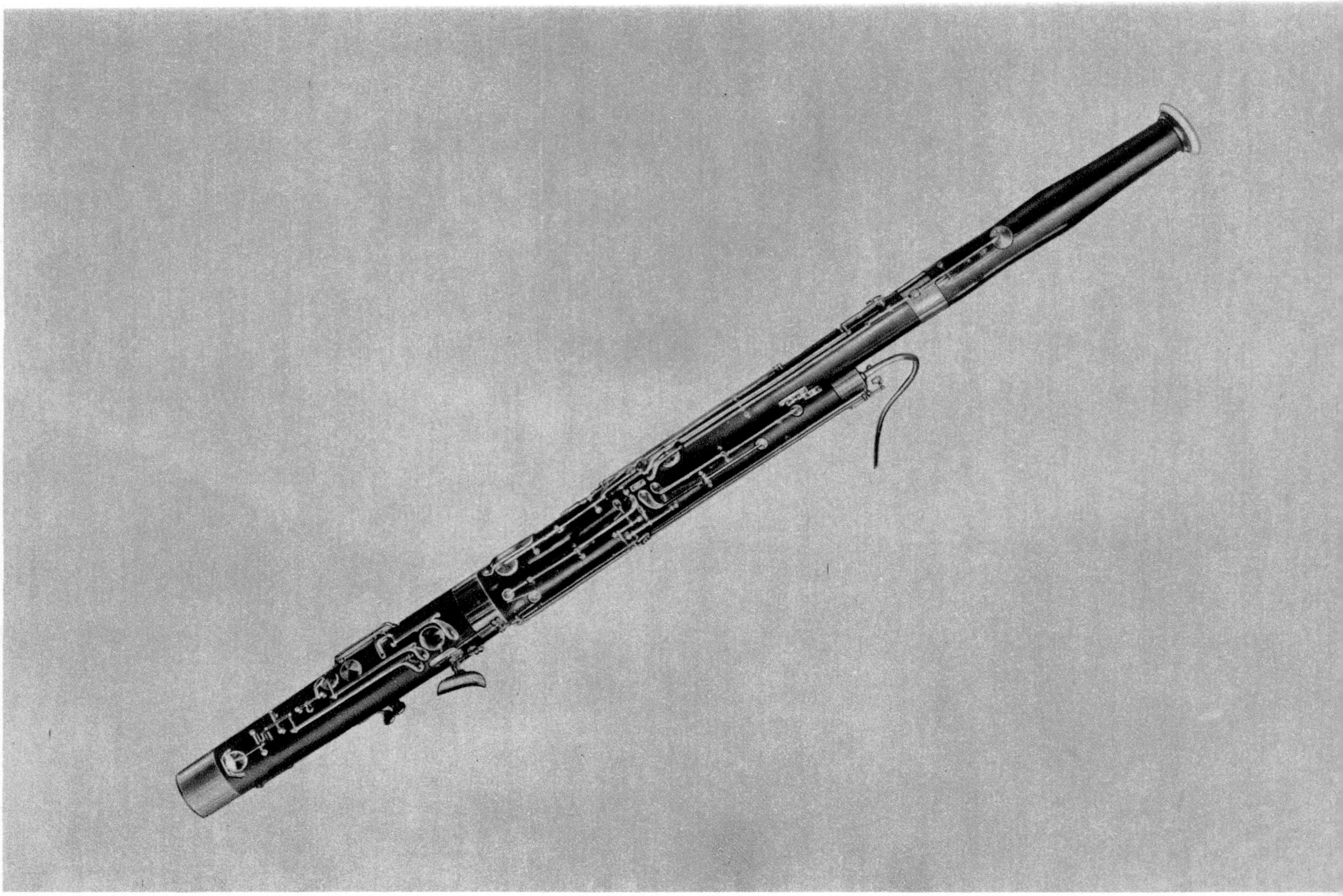

279—280 English horn (cor anglais) and bassoon of modern manufacture.

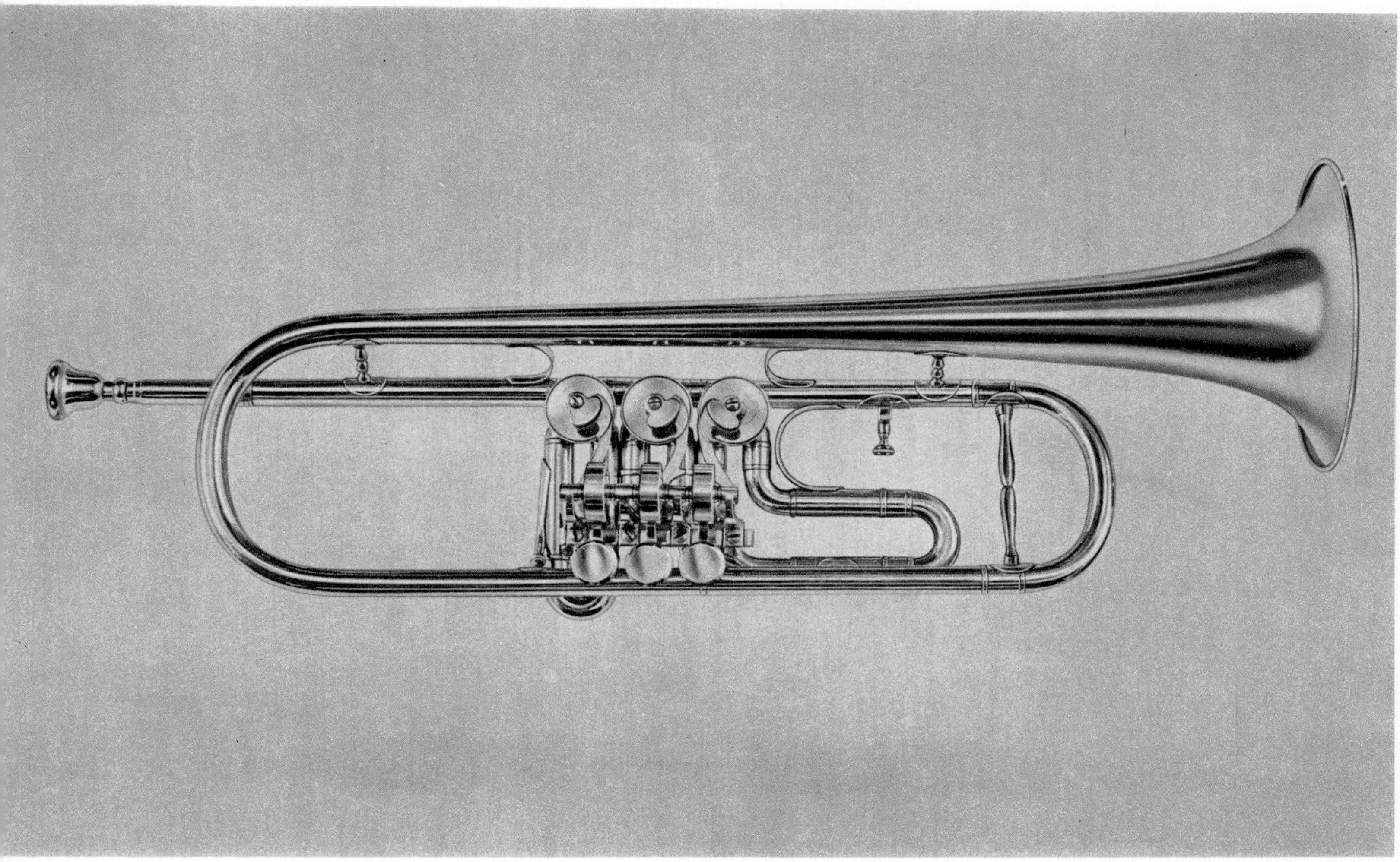

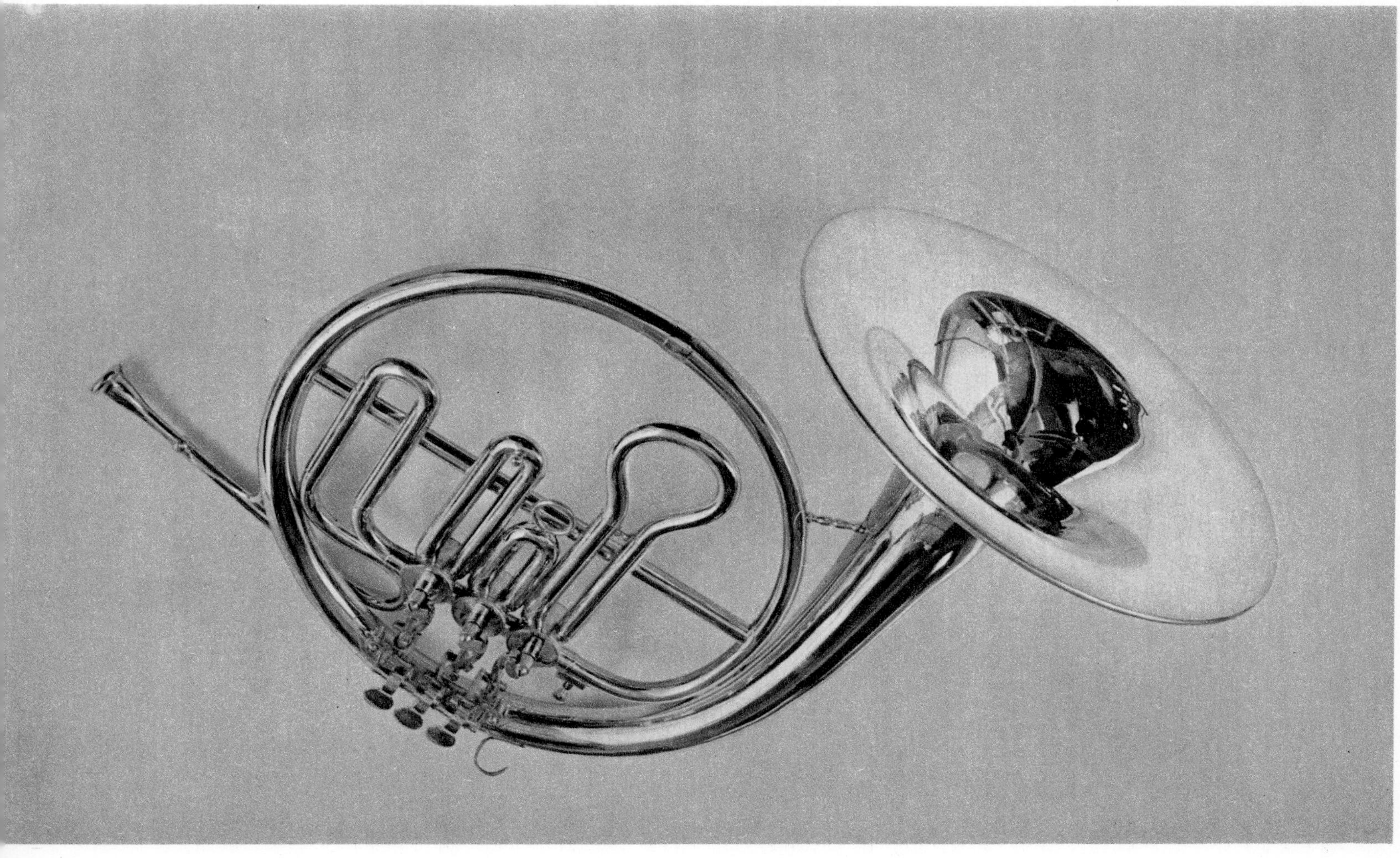

281—282 Trumpet and French horn of modern manufacture.

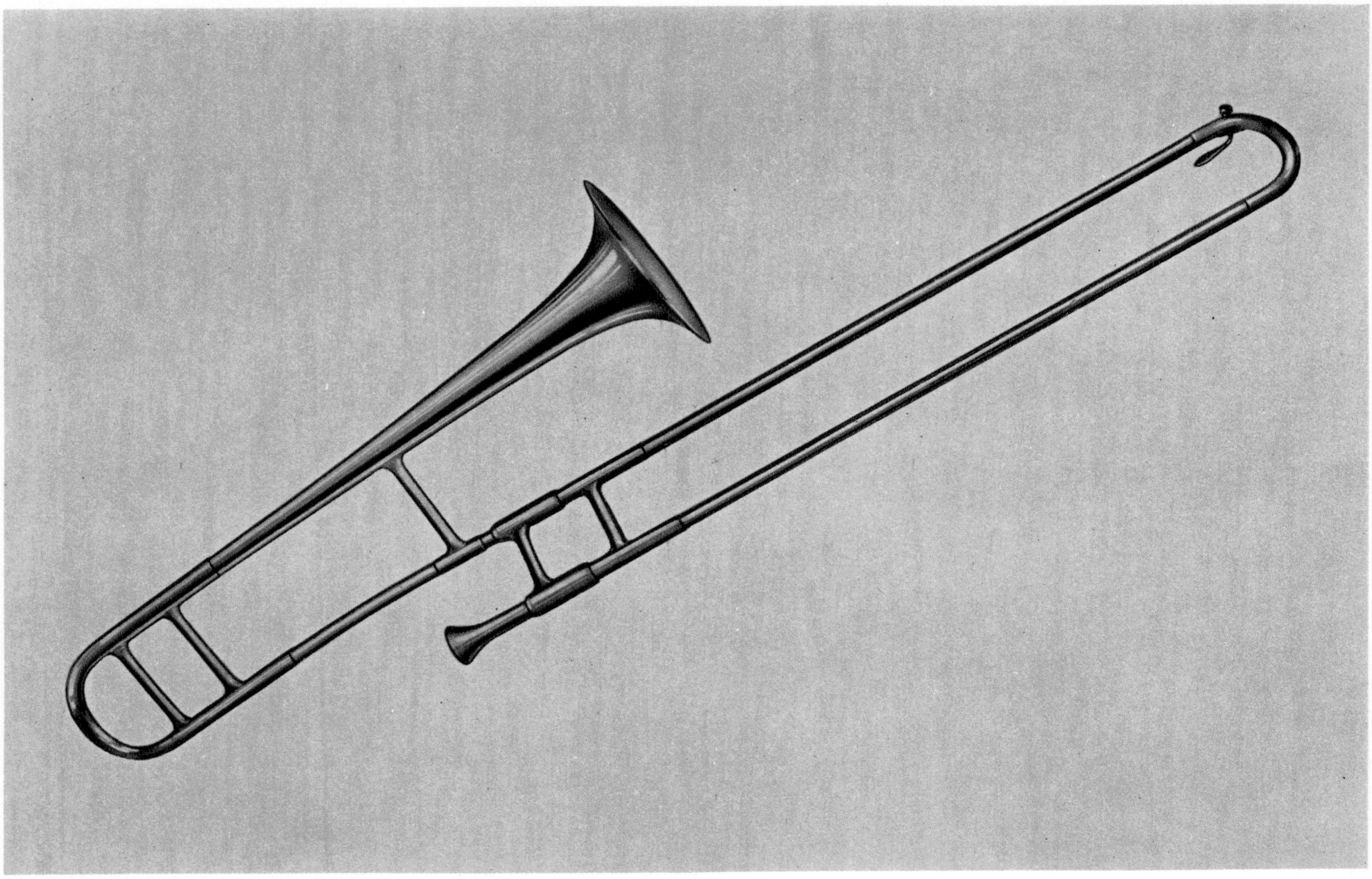

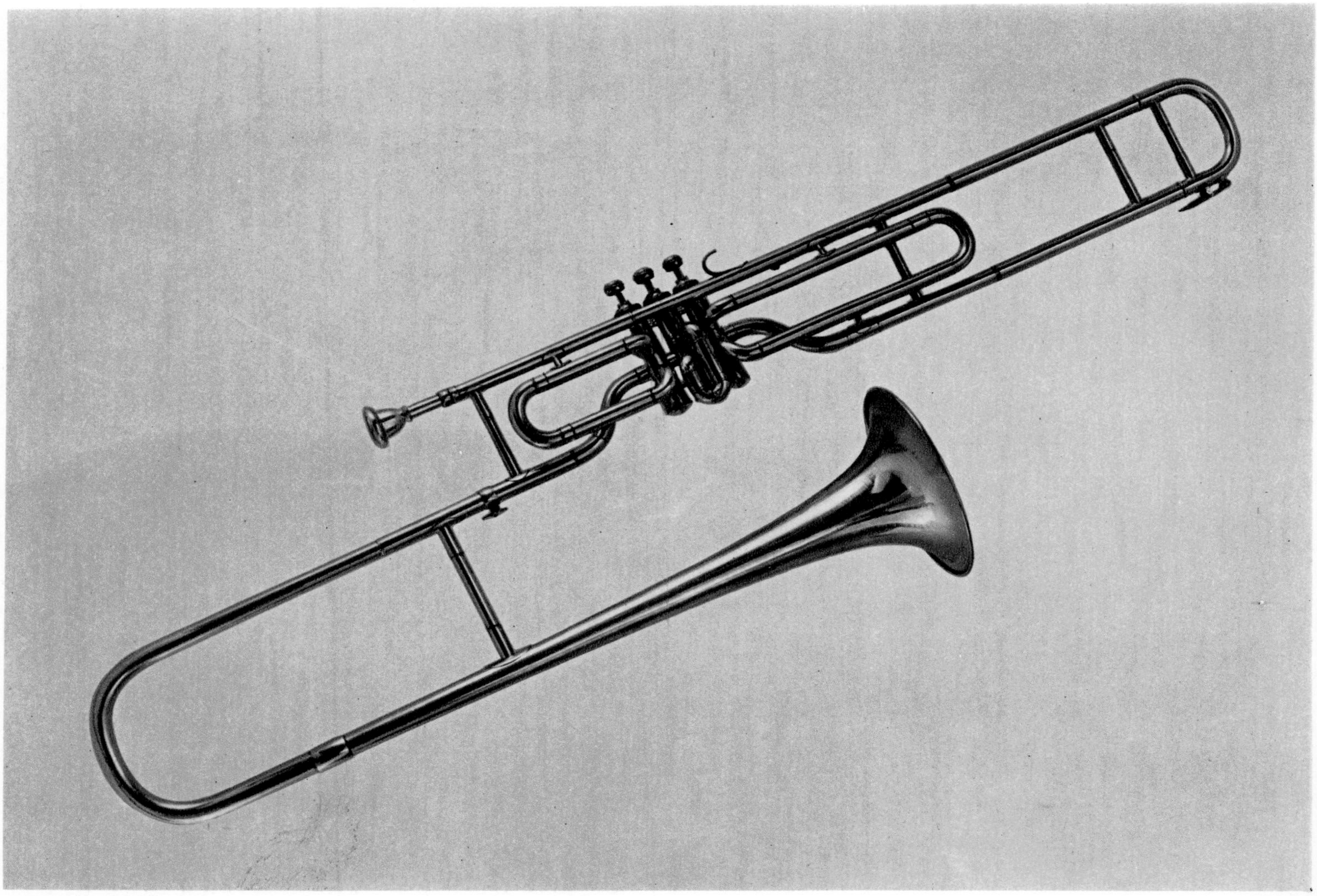

283—284 Slide trombone and valve trombone of modern manufacture.

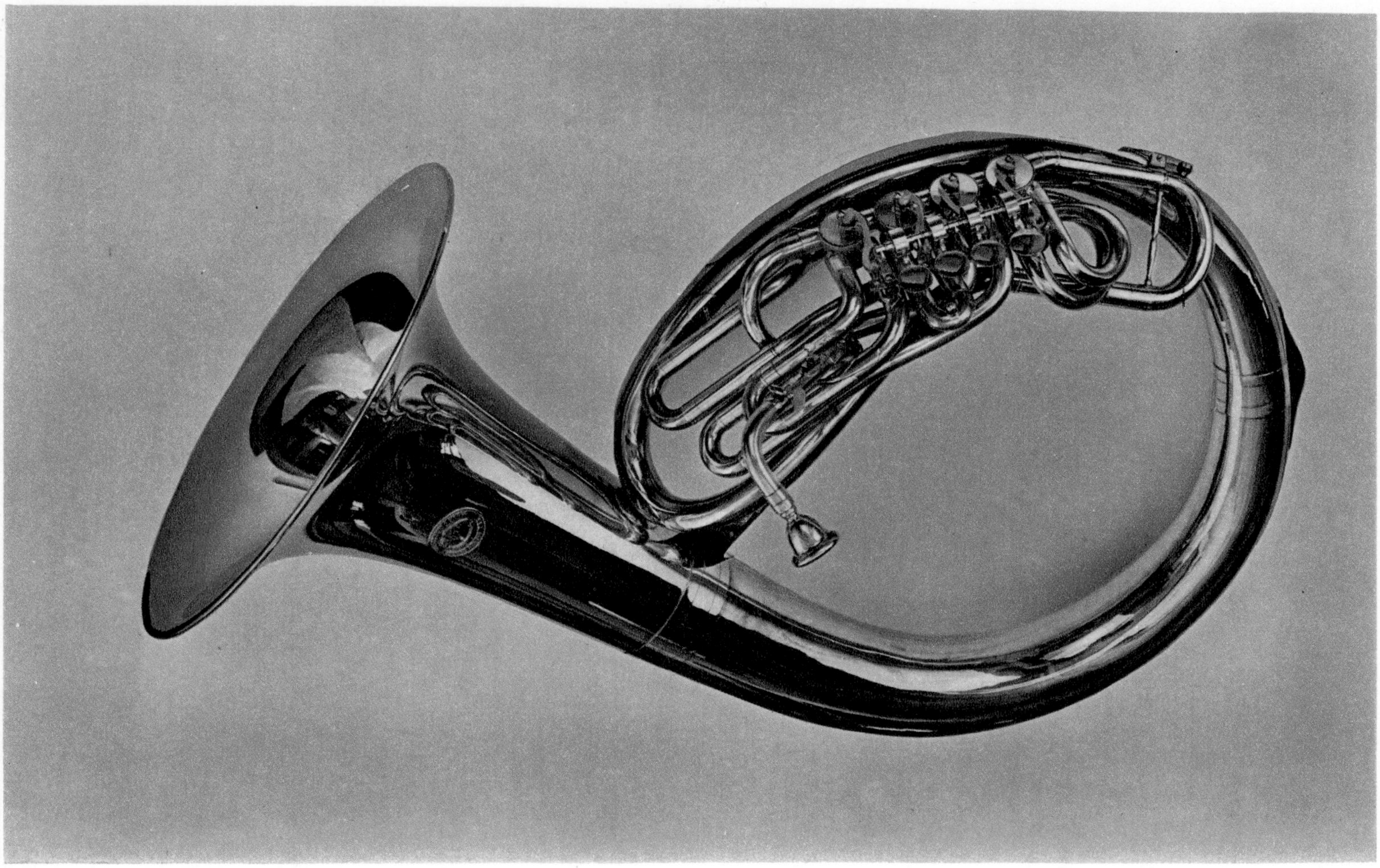

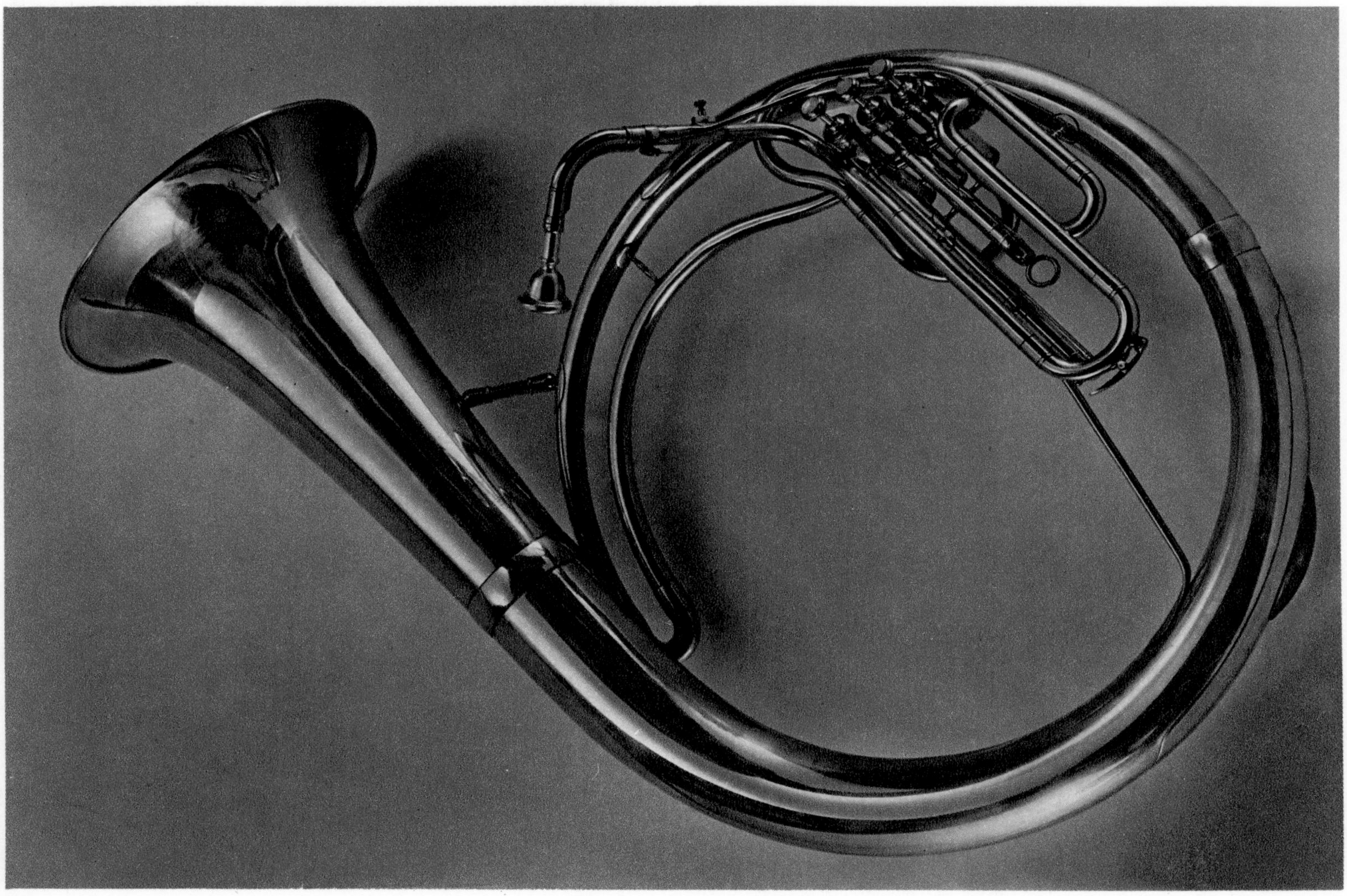

285—286 Rotary valve helicon and piston helicon of modern manufacture.

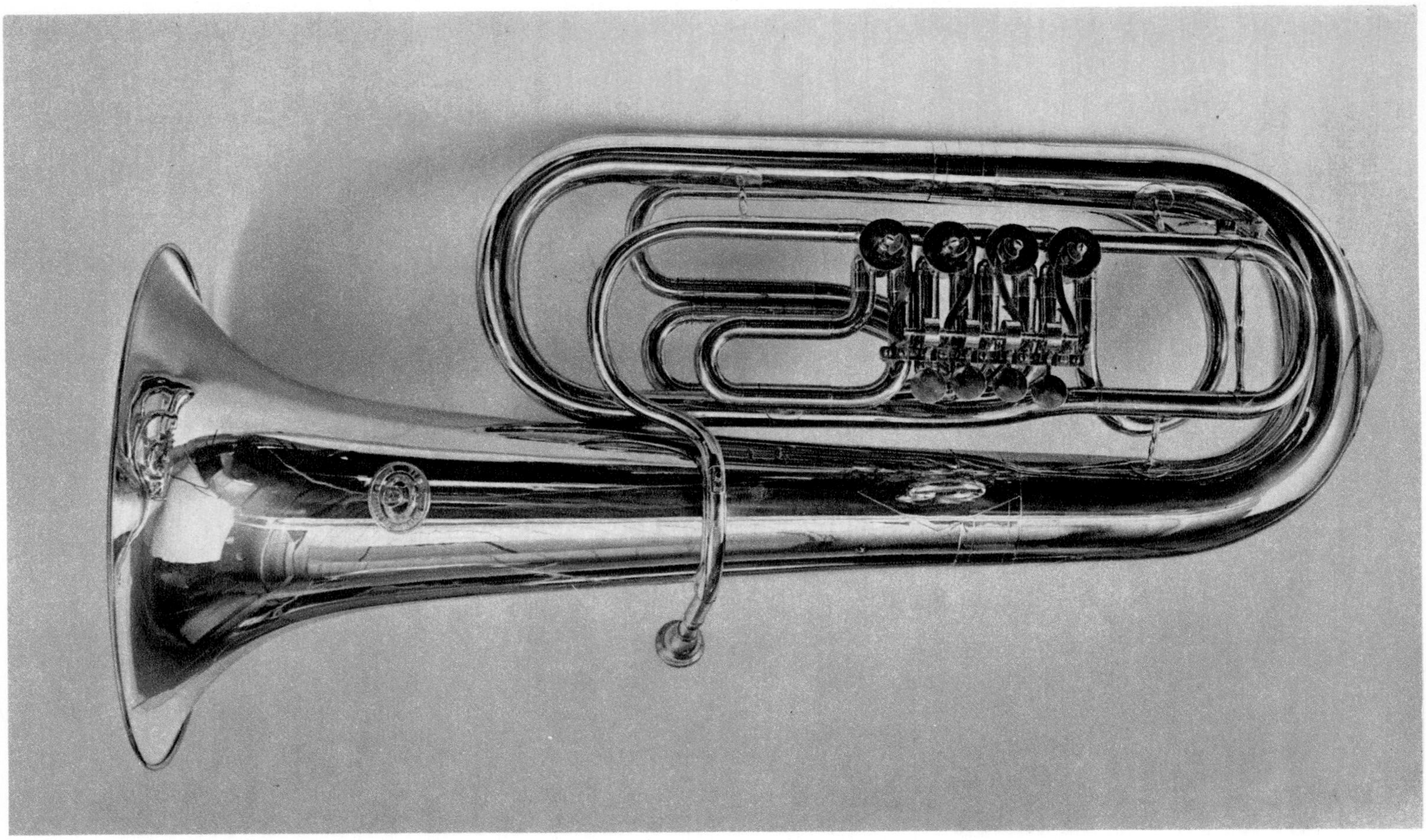

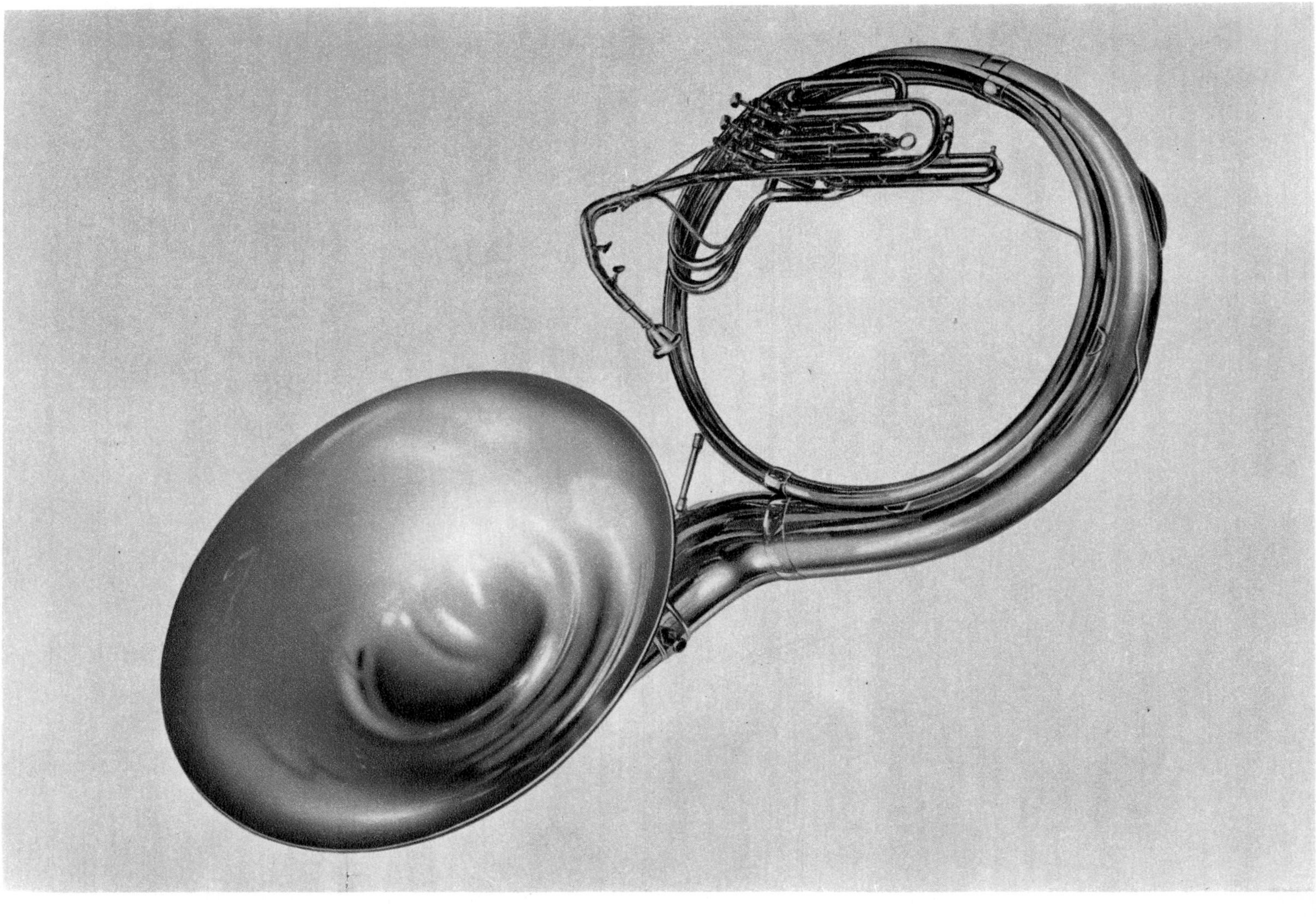

287—288 Bass tuba and sousaphone of modern manufacture.

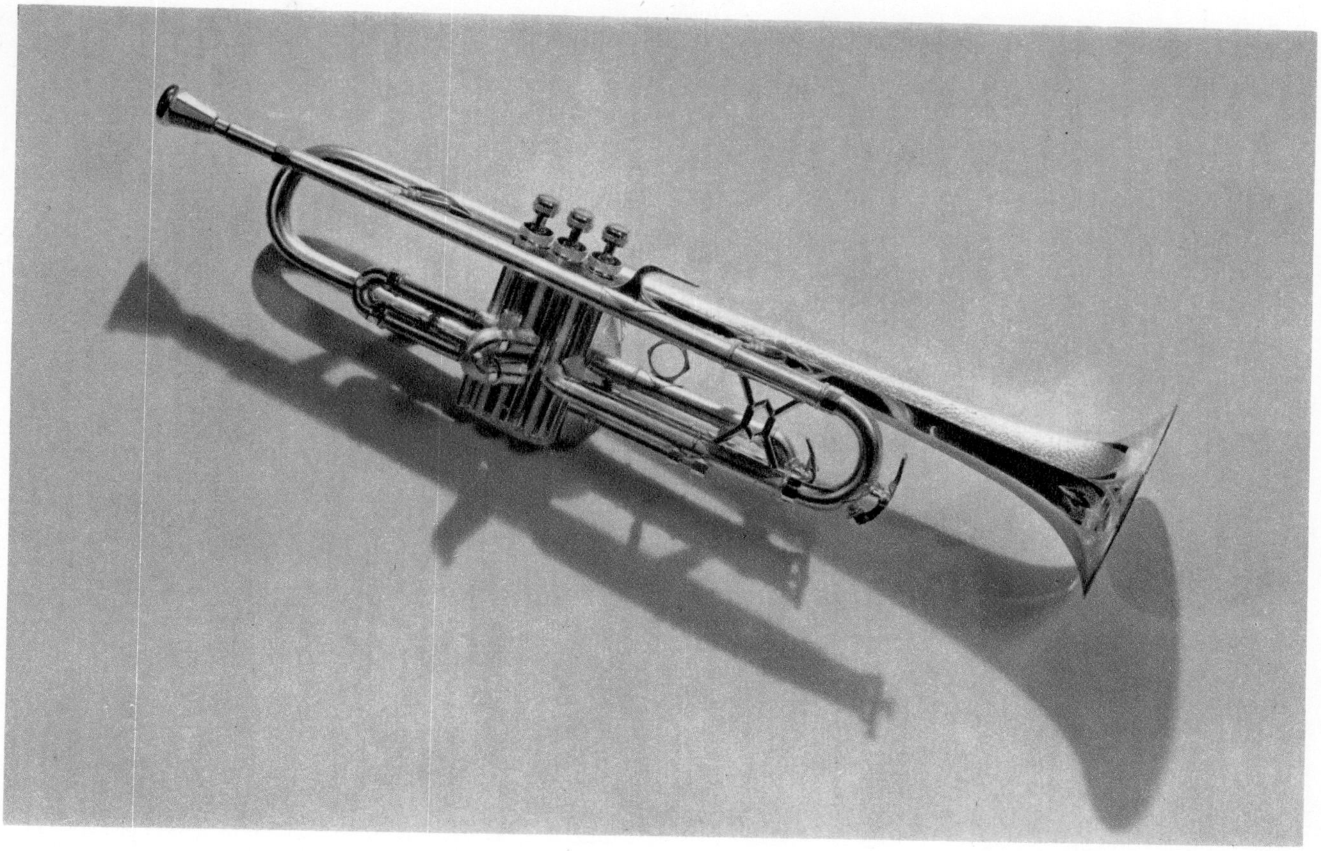

289—290 The piston-trumpet of dance orchestras and a piano accordion of modern manufacture.

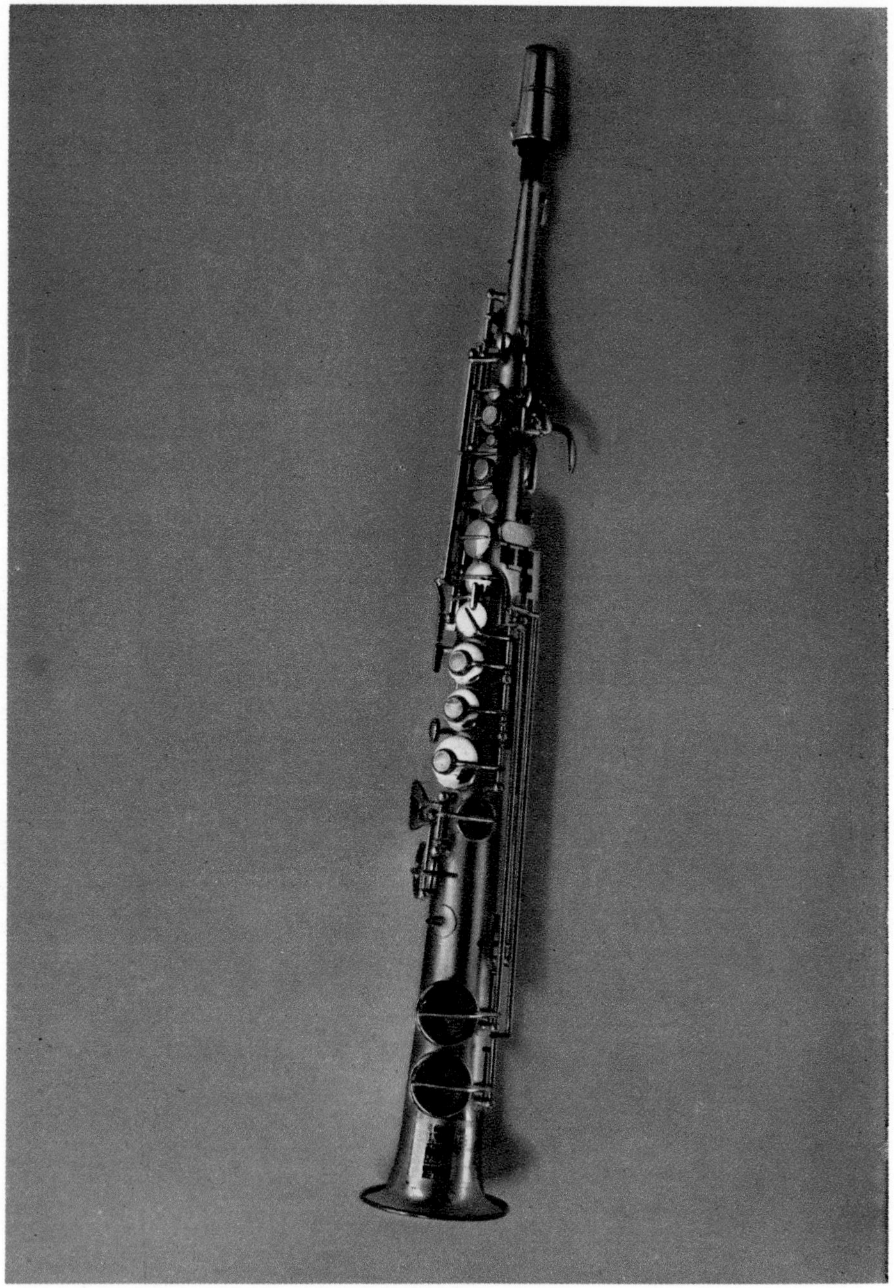

291—292 Soprano and tenor saxophone of modern manufacture.

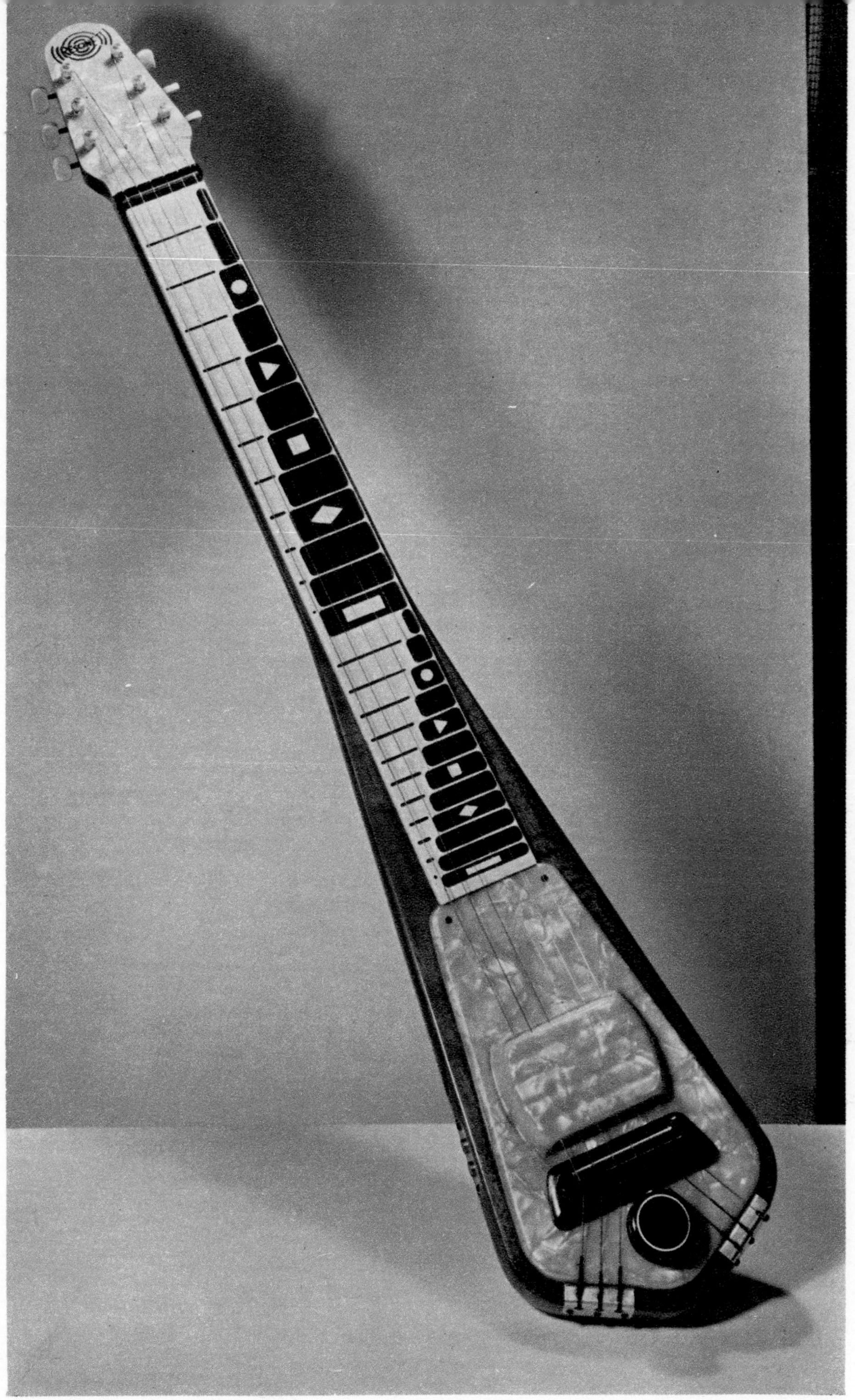

293—294 Guitar of the Gibson banjo type and an electric guitar of modern manufacture.

295 A set of percussion instruments (drums and cymbals) of modern manufacture.

296 Rattle *(tragach)* from Velká Vrbka near Strážnice, Moravia. National Museum, Prague.

Peint par G. Schalken.
Gravé par J. G. Wille Graveur du Roi.
JEUNE JOUEUR D'INSTRUMENT
Dédié à Monsieur G. N. de Merz, Negociant à Nuremberg.
Par son Ami et Serviteur Wille.
Gravé d'après le Tableau Original de même grandeur qui est dans le Cabinet
de Monsieur Damery, Chevalier de l'ordre Royal Militaire de S.t Louis.
A Paris chez Wille, Quay des Augustins.

297 *Bukal*; eighteenth century French engraving. National Museum, Prague.

298 Jew's harp. Detail of a mechanical pointed harp from the end of the eighteenth century. National Museum, Prague.

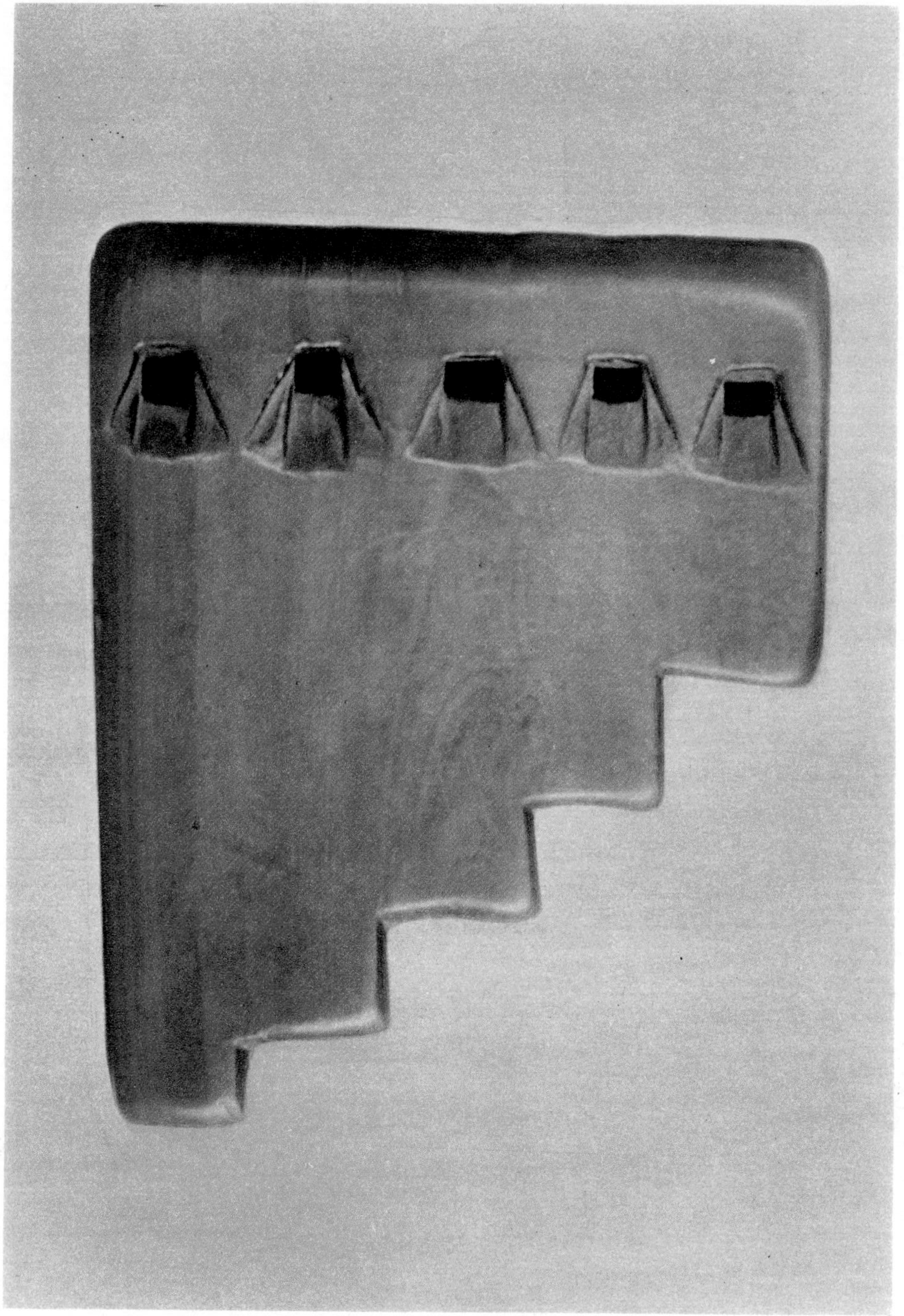

299—300 Panpipes from Příkaz, Moravia, and a rubbed drum from South Bohemia. National Museum, Prague.

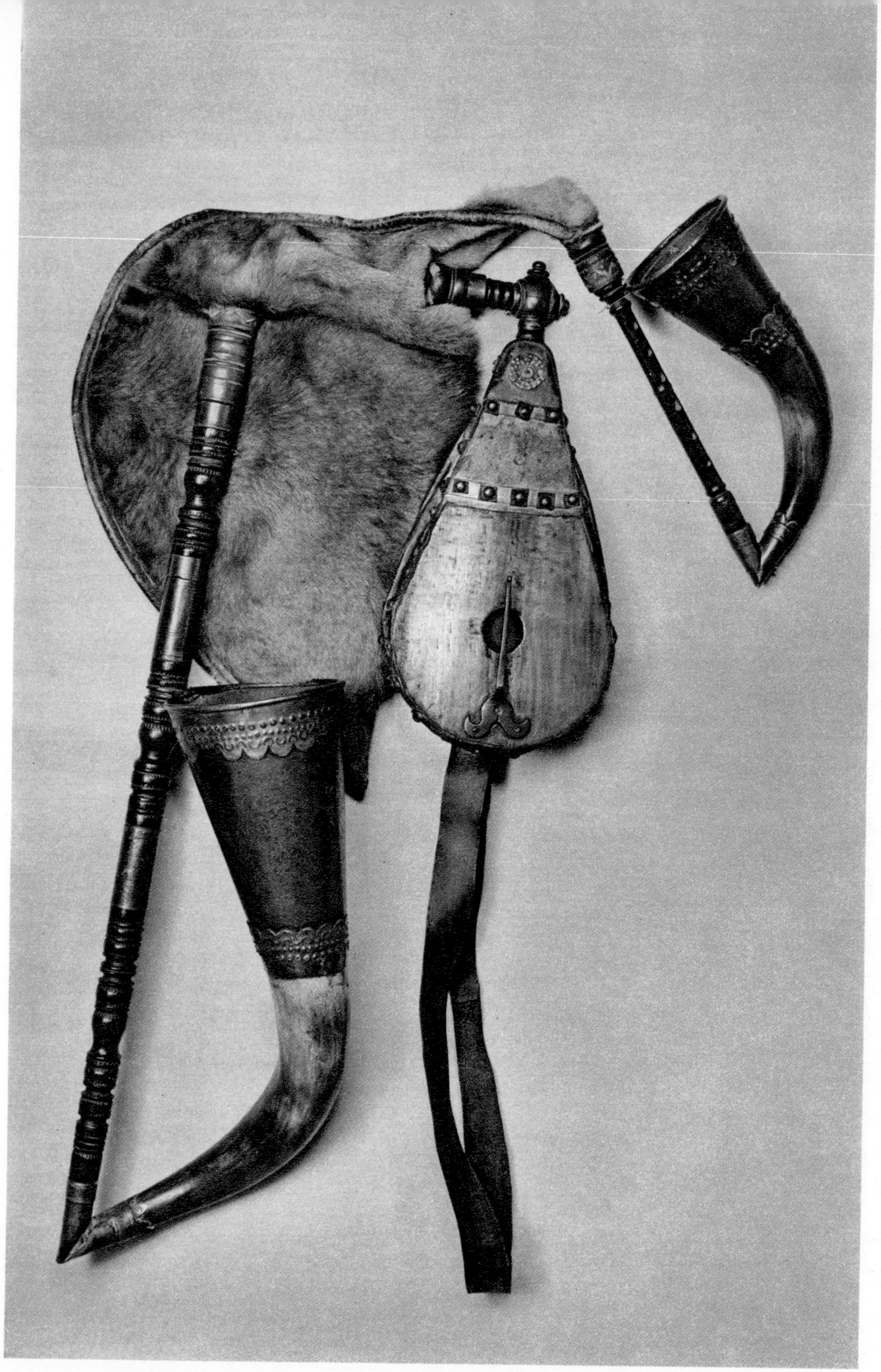

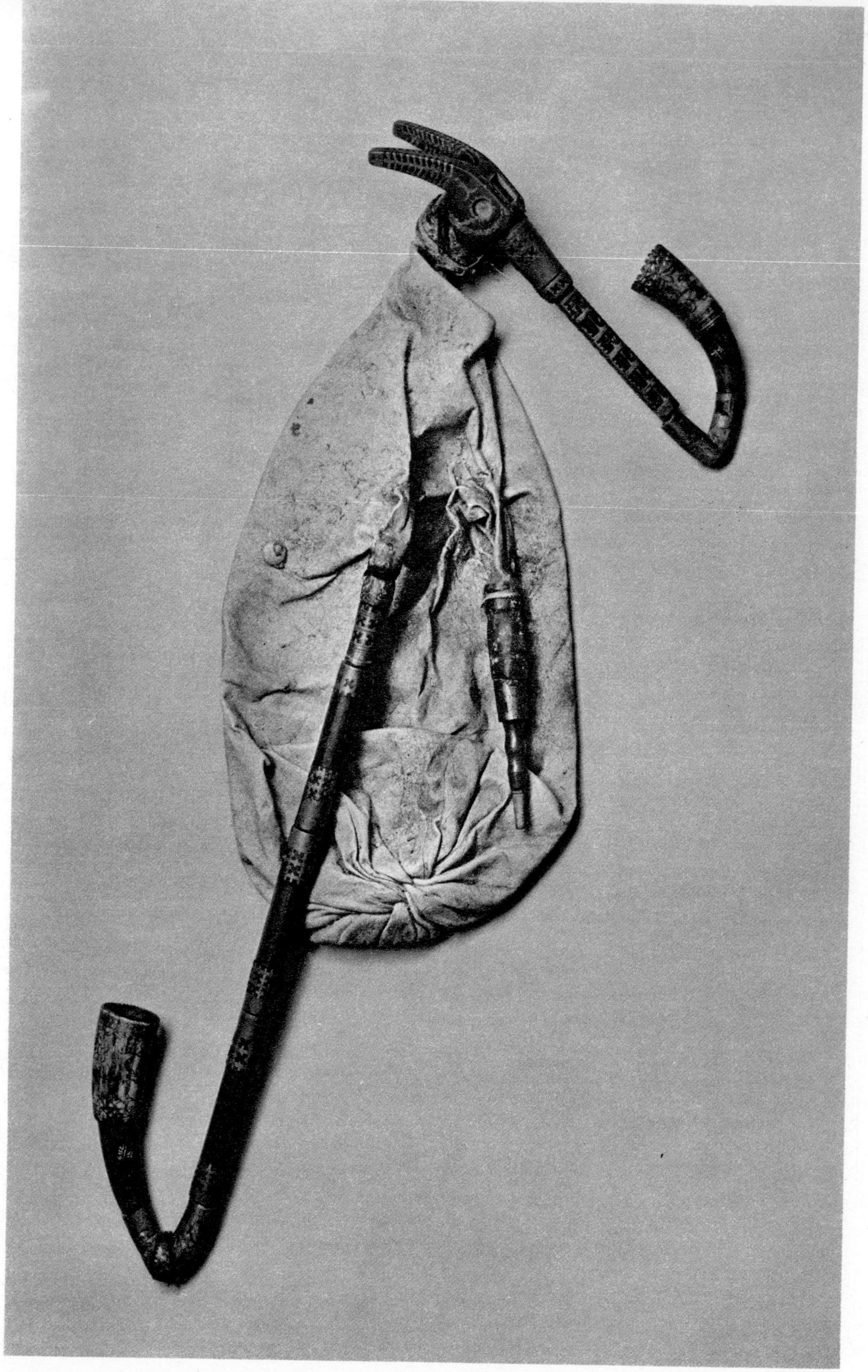

301—302 Czech and Slovak bagpipes. National Museum, Prague, and Slovak National Museum, Martin.

303 Shepherd with a shawm; Viktor Barvitius, 1834. National Gallery, Prague.

304 A bagpiper; Joža Uprka (1861—1940). Brno Gallery.

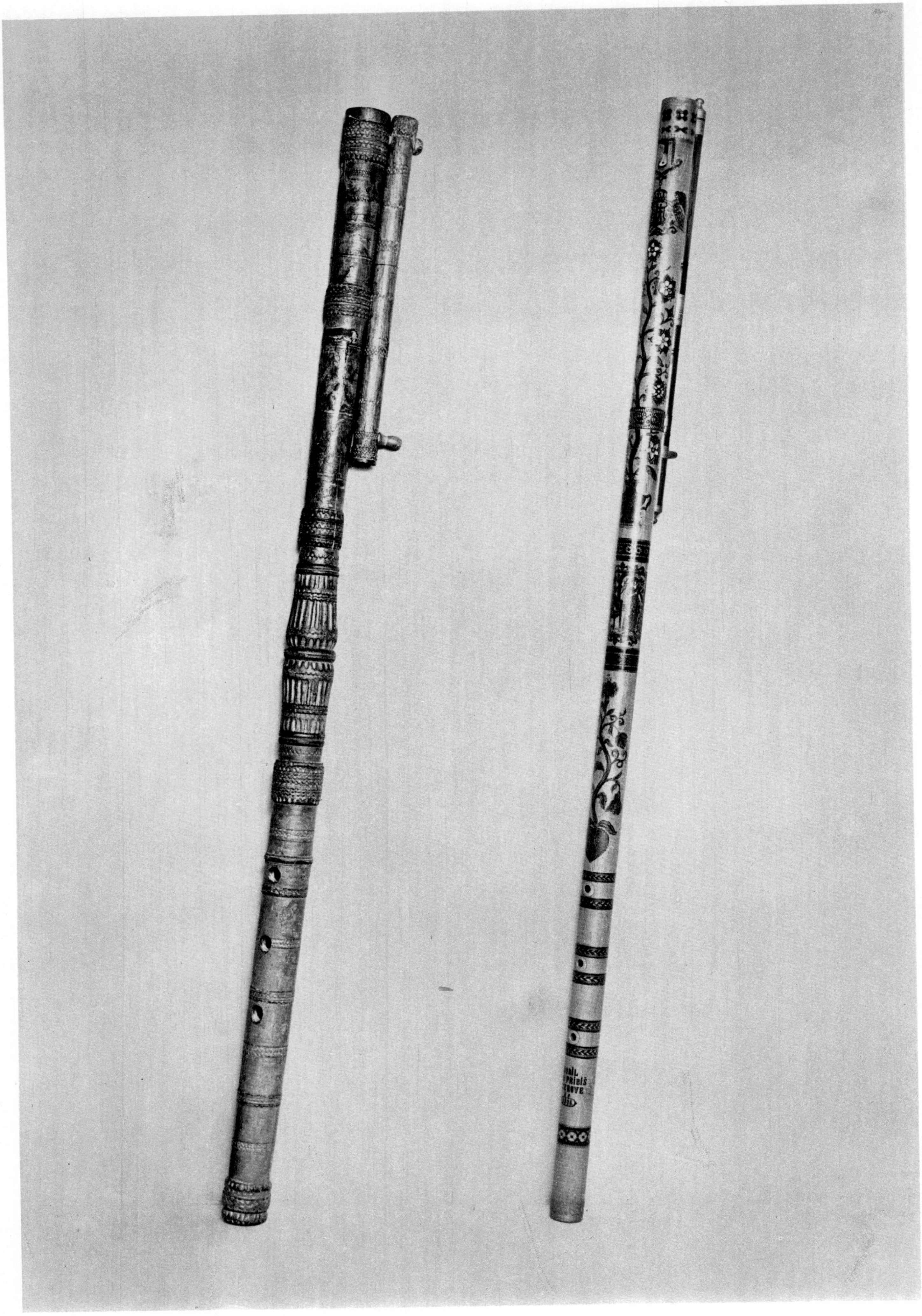

305—306 *Fuyaras* from Detva. This instrument, ornamented with pokerwork and beaten metal, was made by Jan Pribiš of Cerov in 1906. Slovak National Museum, Martin.

307 *Fuyaras* from Detva. Tempera. Janko Alexy.

308 Slovak *fuyara*, bagpipes and pipe. Sketch for sgraffito work on the bridge in Piešťany, by State Prize laureate Martin Benko. Private collection.

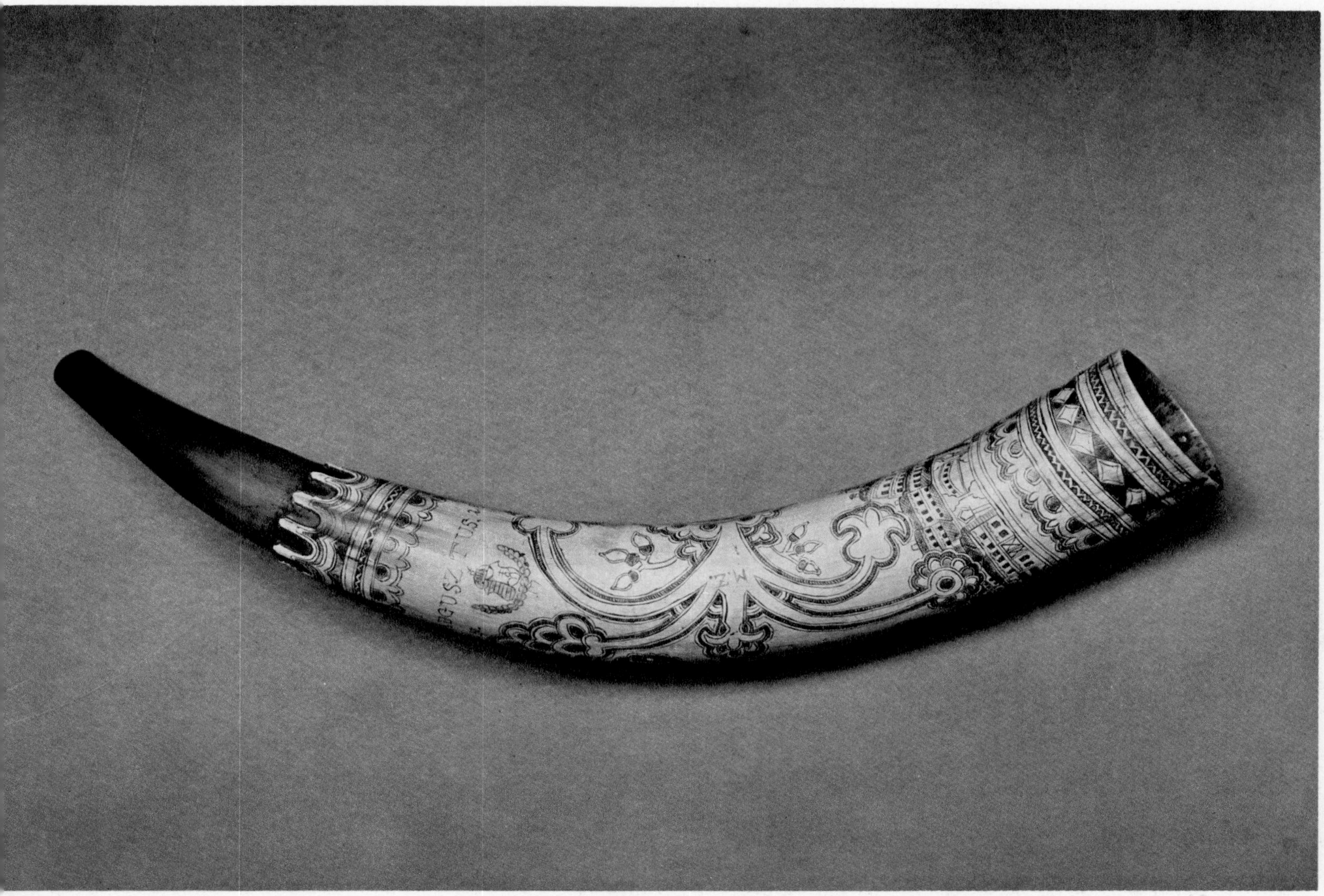

309 Shepherd's horn from Eastern Slovakia, made by Jan Vološin in 1885. East Slovakia State Museum, Košice.

310 Bagpipe and hurdy-gurdy; wooden gingerbread mould, eighteenth century. East Slovakia Museum, Košice.

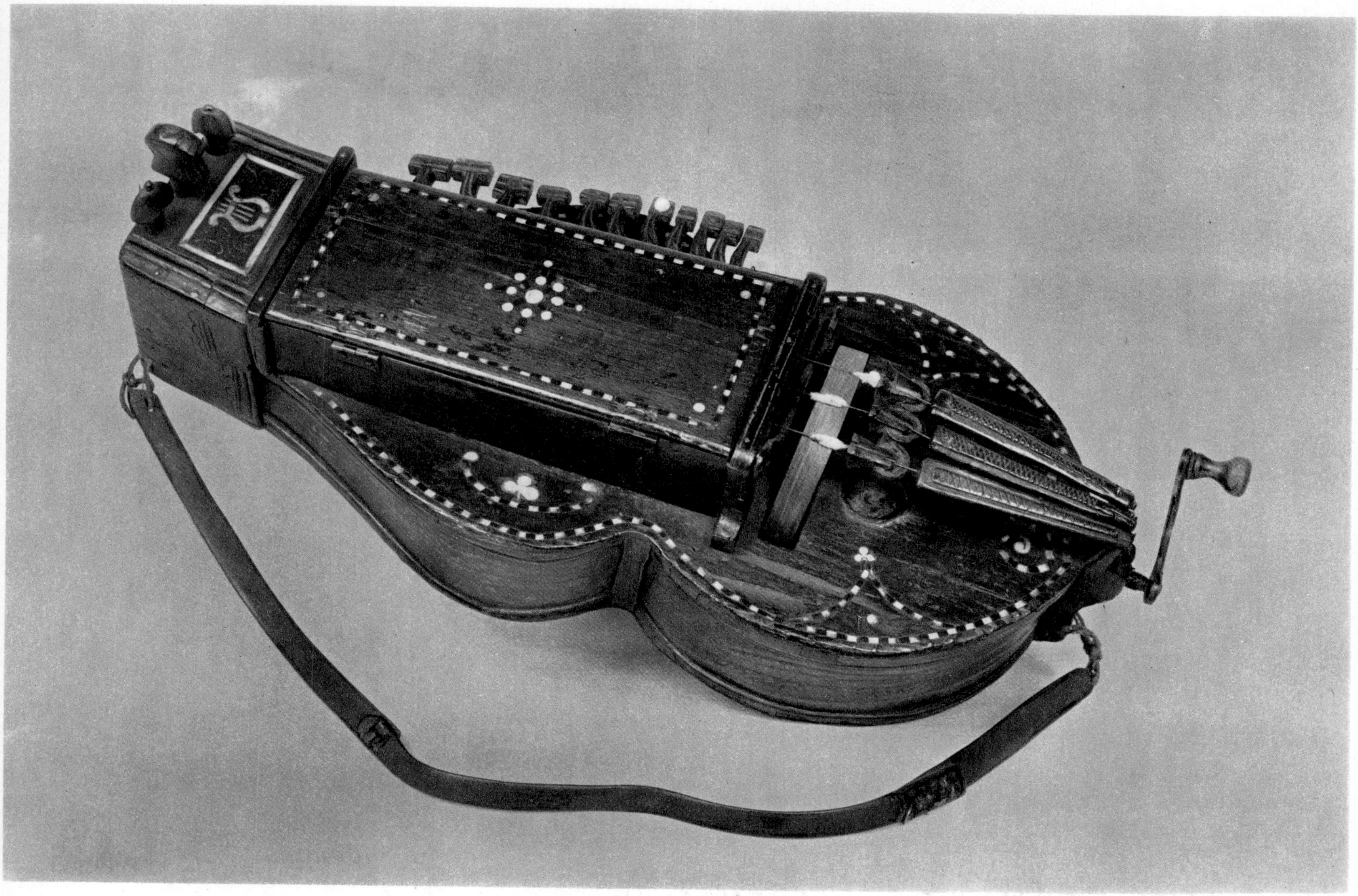

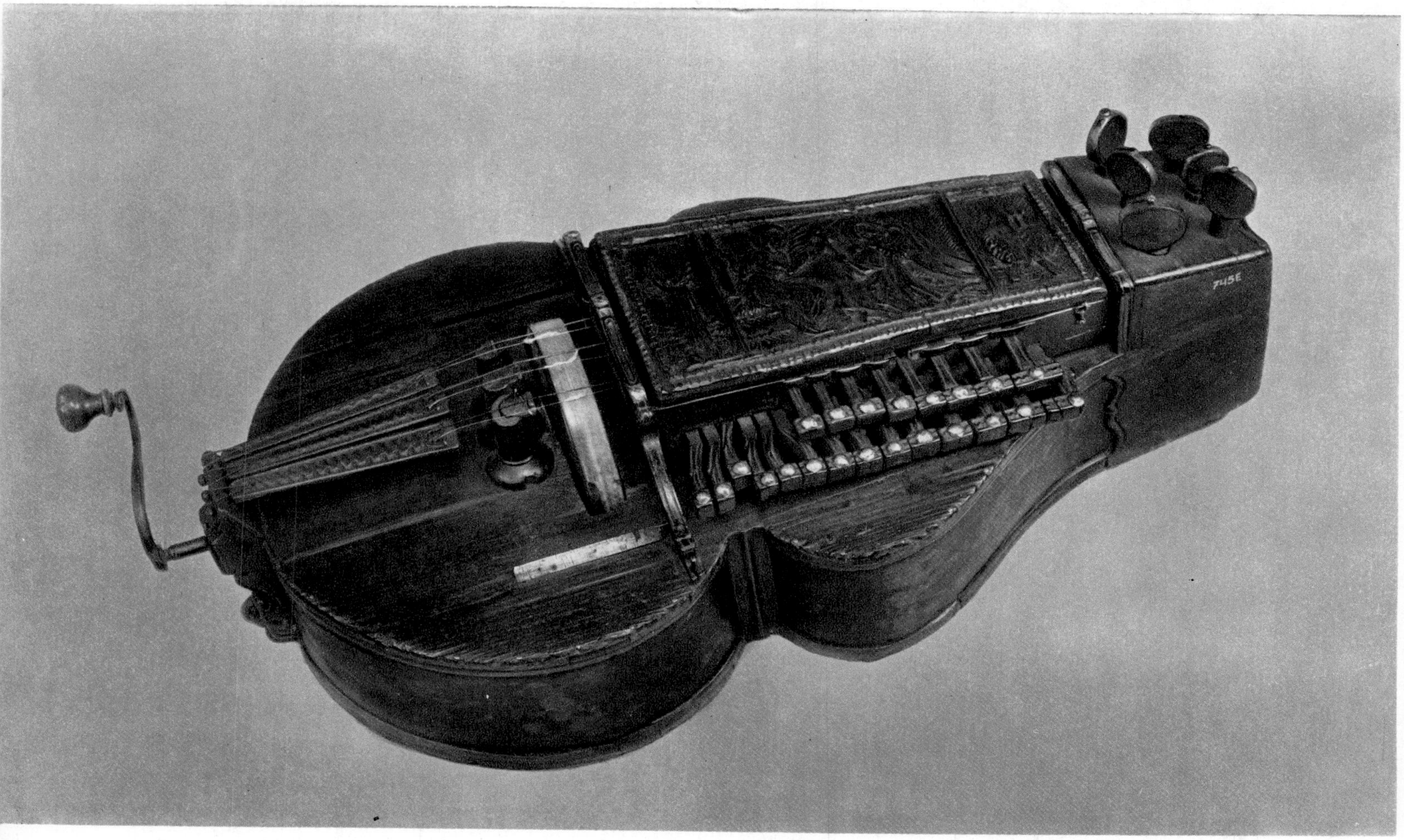

311—312 Czech hurdy-gurdies of the eighteenth century. National Museum, Prague.

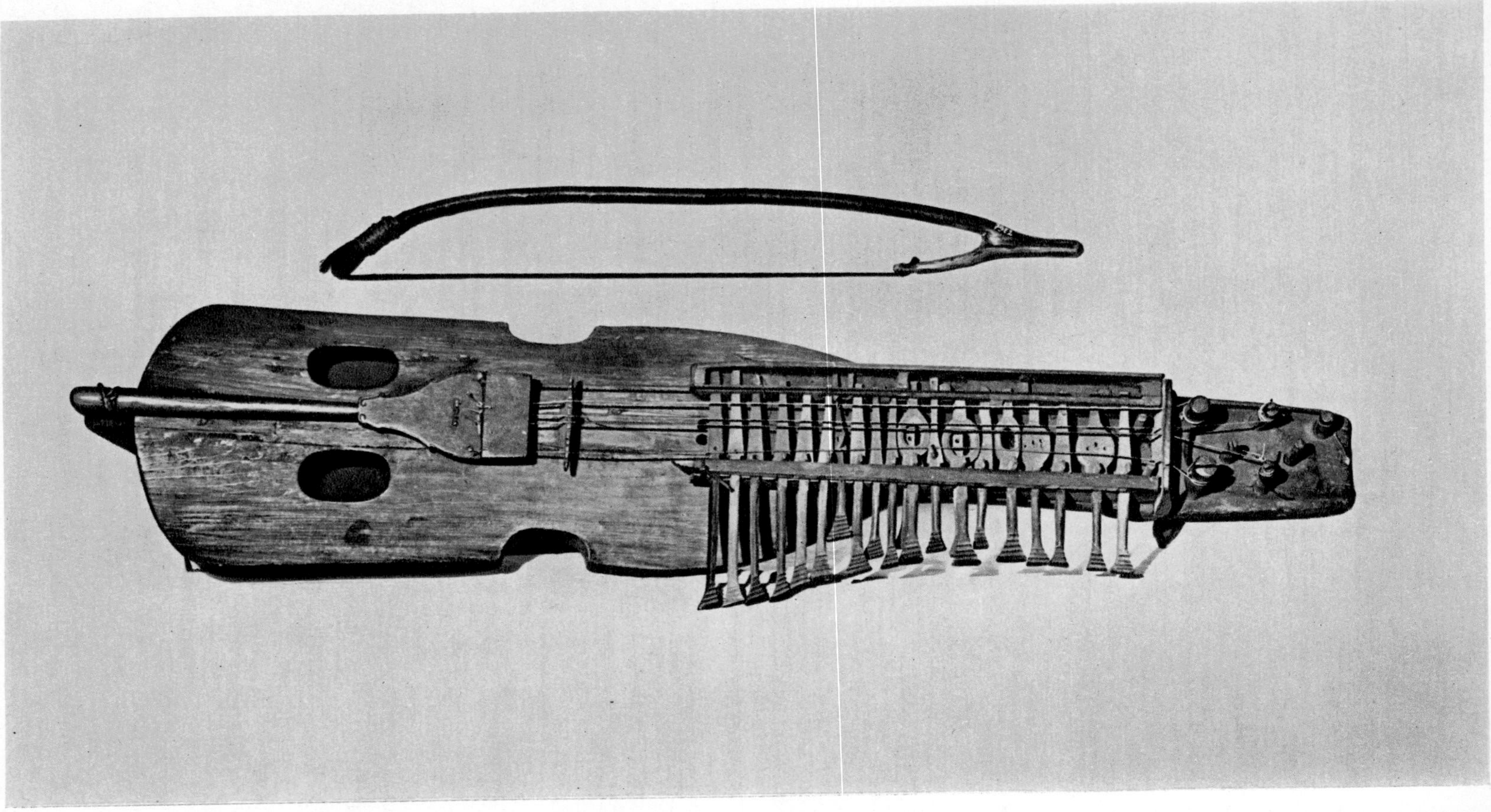

313—314 Swedish bowed hurdy-gurdy, the *nickelharpe*, and Norwegian folk violin *hardangerfelen*. National Museum, Prague.

315 Violin from Horní Lužice; Ludvík Kuba. National Museum, Prague.

316—317 Yugoslav *gussly* and detail of the neck. National Museum, Prague.

318 Russian *gussly* players; Victor Mikhailovitch Vasnietzov (1848—1926).

319 Musicians from Hroznová Lhota; clarinet, violin and double bass. Joža Uprka (1861—1940). National Gallery, Prague.

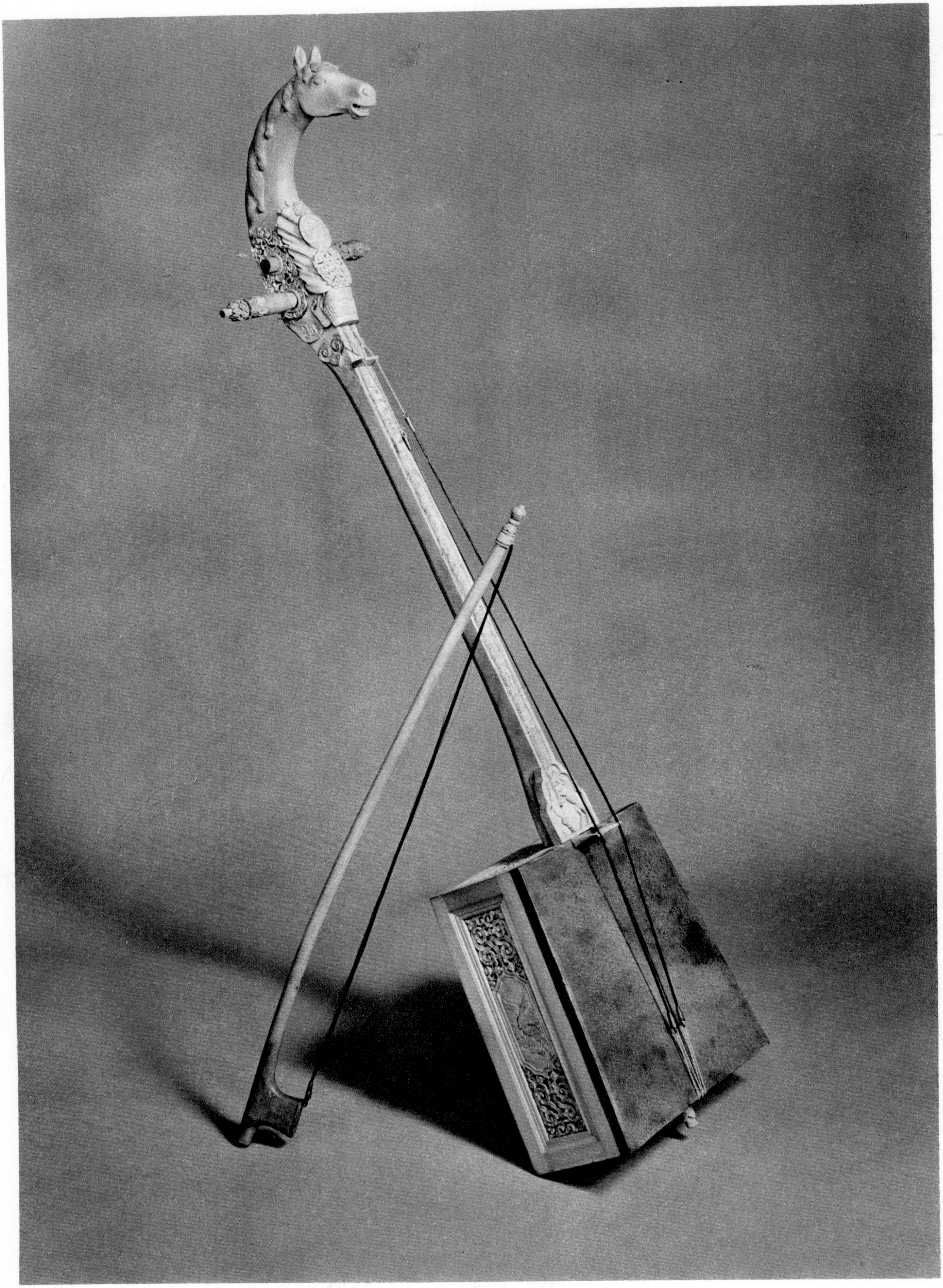

320—321 Mongolian stringed instrument called *morin chur* (horse's head) and detail of its neck. National Museum, Prague.

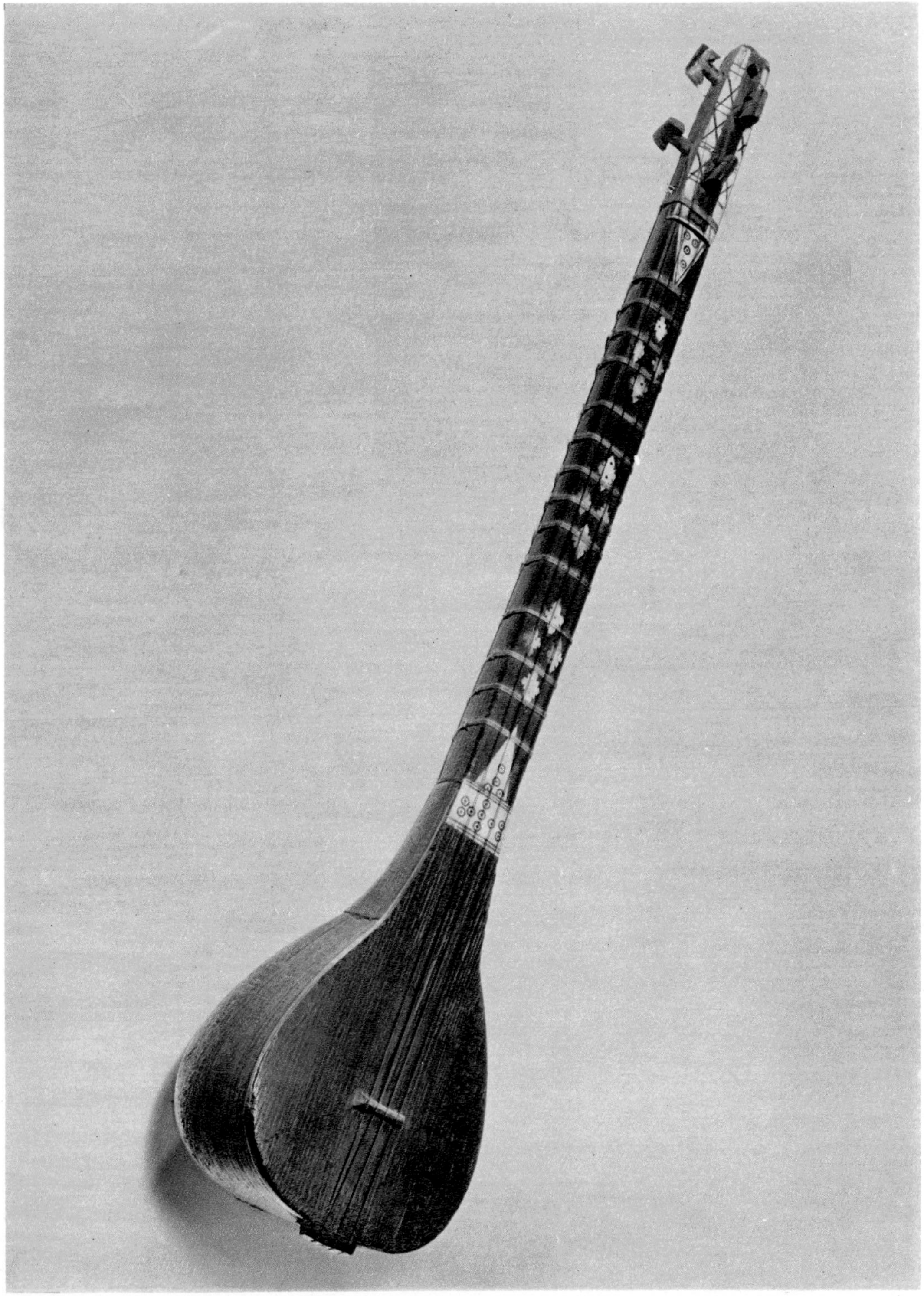

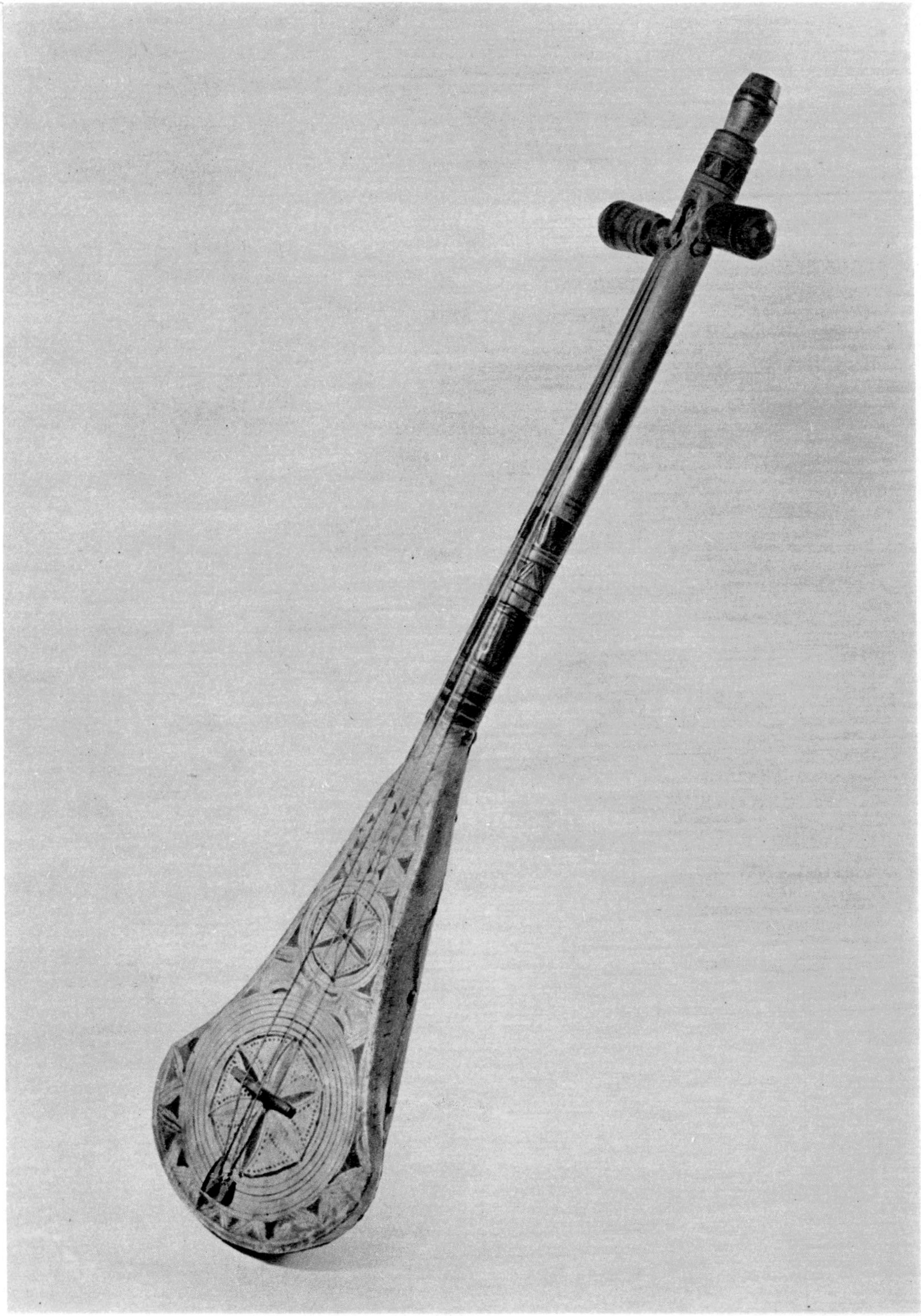

322—323 *Tar* from Transcaucasus and Kirgiz *kobuz*. National Museum, Prague.

# INDEX TO THE ILLUSTRATIONS